SOUTHERN SPAIN

A Travellers' Guide

SOUTHERN SPAIN

A Travellers' Guide

ELISABETH DE STROUMILLO

Distribution:
Distribution in Great Britain and the Commonwealth by
Roger Lascelles, 47 York Road, Brentford, Middlesex TW8 0QP
Telephone: 01 847 0935

ISBN 0 902726 44 7

Distributed in the United States and Canada by
Hippocrene Books Inc., 171 Madison Avenue, New York, NY 10016

US ISBN 0 87052 854 8

Published by Thornton Cox (1986) Ltd.,
4 Baches Street, London N1 6UB

Published in the United States and Canada by
Hippocrene Books Inc., 171 Madison Avenue, New York, NY 10016

Drawings by Alison Cotton
Maps by Tom Stalker-Miller, MSIA
Cover design by Eric Rose
Series editor: Kit Harding

Cover: Vélez Blanco Castle, Andalusía. Photograph Elisabeth de Stroumillo

Inside colour photographs by Elisabeth de Stroumillo with the exception of: Puente San Martín (page 66), Arcaded plaza, Zafra and Roman theatre, Mérida (page 67), Mezquita arches, Córdoba and Torre del Oro, Seville (page 68), Plazuela del Potro, Córdoba, Semana Santa procession, Baeza, Lagunas de Ruidera, Albacete (page 161), Explanada de Espana, Alicante, and Jávea port (page 164) by courtesy of the Spanish Tourist Office, and Torre de Damas, Granada, (page 162) by Christopher Kyd.

Set in 9 on 10 pt Univers by Alderney Printers, Alderney, Channel Islands
Printed in Great Britain by The Guernsey Press Company Limited,
Guernsey, Channel Islands

Thornton Cox Guides:

Titles in print in this series include:

Ireland	**Egypt**
Greece	**Mediterranean France**
Portugal	**Southern Africa**
Malta	**Kenya and Northern Tanzania**

Pilgrims to the El Rocío Whitsun Festival, Huelva

Contents

The Author

Elisabeth de Stroumillo has been a travel journalist for over 25 years, both as a freelance and as Travel Correspondent and Travel Editor of The Daily Telegraph, London.

Born in Paris and briefly resident there from time to time since, she has been on the move since her earliest childhood, living variously in India, Egypt, the United States and Europe.

She has five other books to her credit: one in this series on Greece, and four in her (now out of print) Tastes of Travel series, covering Normandy and Brittany, Western Loire and Aquitaine and North and Central Spain, all including sections on regional gastronomy, plus a guide to Paris.

Her awards include being chosen as Britain's Travel Writer of the Year in 1986 and Ski Journalist of the Year (the Ski USA/Michelob Award) in 1987.

She lives in London and is married to sculptor Philip Turner; they have two daughters.

Ruined fortress at Almeria

Foreword

Spain is probably the most popular holiday country in Europe and, perhaps in consequence, the least known. 'Costa', the Spanish word for coast, is used in English nowadays to convey a tasteless setting for mindless mass tourism and the names of many Spanish resorts have become bywords for the opposite extremes of cafe-society chic and seaside-ghetto horror in the holiday lexicon. The Spain behind the coasts on the other hand, although at least as beautiful, rich in history and interest as any country in Europe, is virtually ignored apart from the trio of cities whose Moorish legacies make them the three points of a well-trodden tourist triangle: Seville, Cordoba and Granada.

Has Spain done herself a disservice by allowing her coasts to become overdeveloped and oversold at the expense of her interior, or has it been a blessing in disguise, keeping the hinterland hidden and unpolluted by tourism? The answer, no doubt, is a bit of both, but recent history has also had something to do with it. For 20 or so years, before and during the Civil War (1936-39) and through the first half of the Franco era that followed it, Spain was isolated from the European mainstream. When I first started going there in the 1950s, British visitors needed visas to enter the country and those with overt left-wing affiliations were denied them. Under the strict Fascist regime, Spain remained largely impoverised and underdeveloped – in today's jargon, 'unspoiled'.

When it became obvious even to General Franco that he must emerge from his isolationist carapace or see his country wither, there began a frenzied race to catch up with the rest of Western Europe. It continued unchecked for the best part of two decades, resulting not only in unplanned, tawdry resort developments but also in ugly and ill-sited industrial ones. Great efforts are now being made to tidy up some of the worst of the older resorts and to upgrade Spain's tourist image by imposing stricter criteria on the building of new ones, but a good deal of unlovely construction is still in progress here and there, along the coasts as well as in the industrial suburbs of towns, probably sanctioned on the principle that the damage has already been done and, since it cannot now be rectified, might as well be compounded. In some cases this is true. In Torremolinos not long ago, for instance, I went in search of the first large hotel to have been built there, the sight of which, so out of scale with that modest fishing village, had shocked me in the early 1960s. It was no longer there: pulled down, I was told, because it had become too small. It was a wry illustration of the gargantuan proportions mass tourism has now reached. Yet for all that there are still some beautiful spots along Spain's coasts and, in the hinterland, hundreds upon hundreds of entrancing towns, villages and castles peppering millions upon millions of acres of glorious countryside. Efforts are being made to open up the interior and restore ancient villages and castles, but the more questing traveller, frequently baulked by inadequate or non-existent signposting, bored functionaries and erractic opening times, could sometimes be forgiven for suspecting a plot to foil their explorations and keep inland Spain, at least, for the Spanish. I am more inclined to see it as a long-ingrained incapacity, only slowly being eradicated, to believe that any stranger could possibly be interested in the country's remoter beauties. Nevertheless, exploring inland Spain remains an infinitely more rewarding than frustrating experience, thanks in no small part to the unfailing kindliness and courtesy of the majority of Spaniards themselves.

Many of them, met by chance along the way, have helped spontaneously and unofficially in my researches for this volume. Among those who have provided official help are local tourist-office personnel in a number of town and cities, notably Madrid, Toledo, Seville and Córdoba, and particularly the staff of the Spanish National Tourist Office in London, among whom I should like to single out for especial appreciation Nicolás Sangines and Charlotte Fenn. My grateful thanks are also due to Christopher Kyd, who relieved me of much of the driving during my most recent tour of Southern Spain.

General Information

The Spanish National Tourist Office has offices in most of the world's main capital cities: in London at 57-58 St James's Street, SW1A 1LD (tel 01 499 0901) and in New York at 665 Fifth Avenue, New York 10022 (tel 4989 260 9570).

How to get there

By Air

Iberia, the national airline, links Madrid (and to a lesser extent Alicante, Málaga, Seville and Valencia) directly with the capitals and main commercial cities of Europe, the Middle East, the United States, South America and Africa. Most of its services are reciprocated by the corresponding foreign airlines; in the case of Great Britain, several airlines. Lowest high-season London-Madrid (and London-Málaga) return scheduled fare is currently £174; lowest comparable New York-Madrid return is currently $783.

In addition, scores of package-tour companies run charter flights to Southern Spain from countries within Europe and outside it, such as the United States and South America, principally to carry holidaymakers on packaged inclusive deals. Seats on these charter flights are regularly sold to individual travellers for considerably less than the cost of scheduled-service tickets, the only disadvantage for the traveller being that charter-flight frequencies are more limited. Thus the time the individual traveller may spend at the Spanish destination is largely determined by the charter operator and corresponds with the standard durations of its package holidays: seven, ten, 14 days, etc.

Buses operate between airports and city centres at Alicante (also to Elche), Almeria, Jerez (also to Cadiz), Madrid, Málaga, Seville and Valencia. Frequency of bus services ranges from every 15 minutes to one per hour from early morning until late at night (less often to less popular destinations, such as Elche). Depending on traffic conditions, journey times last up to 40 minutes. Fares are reasonable: for example, from Madrid Airport to either Plaza de Colón or Plaza de Cibeles, in the city centre, a distance of 13 km (about eight miles), it is currently 200 ptas one-way.

By Land

Rail services operate via Paris from London to Madrid (and on via Córdoba to Algeciras); the total journey time is about 24 hours plus the time needed to make the connection in Paris. The London-Madrid second-class return fare is currently about £144; couchettes (£7.50 each way) and sleepers (from £37.40 each way) are extra. RENFE, the Spanish railway authority, has no London office but bookings can be made through the European Rail Travel Centre, PO Box 303, Victoria, London SW1 1JY (tel 01 834 2345, enquiries only), and major travel agencies such as American Express, Thomas Cook, YHA Travel. It is advisable to book at least one month in advance.

Bus services from Britain to Southern Spain are operated by Euroways Express Coaches, 52 Grosvenor Gardens, Victoria, London SW1 (tel 01 730 8235) over two main routes: London-San Sebastián-Vitoria-Burgos-Madrid-Córdoba-Málaga-Algeciras (journey time, 28 hours, fare currently £117 return) and London-Gerona-Barcelona-Castellón de la Plana-Valencia-Benidorm-Alicante (journey time, 29 hours, fare currently £124 return). Frequencies are up to four times weekly, depending on season.

By Sea

Among regular shipping services to Spain, the one of most use to travellers from Britain is the ferry from Plymouth to Santander in the north, now operated by a brand-new, 23,000-ton purpose-built ship, the 'Bretagne', carrying up to 580 cars and 2,030 passengers in considerable comfort: she has 1146 sleeping berths and over 400 reclining seats. Journey time is 24 hours. The 'Bretagne' carries passengers both with and without cars; fares for the former depending on the size of vehicle, time of year, type of cabin occupied, etc. Fares for foot-passengers are from £55 one-way, and there are three trains a day between Santander and Madrid. There are also regular shipping services from Cádiz to the Canary Islands; from Algeciras to the Canaries, Tangier and Ceuta in North Africa, and from Almeria and Málaga to Melilla (North Africa); from Almeria, Málaga and Valencia to the Balearic Islands (Majorca and Ibiza), plus summer hydrofoils between Alicante and the Balearics.

Travel within the Country: public transport

Air

Iberia and its subsidiary, Aviaco, between them maintain a country-wide network of domestic air services, each as a rule serving different destinations. Most flights are one-class and reservations should be made at least two or three days in advance. Sample fare: Madrid-Seville is currently 19,800 ptas return.

Buses

The bus system is well organised, reasonably comfortable and punctual, but slow thanks to the mountainous terrain and heavy traffic. Long-distance bus services, often with intermediate stops, cover the entire country; information is best obtained at the local tourist office in your city of departure. Tickets must be bought and reservations made at the local bus terminal, preferably a couple of days before you intend to travel. Fares are very reasonable.

Rail

Spain's rail network covers most of the country at reasonable cost but is on the whole old-fashioned. The fastest trains are the Talgos, between Madrid and major provincial capitals, and the electrified Ter between Madrid and Valencia. Next fastest are the *expresos;* the *rapidos* are perhaps mis-named and the *correos* even slower. On most long-distance trains there are two classes, and there is sleeping accommodation on overnight trains. The fare structure is complicated by the number of special deals and discounts on offer and the supplements charged on certain trains. RENFE, the railway authority, also runs a number of 'Tourist Train' excursions from Madrid to Extremadura, La Mancha, etc., and also the luxury 'Al Andalus Expreso' rail cruises, aboard an old-style train, between the principal cities of Andalusía. Information about rail services is available from the Spanish National Tourist Office. Madrid's main railway stations are El Norte (for the northern routes, including Santander), and Atocha (for southern routes).

Taxis

Metred taxis, of which there are plenty in most big towns, can either be found at taxi ranks or hailed while cruising. They normally display a green light on the roof when free and in daylight, when the light is not easily visible, a card inside the windscreen that reads LIBRE. Fares vary in different areas but are reasonable; there are supplements for weekend, public-holiday and night-time journeys, and for trips outside city limits (roadside signs on the outskirts of cities show where excess fares start to apply).

Travel within the country: private transport

Car-hire

The international companies like Avis and Hertz have offices in all major Spanish cities; ATESA (at 7a Henrietta Place, London W1; tel. 01 493 4934) and MELIA (at 12 Dover Street, London W1X 3RA; tel. 01 499 6731) are the principal Spanish car-hire firms. Prices vary with the season and type of car and are not cheap. As a guide, a small Hertz car currently costs £120-£132 (depending on season) for a week, including Collision Damage Waiver, tax and unlimited mileage.

An International Driving Licence is still required for driving in Spain; hirers must be over 21 years of age and private motorists over 18.

Private cars; insurance
Private cars may come into Spain with minimal frontier formalities. A sticker showing the car's country of origin and third-party insurance are mandatory. Private motorists are also strongly advised to obtain a Green Card from their own insurance company, though it is possible to take out insurance at certain border posts to cover third-party risk. It is also compulsory to have a Bail Bond which covers drivers for Accident and Legal Defence.

Rules of the road
The rule of the road is to keep to the right and to give way, except on roads marked as having priority, to traffic coming from the right. Seat-belts are compulsory outside city limits; speed limits are 100 km per hour (just over 60 mph) on main roads unless otherwise specified, and 120 km (75 mph) on motorways.

It is frequently forbidden to make a left or U-turn on main roads; instead, small loop-roads (indicated by the words *"Cambio de Sentido"*) take drivers off to the right and bring them back to cross at right angles.

Flashing orange lights suspended above a road indicate traffic signals ahead that may not yet be visible. If an oncoming car flashes its lights at you, the chances are that a road-police patrol is ahead of you.

Road quality, petrol
There are three motorways *(autopistas)* in the south: one that parallels the Mediterranean coast, entering the Levante near Vinarós and running past Alicante, after which it is still being extended; and two that link Seville with Huelva and Cádiz respectively. Tolls are expensive: coming back from the south towards Santander and the ferry in May, 1989, 180-odd miles (290 km) cost me just under 3,000 pesetas: over 16 pesetas per mile, 10 per kilometre. The advantage was that most vehicles, especially the heavy ones, chose to use the main road instead.

Main-road improvement has not kept pace with the rapid increase in traffic but much building work is taking place everywhere (which can often lead to delays) and surfaces, even on minor roads, are on the whole good. To compensate for the narrowness of so many roads, stretches of uphill gradient often have an extra lane on the right for slow vehicles; even cars should stay in this unless overtaking. A pleasant surprise for foreign motorists is that most drivers of heavy vehicles are scrupulous about helping following motorists by signalling, with the right-hand indicator, when it is safe to overtake.

Heavy traffic chokes most of the bigger towns and cities; bewildering one-way systems are in operation; signposting is woefully inadequate and parking as nightmarish as in any other country.

Petrol is sold by the litre and the price varies slightly according to location: higher in remote areas and on motorways, but at the time of writing averaging 78 pesetas per litre for super-grade, slightly more for the (still rare) lead-free, or *sin plomo.*

Security

As in other countries, theft and vandalism are also increasing in Spain. A new form of urban villainy consists of smashing the windows of cars that are stationary at traffic-lights, and grabbing anything promising off otherwise-empty back seats, so keep valuables (cameras, handbags) with you in the front or, if that is not possible, on the floor at the back. When parking, remember that foreign cars are especially attractive to thieves. Drivers of British-registered vehicles are advised to park tail-in wherever possible, as the yellow rear number-plates proclaim their origins all too clearly. All drivers should be meticulous about removing valuables when they leave their cars, even for a short time, and to make sure that nothing is lying about visible inside the vehicle. When stopping overnight, empty the car and, if possible put it in a garage. The extra cost is worth it for peace of mind.

Equivalent services to Britain's Automobile Association and Royal Automobile Club are provided by ADA, Anastasio Herrero 19, Madrid (tel. 261 1255 for Madrid and environs; 450 1000 for the rest of Spain) and RACE, Jose Abascal 10, Madrid (tel. 447 3200).

Moped and Bicycle Hire

Scooters and bikes can be rented in most popular resorts. Crash helmets are mandatory but not driving licences if the vehicle is under 75cc. The minimum age for riding such vehicles is 14. It would be foolhardy to rent one, however, unless you yourself had full insurance cover.

Accommodation

Hotels

The 1913 edition of Baedeker's "Spain & Portugal" warns the traveller not to expect too much of hotels. "The Spanish landlord," it continues, "as a rule has no idea how to run a comfortable hotel on modern lines", warning that "a supply of insect powder is desirable... and sanitary arrangement are often very unsatisfactory."

The hotel scene in Spain has changed greatly since then, thanks partly to the example set by the State with its Paradors, of which more later, and partly, of course, to market pressures exerted by the packaged-holiday industry. Hotels are officially classified from one to five stars, and a few are super-classified as *gran lujo* (grand de luxe); the more modest *hostáls* (inns, or pensions) are classified from one to three stars. *Residencias* normally provide no food, not even breakfast, though there may be a cafeteria in the same building, or nearby. Two- and one-star *hostáls* will not normally have private bathrooms.

As a general rule, lower-rated hotel and *hostál* accommodation is of a higher standard in cities and resort areas, where the competition is stiffer. The independent tourist will also feel closer to the 'real' Spain in this sort of budget accommodation because all the fancier resort hotels, right up to the *gran lujo* class, nowadays take package-holiday groups and are mainly geared to coping with mass arrivals and departures, standard meals, and so on. In cities, the higher-class hotels are also catering for business travellers as well as packaged tourists and are consequently much more impersonal than the smaller, perhaps family-run, *hostál.*

In smaller towns further off the beaten track, and along main highways, you could find the lower-rated hotel decidedly basic, but in many such places there are few alternatives. However, they are almost always clean and adequate for an overnight stop and, if you are in any doubt, the hotelier will probably allow you to look at the room before you decide.

Paradors

It has become fashionable to decry Paradors as being too obviously touristy but, bearing in mind the remarks in the previous paragraph, this is merely snobbery in reverse. Anyone whose budget will run to them cannot do better than the best of them, located as they often are in converted castles or other historic buildings in places of great interest, and furnished as far as possible in the style of the original building. Even the least atmospheric of the Paradors (amd some are modern) are rarely bad, and their dining-rooms do make an effort to include some regional dishes on the menu, which cannot often be said of the vast majority of hotels or even restaurants.

Bed and breakfast rates, per person, currently vary between about £20 in low season at one of the more modest establishments, up to

£42-odd at the magnificent ones such as the Parador S Francisco in Granada.

Paradors can be booked in advance in Britain through Keytel International, 402 Edgware Road, London W2 (tel. 01 402 8182); some also feature in pre-booked itineraries for independent motorists, offered by Brittany Ferries and tour firms specialising in Spanish holidays for the more discerning traveller.

Apartments and villas
Thousands of these have sprung up along the Costas in recent years, and a few tourist apartments are making their appearance in the big cities too. Most of those in resort areas are packaged by tour operators, but the Spanish National Tourist Office has a list of firms that includes several through which accommodation can be rented independently.

Farmhouse accommodation
A booklet entitled *'Vacaciones en Casas de Labranza',* is obtainable from the Dirección General de Empresas y Actividades Turisticas (Seccion de Alojamientos no Oteleros), Avenida de la Industria 19, Alcobendas, Madrid. It gives details of approved rural accommodation throughout the country, some of which is also offered through holiday firms specialising in 'offbeat' Spain.

Camping and Youth Hostels
Camping is well-organised: the hundreds of sites are inspected and classified into luxury, first, second and third classes. Most are on or near the coast and tend to get crowded in summer, but there is also a scatter of sites inland in areas of natural beauty. The Spanish National Tourist Office issues lists of approved campsites.

There are over 20 Youth Hostels in Southern Spain, most only open in high summer and perhaps over Christmas-New Year and Easter. Those open for most of the year are at Albuquerque (Extremadura), Alicante, Benicasím and Valencia (Levante), Granada, Jaén and Málaga (Andalusía), and Madrid. The head office is: RED Española de Albergues Juveniles, Calle Jose Ortega y Gasset 71, 28006 Madrid.

Choosing Hotels and Restaurants - and Complaining
Although the annual Red Michelin Guide 'España - Portugal' is not as infallible in Spain as in France or Britain, it is the best selective accommodation guide available and it would be unwise of motorists touring extensively to try to do without it. Most other guides, including this one, only have the space to mention a few favourite hotels and restaurants in the big cities; Michelin covers a host of smaller places,

often in out of the way locations.

If you are dissatisfied, remember that Spanish law requires all hoteliers, restaurateurs, campsite and even petrol-station proprietors to produce complaint forms on request. If they cannot do so, then the local Tourist Information Office will be able to supply them; they should be filled in as soon as possible and sent to the Dirección General de Turismo of the province concerned (see addresses below).

Church Services

The vast majority of Spaniards are of the Roman Catholic faith and, outside Madrid (where the Church of England (Anglican) church is on the corner of Calle Nuñez de Balboa and Calle Hermosilla), Protestant church services are held only along the Costa del Sol (Málaga, Almuñecar, Algeciras, Estepona, S Pedro de Alcántara, Fuengirola and Benalmádena).

Climate

From late May until the end of October sunshine and blue skies are the norm along the Costas of Southern Spain. Showers and even grey days are rare: the average number of rainy days per year ranges from 62 in Malaga up to 98 in Madrid. Average coastal temperatures vary from 6°C (41°F) in Murcia in January up to 32°C (90°F) on Alicante's Costa Blanca in August. In the mountains – and you are never far from mountains in Spain – it is invariably cooler and fresher: one of the country's premier ski resorts, Solynieve, lies above Granada in the Sierra Nevada mountains. In Madrid, at an altitude of 646 metres (2,100 ft) the minimum average January temperature is 1°C (34°F) and snow is not uncommon; the capital's summer temperatures go up to an average of 30°C (86°F) in August. Hotter still is the Guadalquivir basin, where Seville's summer temperatures average 36°C (97°F).

If your main objective is to explore rather than to bask on a beach then April, May and June are the best months, not only for weather but also for the myriads of wild flowers, followed by September and October. Even in the winter months the climate along the Mediterranean can be benign: maximum January temperatures average between 15° and 17°C (59° and 63°F) on the Costas Blanca (Alicante), Cálida (Murcia), del Azahar (Valencia), de la Luz (Cádiz) and del Sol (Málaga).

Currency, Credit Cards and Banking

The currency unit is the peseta (abbreviated to pta/ptas). Coins are issued to the value of 1, 5, 10, 25, 50, 100 and 500 ptas; notes to the value of 100, 200, 500, 1,000, 2,000, 5,000 and 10,000 ptas. Visitors are allowed to bring in any amount of foreign currency and Spanish banknotes, and to take out up to 100,000 ptas in notes. Most banks and tourist-orientated hotels will change money and travel-cheques at the prevailing rate.

Banks are open six days a week: Mondays to Fridays from 0830 to 1400 and Saturdays 0830 to 1230 (in summer, 1300 in winter).

Credit and charge cards (Access/Mastercharge, Barclaycard/Visa, American Express and Diners Club) are widely accepted in hotels, restaurants and shops – though it is wise to check in advance if you do not see a sign displayed – but petrol stations rarely take plastic.

Eurocheques are accepted at most banks and at many shops.

Customs, Immigration and Health

As well as currency, referred to above, every traveller may bring in one litre of spirits and 200 cigarettes, or the equivalent in cigars and pipe-tobacco. There is no limit on valuable personal possessions (cameras, binoculars, sporting equipment, etc) that may be imported for your personal use; no limit, either, on how much you may take out of Spain in the way of purchases.

A valid passport is all that is required of citizens of EEC countries, the United States and Japan; citizens of other countries need visas. Those intending to stay for longer than three months normally need a police stamp on their passports. After six months, residency must be applied for, though if the intended stay is not likely to be much longer than that limit, many prefer simply to leave the country for a day and return.

British visitors covered by Britain's National Insurance qualify for free treatment under Spain's health service on presentation of Form E111 (available through your local DHSS office in Britain), but comprehensive personal insurance cover is wise nonetheless. The two most common ailments to afflict holidaymakers are sunstroke or sunburn and stomach upsets. These can be avoided by accustoming yourself gradually to the sun, and by avoiding highly-spiced or uncooked foods in humbler restaurants, and rationing your intake of shellfish and wine. Although tap-water is normally safe, it is prudent to stick to bottled water and to go without ice-cubes in your drinks.

Dress, Cosmetics and Medicaments

The days are long gone when women's bathing-suits had to have skirts and men's to incorporate vest-like tops; bikinis and even toplessness are the norm on the beaches of Southern Spain and there are a few nudist beaches. But although women no longer have to wear hats or *mantillas* in churches, the authorities are strict about forbidding you to enter a religious institution with legs bare above the knee or bare shoulders: skirts or trousers rather than shorts is the rule, and sleeves.

Cosmetics and most internationally-marketed patent medicines are to be found in most towns and resorts, at roughly equivalent prices to what you would pay at home. In addition, certain patent medicines available in Spain may be unfamiliar but more efficient than the equivalent at home, so it is worth asking a chemist's advice.

Hairdressers for both men and women, and beauty salons, are plentiful.

Embassies and Consulates

Australia: Paseo de la Castellana 143, Madrid (Embassy and Consulate)
Canada: Nuñez de Balboa 35, Madrid (Embassy and Consulate)
Irish Republic: Hermanos Becquer 10, Madrid (Embassy and Consulate)
UK: Fernando el Santo 16, Madrid (Embassy and Consulate);
Avenida Fuerzas Armadas 11, Algeciras (Vice Consulate);
Plaza Calvo Sotelo 1-2, 1 Aptdo, Correos 564, Alicante (Consulate);
Edificio Duquesa, Calle Duquesa de Parcent, 4, Málaga (Consulate);
Plaza Nueva 8, Seville (Consulate).
USA: Serrano 75, Madrid (Embassy and Consular Section)

Etiquette and social customs

Although Spanish women are now thoroughly emancipated and the legendary gallantry of the Spanish male more wavering than of yore, Spaniards remain a proud and inherently courteous people. George Borrow, who travelled extensively in the Peninsula during the first half of the 19th century on three separate missions to distribute and sell Bibles and "to visit the people in . . . secluded spots, to talk to them of Christ, to explain . . . the nature of His book" prided himself on being able to communicate with all classes of people by exhibiting faultless courtesy at all times (it sometimes got him out of potentially nasty spots).

The 1913 Baedeker advises travellers against brusqueness, exhorting them to "be prepared to lose a little time in the exchange of compliments" . . . (and) . . . "to maintain a certain courtesy of manner towards even the humblest individual." A less elaborate application of the same policy holds true today: the greetings *"buenas días"* or *"buenas tardes"* ("good day" and "good afternoon/evening") exchanged with shop assistants, petrol-pump attendants and waiters never come amiss and are often used between strangers – in lifts or on trains, for instance.

When asking for directions, or anything else, you get better results if you preface your question with *"Perdón, por favor"* ("Excuse me, please"), and it is hard to overdo the *"muchas gracias"* (many thanks). You will also establish many a rewarding cordial relationship, however brief, by admiring someone's child for Spaniards are devoted to children.

On the other hand, they have no concept the desirability of keeping their voices down for the sake of other peoples' conversations, or of meekly queueing for buses or postage stamps, or of refraining from smoking in restaurants (or anywhere else). And, particularly in the south where there is a large, impoverished gipsy population, young hustlers trying to thrust their services or wares upon you can seem faintly menacing. Rather than buy something I do not want, I have found it expedient to offer something instead: sweets, perhaps, or fruit. They do not expect it, and it can change their attitudes dramatically.

In general, Spaniards are not curious about foreigners – or are too polite to exhibit curiosity. By the same token, asking personal questions of slight acquaintances is to be avoided, as are searching conversations about politics (especially the Gibraltar question) and religion. Even a woman travelling alone will not be asked whether she has a husband lurking in the background; nor will she be subjected to unwelcome insinuations; nor will she be made to feel a freak entering a restaurant alone. It would be unwise, however, for a woman, or even a couple of women, to try hitch-hiking, which is discouraged in Spain anyway.

The Siesta

The custom that most travellers find hardest to adjust to is that of the *siesta* and its effect on their schedule. Even now, although large department stores, hypermarkets and factories no longer close for three or four hours at lunchtime, the vast majority of shops, museums and tourist sights do, which can complicate the planning of a tour or sightseeing programme; and many offices, including tourist information offices, do likewise – or are open only until 1430 or 1500. Not that most Spaniards actually sleep during siesta-hours: the long midday break is simply a habit that dies hard. Those who do not nod off after lunch seem to manage on next to no sleep, for they are up early and neither for their own sakes nor those of their adored children would dream of thinking about the evening meal until 2100 or later; moreover they are still enjoying the night-time coolness, strolling or sitting and chatting until midnight and after.

Festivals and Entertainment

Theatre and Music

Theatre, opera and concerts go on year-round in Madrid, and most provincial capitals have regular seasons of theatre, dance and music; these are well advertised locally and tourist information offices can also give you details.

That 20th-century hub of nightlife, the disco, is ubiquitous even in small towns, and in tourist areas there are *flamenco* and other folklore shows on most nights pretty well all year round.

Cinema, Television

Most towns of any size have a cinema, but foreign films are likely to be dubbed into Spanish. If your hotel room boasts a TV set, you may be able to get one of the English-language channels but, except for an early-morning news roundup, their output is not apparently concerned with increasing the prestige of the programme-makers in English-speaking countries. In bars and similar public places, Spanish TV is on at maximum volume for sporting events, often competing with the jingling noises emitted by electronic games machines.

Festivals

In addition to the national public holidays listed later in this chapter, regional or municipal governments may add another two public holidays on dates of parochial interest. The principal local celebrations, or *fiestas,* in Southern Spain are the January 5 Eve of Epiphany parade that takes place in most big cities; the February pre-Lent carnivals at Cádiz, and at Villanueva de la Vera in Extremadura; the *fallas* in Valencia in honour of St Joseph in mid-March; the Holy Week celebrations in Seville, Málaga, Jerez and Cuenca in March/April; the holy Thursday procession at Valverde de la Vera in Extremadura in March/April; Seville's post-Easter Spring Fair; Madrid's San Isidro festival, from mid-May for a month; Jerez de la Frontera's Horse Fair and Alcoy's Moors and Christians *fiesta,* both in May; the San Juan celebrations on the Costa Blanca in June; the El Rocío Whitsun pilgrimage in June; Toledo's Corpus Christi processions, also in June; the Virgen del Carmen *fiestas* along the Costa del Sol and at San Fernando (Cádiz) and San Pedro del Pinatar (Murcia) in July; the Moors and Christians festival at Villajoyosa (Alicante) at the end of July; the Elche mystery play at Elche (Alicante) in mid-August; Sanlúcar de Barrameda's Guadalquivir river-festival in early September; Jerez de la Frontera's Grape

Harvest festival and Ronda's 18th-century bullfight re-enactment, both also on moveable dates in September. For more parochial festivals, ask at the local Tourist Information Office.

Bullfights

The most traditional of all Spanish entertainments, of course, is the bullfight, and one or more form part of most festival celebrations. The concept of men ritually slaughtering animals is anathema to most foreigners, even those who regularly hunt, shoot or fish, and even if they go regularly to boxing-matches but have never watched a good bullfight. There is also a small anti-*corrida* faction in Spain itself, but it has little popular support; the bullfight or *corrida,* from being a sport of noblemen in past centuries, has evolved into a professionally-organised spectacle of skill and bravery that continues to draw enthusiastic crowds of *aficionados.* At its worst – and there are many bad bullfights – it does seem like ritualised butchery; at its best, it is more akin to a ballet than to a fight: a highly stylised series of dance-like movements, in three separate and strictly-defined 'acts', to which the elements of unpredictability (on the part of the bull) and danger (for man as well as bull) add an intensely dramatic quality.

It is vital that your first bullfight, if you are enquiring and courageous enough to risk the experience, should be a first-class one. Try to enlist the advice, and preferably the company, too, of a true *aficionado,* who will be able to advise you in advance not only about the ranking of the *toreros* or bullfighters (generally three per fight) but also about the provenance of the bulls. They are bred for their strength, speed and ferocity and, until they reach the bullring, have never faced a man before: their willingness and capacity to charge, fast and straight, is determined by testing potential dams and selecting only the most suitable. A knowledgeable companion will also help you to appreciate the spectacle: to quote the 1913 Baedeker again, "the finer points of the sport . . . will generally escape the novice, unless he has an expert *(aficionado)* at his elbow."

The essence of the fight itself (and there are usually six bulls involved, two for each *torero*) is for the man, by force of his personality as well as his skill, to dominate the bull to such an extent that man and animal seem to become partners in the three-act ritual. In the first 'act', or *suerte,* the *torero* and his assistants make passes at the bull with big, swirling capes, mainly to determine how the animal charges and how fearless it is, and the mounted *picadors* make a few jabs at its powerful neck and shoulder muscles with their lances to make the bull lower its head. (It is the sight of the *picadors'* usually clapped-out old horses, wrapped in protective padding but occasionally thrown to the ground or injured by the charging bull, that particularly disgusts foreigners, and an over-aggresive *picador* will be booed by Spaniards too. But there were always cheers for a Mexican woman bullfighter who performed much of the *corrida* from the back of an un-padded horse some years ago.)

There are more passes with the cape, generally by the *torero* alone, in the second 'act', when either he or one of his assistants, holding two decorated barbs or *banderillas* in his hands, will incite the bull to charge him and, as he deftly makes a last-minute move to avoid it, plunge the barbs into its back.

In the final 'act', the *faena,* the *torero* exchanges the cape for the *muleta,* a small, scarlet cloth which he hangs over his sword, and makes a series of ever-shorter, ever-closer passes aimed at manoeuvring the bull briefly to an angry, puzzled standstill, with its head lowered, just in front of him; at this point he can take aim with his sword and, as the bull makes its final charge, plunge the sword into its neck just behind the horns to finish it cleanly and swiftly.

Food and Drink

Various dishes

Mass catering for mass tourism has eroded the genuine cuisine of Southern Spain and substituted bland, 'international' cooking. The only truly Spanish dishes the average tourist will come across are the *tortilla,* or potato-and-onion omelette, which is not native to any particular part of the country, and two that actually originated in the south: the *paella,* born in the rice-growing areas around Valencia, and *gazpacho,* the ice-cold vegetable soup invented by the Moors of Andalusía. There are, however, many more regional dishes that I shall mention in their geographical contexts, and many that can be found throughout the country at the proper season but need to be asked for by name. In spring, for instance, *habas* (broad beans), *guisantes* (peas) or *alcachofas* (small artichokes) *con jamón* – tossed in olive oil with garlic and small pieces of the delicious smoked ham that is to be found all over the south. The best is from Extremadura, which also boasts some of the best *chorizos* and *morcillas* (red and black salami-type sausages).

If you pass up hotel breakfasts, another southern speciality much favoured for morning snacks as well as breakfast is the *churro:* a sausage-shaped length of light batter that is crisp-fried in hot oil and lightly sprinkled with sugar. Frying in oil is the basis of a great many southern dishes – in a climate where long, slow cooking is to be avoided – but when properly prepared they are not 'greasy' and the oils (sunflower and other vegetable oils as well as olive oil) are healthy and easily digestible.

Fresh vegetables and fruits are abundant in their proper seasons, and delicious; look for them in shops and markets if you cannot find sufficient variety on the table. Other desserts, apart from the inevitable *flan* (caramel custard) and ice-cream, are few. Cheeses mostly come from La Mancha and go under the collective name of *manchego;* except for the softer and milder *fresco* they are firm and dryish with a piquant flavour.

Tapas

If you are timid about trying unknown dishes at a restaurant, you will find that the most painless way of experiencing the huge variety of local cuisine is to get the *tapas* habit. *Tapas* are tiny bar-counter servings *(raciones)* of all sorts of foods to go with drinks - which can be soft drinks, or even coffee at a *bar-cafeteria,* as well as wine, beer or spirits. Their range is almost endless, from stuffed mushrooms and other vegetable dishes to little morsels of fried liver, marinated fish or shellfish, pieces of ham skewered to little squares of bread, mini-*chorizos* or tender pieces of stewed tripe. Some *tapas,* obviously, come straight out of tins; others are prepared in-house and dishes of them are set under glass along the bar counter. The best variety appears soon after midday when Spaniards, having sustained themselves throughout the morning on coffee and *churros,* still have a couple of hours in which to face starvation before it is lunchtime.

The microwave oven has been a boon to *tapas* enthusiasts who previously had to accept the fact that everything was going to be cold; nowadays the dishes meant to be eaten hot can be re-heated for a second or two on their saucers before being served, and taste much better for it.

For touring motorists, *tapas* are a real blessing: no need to waste time over long lunches, nor to feel sleepy after them. The *tapas* will be on display all afternoon and well into the evening, and you can stop and stoke up briefly (and extremely reasonably) as often as you like. *Tapas*-bars are sociable places, too, where everyone exchanges greetings and you can easily get into pleasant conversations.

Restaurants

Restaurants, on the other hand, even the more modest ones, tend to be fairly formal with clean white tablecloths and punctilious, if not always swift, service. Menus are often dauntingly long (you can be forgiven for wondering how on earth all those dishes can be freshly-prepared) and, if none of the staff speaks English, a dictionary or the brief lexicon at the end of this volume will help. Eating-hours are late: any time between 1300 and 1600 for lunch; not before 2100 for dinner, except in tourist areas where they expect famished foreigners to appear before that.

Apéritifs

Sherry, best known of Spanish apéritifs, comes of course from the area around Jerez de la Frontera, southwest of Seville. It is produced from the Palomino grape, fortified after up to two years' storage, and eventually matured by judicious blending, using the traditional *solera* method by which older barrels are topped up from younger ones. There are three main varieties: the pale, dry *fino,* the medium-dry *amontillado* and the brown, heavier *oloroso.* Manzanilla, which is very akin to sherry, comes from the district around nearby Sanlúcar de Barrameda.

Spirits

Spain produces her own brands of gin (Larios is the best known), whisky (Dyk) and brandy under many labels, much of it produced in the Jerez region. Thanks to low taxation, they are all very reasonably-priced by comparison with what you buy in Britain; in fact even Scotch whisky is often cheaper in a Spanish grocery than it is in a British duty-free outlet.

Wines

Rioja, in the north, is the most prestigious Spanish wine-name but good, often stronger, ones are produced in the south, most of them red: Valdepenãs and Manzanares from La Mancha, the most abundant of all Spanish wine-producing areas; Almendralejo and Castillo de Medellin from Extremadura; the heavy, sweetish dessert wines of Málaga; the smooth Jumillas and Yeclas from the northern part of Murcia province; the heady Montilla from the Córdoba area. Perhaps because it lacks light table wines, Andalusía is credited with having invented *sangría,* that refreshing, well-chilled mixture of red wine, soda water and a dash of brandy, to which slices of fruit are added.

Gratuities and Bargaining

Hotels and restaurants

In hotels and restaurants, bills include by law a percentage to cover service even though it may not be itemised (as is VAT, known in Spain as IVA), but it is still usual to leave around ten per cent on the table in a restaurant, a few pesetas in a bar, and to tip individual hotel staff (porters, chambermaids) for services rendered. Chambermaids expect nothing if you only stay a night or two but they work hard and an average of 100 ptas per night for longer stays in appreciated. The concierge in a large hotel who arranges excursions or hire-cars for you is probably getting a commission from the supplier, but if he exceeds himself by managing to procure at box-office prices a hard-to-get ticket for the ballet or a bullfight, a tip is in order.

Taxis

Taxi-drivers should get about ten per cent of the fare but if, perhaps on your first ride in from an airport, you have no small change and the driver claims not to have any either, just pay the fare and he will not grumble. He has gambled on your handing over a note for much too much, and lost, and will be philosophical about it.

Porters; parking attendants

Porters at airport and railway stations should get up to 100 ptas per piece of baggage carried; the man with an air of self-importance who waves you into a parking space in a public square may be the official car-parking attendant, in which case he will present a small ticket and tell you how much he expects for it; if he doesn't, but looks expectant, try him with 25 ptas.

Hairdressers

Hairdressers and barbers expect about 15 percent of the bill and it is customary to give a small tip to theatre usherettes and cloakroom attendants.

Bargaining

Bargaining is not the custom in shops, nor in food markets, but you are expected to haggle a bit in a flea market, especially when it comes to 'antiquities'. There are no hard-and-fast rules: you decide how much a thing is worth to you, and remain politely firm. Shaking your head sadly and walking away has often worked wonders by the time you saunter past the stall for the second time.

Language

Pronunciation

Outside the main resort areas, few people speak English, so it is worth trying to master some basic Castilian Spanish which everyone will understand even if they themselves speak with regional accents. It is not a difficult language to pronounce, nor to read, since words are pronounced as they are spelt. Stress is normally laid on the penultimate syllable of words ending in vowels, or their plural forms *(alcachófas)* or on the final syllable of words ending with consonants. Where these rules vary, an accent indicates where to lay the stress *(Andalusía).* The vowels are pronounced 'ah, eh, ee (there is no long i), oh and oo', and there is no 'silent' e. The letter B tends to be gobbled rather than emphasised and consonants at the ends of words are also frequently gobbled or dropped altogether; 'Madrid' sounds like 'Madree'. C is hard, except before an e or i, when it is lisped, as in 'thing' in Madrid and surrounding areas, and becomes a sibilant 's' in the far south. Ch is pronounced as in church, G is hard, as in Granada, except when followed by e or i, when it resembles the Scottish ch, as in 'loch'; Generalife, for instance, is pronounced Kheneralife. Putting u between G and an e or i hardens the G but is not pronounced itself; in *guisantes* (peas), the 'gui' sounds like the first two letters of 'give'. H is normally not pronounced at all; J is coughed out like the G in Generalife (Jerez, for instance, is Herez); LL is pronounced rather like the Y in 'yellow'. The accented N has a 'ni' or 'ny' sound to it, as in 'vineyard'; Qu is pronouced like K; R is pronounced with a roll of the tip of the tongue and RR is rolled even more vigorously; Z, like the soft C, is lisped in northerly areas and hissed in the south.

Vocabulary
A dictionary or phrase-book is invaluable, and once you have mastered the pronounciation you will sound so convincing, however meagre your vocabulary and grasp of grammar, that one of the first Spanish phrases to learn by heart is *por favor, puede usted hablar mas despacio,* meaning 'please speak more slowly' - especially in Andalusía, where the strong local accent compounds to the point of confusion the national habit of talking like a rattle of machine-gun fire.

Lavatories

Public conveniences *(servicios, aseos)* are virtually unknown. There used to be one in the main square in Toledo but it has now gone: it was "seenking," I was told. There is one in the main square at Alcalá del Júcar and a rather pretty folly of one in Requeña; if there are others, I didn't see them on my most recent, extensive trip. But every museum has a very acceptable loo and so do showplaces like Madrid's Botanical Gardens. Bars, cafeterias, restaurants and petrol stations have them, their standards of cleanliness usually reflecting the grandness of the establishment; big department stores also have them. It is wise (for men, too) to carry a supply of lavatory paper or paper handkerchiefs, however, for many places do not run to paper at all and others only seem to provide it for women.

Photography

In the main cities and tourist areas, black and white film can only occasionally be found but colour film is available everywhere, at roughly comparable prices to those you pay at home. Processing can, of course, be done in Spain but unless you are staying in one place for more than a day or two, it is best to wait until you get home. Thanks to the strength and angle of the sun's light at midday, which tends to 'flatten' subjects and drain them of colour, you will get best results if you take your pictures early or late.

Post and Telephones

Post offices are normally only open from 0900 to 1400 except in main cities where the central post office stays open all day long, often until 2000 (though certain counters may close for a break in the afternoons). The smaller offices can take registered mail and parcels and deal with money orders as well as selling stamps (but these are more easily bought from tobacconists); the central post office will also have telex, fax and poste-restante facilities (such mail should carry the recipient's name, followed by the words *lista de Correos,* followed by the names of the town and the province), and can cash British National Girobank postcheques.

Public telephones

Some post offices may have public telephones but the two services are entirely separately run, so this is not always the case. The automatic telephone system is reliable and there are plenty of telephone kiosks in towns and resort areas. To make an international call, look for one marked *Telefono Internacional* and have plenty of 50 and 100-pta coins handy. Put one in the slot (or groove sloping down to the slot), dial 07 and wait for a shriller tone, then dial the country code (a list is normally displayed) and number you want. You cannot reverse the charges from a public telephone box; instead, ask for the telephone company's office and do it from there. International calls are more expensive from Spain to Britain than vice-versa (during off-peak hours) so get yourself rung back if you can.

Public Holidays

There are seven national public holidays in the Spanish calendar: New Year's Day, Good Friday, May 1 (Labour Day), August 15 (Assumption of the Virgin), October 12 (National Day, feast of the national patroness, the Virgen del Pilar), December 8 (Immaculate Conception) and Christmas Day. Five more are observed in most, but not all, provinces (regional authorities may substitute dates of more local significance for some of them): January 6 (Epiphany), March 19 (St Joseph), Thursday in Holy Week, Corpus Christi and July 25 (St James, or Santiago, Spain's patron saint).

Shopping hours

Most shops, including food shops and tobacconists, are open from 0930 or 1000 until 1330 or 1400 and then from about 1700 to 2000 or 2030. Only the big department stores, such as the Corte Inglés chain, and big hypermarkets do not observe the practice of the long *siesta.* Most shops are closed on Sundays. Petrol stations remain open all day long and tend to stagger their closing-days in each district or township.

Open-air markets, which are held at least once a week in most towns and villages, normally only function in the mornings, until about 1400. In strongly tourist-oriented cities and resort areas, some souvenir shops at least will be open all day long, seven days a week; food shops on camping sites and in villa or apartment developments may open on Sundays but will normally shut for the midday *siesta.*

The particular specialities of a town or area are mentioned in their contexts; as a general rule, best buys are leather goods of all descriptions, including clothing and shoes; ceramics; Havana cigars; tinned olives and olive oil (the best is labelled *Aceite Virgén de Oliva);* pure saffron and other herbs.

Sightseeing hours

Nearly all museums and other sights are closed on Mondays and many close on Sunday afternoons as well; except where this practice varies, I do not specify it in the text. Many are only open in the mornings: from 0930 or (more often) 1000 until 1330 or 1400 (in the local contexts, I say 'mornings only'). Some re-open in the late afternoon, perhaps from 1700 or 1800 to 1900 or 1930 (in the text, 'mornings and afternoons'). If they open earlier, or stay open later (the Roman theatre in Mérida, for instance), or if they do not close for lunch (the Prado in Madrid), I say so. Even so, local authorities have a way of altering the hours without warning, so although my information was correct at the time of writing, it is worth checking with the local tourist information office if you are on a tight schedule. Public-holiday opening hours are usually the same as on Sundays, but on the main festival days many a place remains closed closed all day.

Entrance fees

Entrance fees also have a way of changing; at the time of writing they varied between about 50 and 400 ptas. Few individual visitors qualify for free admission, though some museums will let you in free on production of a student card (it is worth a try) and a few allow free entrance to foreigners resident in Spain.

Sports

Water Sports

Just about every type of water-based sport is available along the Costas, Mediterranean and Atlantic alike, and on many of the man-made lakes inland, particularly those within easy reach of Madrid. From swimming and pottering about in humble pedalos to yachting and dinghy sailing, paragliding, water-skiing, windsurfing, snorkelling and sub-aqua diving – the choice is wide. Marinas, sailing clubs and schools and windsurfing schools abound, and many British tour-firms operate specialist sport-based package holidays.

Tennis, riding, golf

The more sophisticated purpose-built resorts (Sotogrande, La Manga) offer tennis, riding and golf as well as water-sports, and there are other golf courses around Madrid (4) and in the provinces of Andalusía (29), Valencia (10) and Murcia (2). For more details, contact the Real Federación Española de Golf, Capitan Haya 9-5°, 28020 Madrid, or ask the Spanish National Tourist Office. Tennis facilities, attached to tourist developments and municipality-owned alike, are ubiquitous. Specialist companies also offer organised riding, walking and other hobby holidays in the Andalusían hills and there are dozens of other sports that you can pursue independently, each of which (including sports for the disabled) has its own national federation. For a list of these, apply to the Spanish National Tourist Office.

Horse-racing

Among spectator sports other than bullfighting, horse-racing is popular (there are race-courses at Madrid, Seville, Sanlúcar de Barrameda and Valencia) and football is a national obsession.

Bird-watching, fishing, shooting

More sedentary tastes for which Britain's specialist holiday firms cater include bird-watching, botanising and painting; for details of who runs all these out-of-the ordinary holidays, including sporting ones, write to the Spanish National Tourist Office. For those of more esoteric bent, Southern Spain offers excellent shooting: not just partridge, quail, water-fowl and other small game but also deer, wild boar, ibex and mountain goat in season; there is also lake, river and seawater fishing. You will need to have a license from the appropriate authority for these activities; again, the Spanish National Tourist Office can advise you.

Skiing

Skiing is becoming increasingly popular in Spain, perhaps thanks to the enthusiastic example set by King Juan Carlos who is often out on the slopes at winter weekends. Most of the more developed resorts are in the north, in the Pyrenees, but there are four within reach of Madrid – of more interest to residents than transient visitors, since snow-conditions can change rapidly – and one important one, Solynieve, in the mountains above Granada, featured by several winter-sports tour operators. The Winter Sports Federation(Federacion de Deportes de Invierno) is at Claudio Coello 32, Madrid.

Tourism: Provincial Departments; Information Offices

Madrid Province
Dirección General de Turismo, Duque de Medinaceli, 2, 28014-Madrid.

Information offices:
Madrid City: Princesa, 1 Torre de Madrid; tel. 24 12 325
Madrid Airport: tel. 205 86 56
Aranjuez: Plaza de Santiago Rusinol; tel. 89 10 427

Castilla-La Mancha
Dirección General de Turismo, Cuesta de Carlos V, 10-2'-45071, Toledo

Information offices:
Ciudad Real: Alarcos, 31; tel. 21 29 25
Cuenca: Dalmacio Garcia Izcara, 8; tel. 22 22 31
Toledo: Puerta de Bisagra, s/n; tel. 22 08 43

Extremadura
Dirección General de Turismo, Cárdenas, 11, Mérida (Badojoz)

Information offices:
Caceres: Plaza General Mola, s/n; tel. 24 63 47
Caya: Menacho, 12; tel. 22 27 93
Badajoz: Pasaje de San Juan, 1; tel. 22 27 63
Mérida: Puenta, 9; tel. 31 53 53

Andalusía
Dirección General de Turismo, Avda. República Argentina, 31, 41071, Sevilla

Information offices:
Almeria: Hermanos Machado s/n, Edificio Servicios Multiples; tel. 23 47 05
Cádiz: Calderón de la Barca, 1, duplicado; tel. 21 13 13
Algeciras: Avda. Marina s/n; tel. 60 09 11
La Linea: Avda. 20 de Abril s/n (Cádiz); tel. 76 99 50
Córdoba: Torrijos, 10; tel. 47 12 35
Granada: Casa de los Tiros, Pavaneras, 19; tel. 22 10 22
Huelva: Vázquez López, 5; tel. 25 74 03
Jaén: Avda. de Madrid, 10; tel. 22 27 37
Úbeda: Pza. de los Caidos s/n (Jaén); tel. 75 08 97
Baeza: Pza. del Populo s/n (Jaén); tel. 74 04 44

Málaga: Marqués de Larios, 1; tel. 21 34 45/27 68 49
Málaga Airport: tel. 31 20 44/31 60 00
Ronda: Plaza de España, 1 (Málaga); tel. 87 12 72
Torremolinos: Bajos de la Nogalera, Málaga, local 517; tel. 38 15 78
Marbella: Avda. Miguel Cano, 1; tel. 77 14 42/77 46 93
Benalmadena Costa: Carretera Cádiz-Málaga, km. 229 (Málaga); tel. 44 24 94
Sevilla: Avenida de la Constitución, 21; tel. 22 14 04

Levante: Alicante
Dirección General de Turismo, Isabel la Catolica, 8, Valencia 46004

Information offices:
Alicante: Explanada de España, 2; tel. 21 22 85
C/Portugal, 17 Estación Central de Autobuses; tel. 22 38 02/22 07 00
Alicante Airport: tel. 28 50 11 ext 100
Altea: Compte de Altea, Apto. 128; tel. 84 74 34
Benidorm: Avda. Martinez Alejos, 16; tel. 85 13 11/85 32 24
Avda. Panamá, s/n; tel. 85 69 86
Calpe: Avda. Ejérictos Españoles, 66; tel. 83 12 50
Denia: Patricio Ferrandiz, s/n; tel 78 09 57 (Munic) 78 07 24
Elche: Paseo de la Estación, Parque Municipal; tel. 45 27 47
Jávea: Plaza Almirante Bastarreche, 24; tel. 07 36

Levante: Castellón
Dirección General de Turismo, Isabel la Catolica, 8, Valencia 46004

Information offices:
Benicarló: Ayuntamiento Municipal, Plaza San Andrés, s/n; tel. 47 31 80
Benicasim: Paseo Maritimo la Corte; tel. 30 02 44
Castellón de la Plana: María Agustina, 5, bajo; tel. 22 77 03

Levante: Valencia
Dirección General de Turismo, Isabel la Catolica, 8, Valencia 46004

Information offices:
Cullera: Carrer del Riu, 56; tel. 152 09 74
Gandia: San José de Calasanz, 7; tel 287 35 36
Parque de la Estación s/n; tel. 284 24 07 (summer only)
Valencia: Paz, 46; tel. 352 40 00
Manises Airport; tel. 153 03 25
Telephone information service – 352 40 00

General Information

Levante: Murcia
Dirección General de Turismo, Isidoro de la Cierva, 10-2°, 30001-Murcia

Information offices:
Murcia: Alejandro Seiquer, 4; tel. 21 37 16
Cartagena: Ayuntamiento; tel. 50 64 83

The Country and its History

The Country

Spain has the second-highest average altitude in Europe, coming second only to Switzerland; it is very nearly true to say that except in the Guadalquivir basin, a V-shaped depression extending inland from the south-western Atlantic coast to well east of Córdoba, you are never at sea-level unless you are almost within sight of the sea itself. This fact is of minimal importance to the sunseekers who flock to the Costas but of great relevance if you plan to tour, because the mountainous terrain is a determining factor in deciding how much distance you can reasonably expect to cover.

There are high plateaux, notably the vast Meseta around Madrid, of which La Mancha is the south-eastern part, but elsewhere the landscape is unremittingly mountainous. Augustus Hare, whose 'Wanderings in Spain' was published in 1873, constantly refers to the countryside as "hideous" ... "desolated and treeless" ... "barren" ... "dull grey"; clearly mountainscapes were wasted on him.

Re-afforestation has transformed them to some extent, but even the most bare of them reflect the changing light in shades of purple or copper, blue or blue-green, grey and pink, and make shapely frames for every landscape. They are home to a considerable variety of wild fauna including rabbit, hare and fox; deer and roebuck; ibex and mountain goat, and myriad birds.

The principal ranges in the south are the Sierra de Gredos, an extension of the Central Cordillera, lying along the western dividing line between north and south, and the Sierra Morena to the south of them; the Toledo Mountains in the centre; the Serranía de Cuenca in the east, at the southern end of the Iberian Cordillera, and the Sierras that form part of the chain running behind the Mediterranean coast, which includes the Sierras Nevada and Bermeja and the Serranía de Ronda.

Cultivation and Climate

Cultivation on the lower slopes of these mountains and of the plateaux they support is intense: vines, olives, almonds and other fruits; grain and vegetables; grazing pastures in areas where rainfall is reliable; specialist crops like saffron, of which Spain is the world's largest producer.

Despite increasing affluence, reflected in the enormous increase in the use of agricultural machinery, mules and donkeys are still ubiquitous, as beasts of burden and for work in fields where the lie of the land makes mechanical methods impractical. Handsome horses are everyday transport for many country people. Pigs are raised in great numbers in Extremadura, renowned for its hams and other charcuterie; large flocks of goats are frequently seen being herded to graze the scrublands; rural householders keep chickens. Lizards are commonplace, as indeed are flies, but poisonous snakes are rare.

The climate is affected by the topography: that of the central Meseta, with its searing summers and bitter winters, is akin to that of Central Europe; south of the mountainous barriers that seal off the Meseta, it is Mediterranean. Rain is scarce; water is assured by the damming of the region's major rivers: the Guadiana and Guadalquivir in the west, the Turia, Júcar and Segura in the east – and in exceptionally dry seasons the Guadiana and the three latter rivers can be reduced to next to nothing by the time they reach the sea. However, care has been taken to landscape and plant the verges of the man-made lakes formed by the dams; many attract numbers of weekenders and holidaymakers. And despite the aridity the variety of flora to be seen in the spring is staggeringly rich: hillsides smothered in cistus and broom sloping down to fields and roadsides brilliantly carpeted with all manner of other wild flowers.

Coastal Regions

Along the coast, over-fishing has depleted stocks in the Mediterranean but Spaniards are great connoisseurs of fish, which they adore, and you can be confident that what is set before you will be fresh. The Mediterranean beaches, with few exceptions, owe their popularity more to their accessibility, climate and amenities than to their inherent qualities; at best their sand is dun-coloured and somewhat gritty; at worst, they are pebbly or stony. The Atlantic beaches are finer, paler and, on the whole less developed, but they are also windier and the sea-currents present more hazards to bathers. Overall, however, the number of Spanish beaches meeting EEC standards of cleanliness is rising steadily.

History

Celts to Carthaginians

That Spain has been inhabited since prehistoric times is evident from the many cave-paintings to be found all over the country and, thanks to its rich mineral deposits, there is evidence of trade in metals between south-western Spain and Brittany, Cornwall and Ireland. Celtic invaders from the north and emigrants from North Africa arrived in mainland Spain between the 7th and 3rd centuries BC to mix with its Iberian population (the Carthaginians, from what is now Tunisia, had colonised the island of Ibiza).

From the Eastern Mediterranean came the Greeks and, in 1000 BC, the Phoenicians, who sailed between the Pillars of Hercules to land at Cádiz and found a colony there. The indigenous inhabitants revolted againsts them in about 500 BC but were crushed with the help of Carthaginian troops from Ibiza; a military expedition that resulted in the establishment (by Hasdrubal, ancestor of Hannibal) of the colony of New Carthage on the mainland, its capital at Cartagena.

Roman rule

Next came the Romans, who were defeated by Hannibal at Sagunto in 219 BC, sparking off the Second Punic War, but who conquered New Carthage in 209 BC and finally routed the Carthaginians for good eight years later. They made Córdoba their administrative capital and ruled Spain for three centuries; three Roman Emperors were of Spanish birth, including Hadrian, best known for the wall he built in his reign across the northern part of Britain. Towards the end of the Roman era, during which Christianity had spread throughout Spain, waves of invaders crossed the Pyrenees, including the Vandals, whose kingdom of Vandalusia is present-day Andalusía, the Goths and the Visigoths.

Moslem invasion

It was the Visigothic King Rodrigo, or Roderick, whose defeat at the Battle of Guadalete in 711 AD opened all Spain to the Moorish invaders from North Africa. The first arrivals came at the invitation of rebellious Visigothic chieftains up in arms against Rodrigo; having helped to defeat the king, the newcomers were so taken with the fairness and fertility of the country that they not only stayed themselves but were followed by a succession of others. The first half-century of the Moorish presence in Spain was consequently marked not just by battles between Moslems and Christians but also by repeated skirmishes between the different tribes of invaders. (It is perhaps worth pointing out here that the name 'Moors', whose use is so widespread that it seems pointless to substitute anything else, is in fact misleading: these invaders were not from Mauritania but from Islamic North Africa.)

In 755, the last remaining member of the Ummayyads (one of the three warring families claiming descent from the Prophet Mohammed) found his way to Spain from Damascus, where the rival Abbasids were in power. This was Abderrahman I, who soon brought Spain's other Moslems to heel and established an Emirate, later to become a Caliphate, with its capital at Córdoba. Under his descendants this lasted for some 250 years, and under Abderrahman III (in whose veins ran more than a little pure Spanish blood, for Moslems and Christians lived in reasonable amity for a long time and much inter-marrying took place) it was the most brilliant and learned court in Europe. But it eventually disintegrated and Moorish Spain split into about 30 semi-autonomous kingdoms, or *taifas,* that spent at least as much time quarrelling among themselves as they did in fighting off the Christians of the north; indeed, it was not uncommon for Moslem and Christian kings to become allies against a common enemy of either faith from time to time.

For a brief period in the 11th/12th centuries the Almoravides, sweeping in from North Africa, managed to reunite Moslem Spain, but within 50 years it had split once more into individual *taifas;* the next tribe of unifying invaders (the fanatical Almohades) were only successful for an equally brief period.

Christian Reconquest

The reconquest of Moslem Spain in the name of Christianity started in the North, where a small part of the country had succeeded in resisting the invaders. The Christian monarchs and their forces were greatly reinforced by the faithful from elsewhere, for whom the religious struggle in Spain not only presented an opportunity to gain distinction (and perhaps rich plunder too) but also took on the nature of a crusade. This was largely thanks to a well-organised campaign by the Church in other Western European countries. The miraculous 'discovery' of the sarcophagus of St James at Santiago de Compostela, and the equally miraculous appearances of the Saint in battle against the Moors, were skilfully exploited to enlist the support of Christian forces from other lands, including Britain.

The Reconquest lasted almost as long as the Moorish occupation – nearly 800 years – during which time cities and even kingdoms frequently changed hands. By 1250 most of Southern Spain had been reconquered except for Granada, but for the next 225-odd years strife between the Christian Kingdoms halted further unified progress in the holy war against Islam.

In 1469 Ferdinand of Castile married Isabella of Aragón, thus uniting the two most important Christian kingdoms of the North under these 'Catholic Monarchs', so-called because neither ranked above the other, and in 1492 they finally conquered Granada and expelled the last Moorish king, Boabdil.

Religious Persecution

It had been necessary to fuel popular Christian fervour by all possible means in order to bring the Reconquest to its successful conclusion, but the consequences of this fanatical crusading were deeply unfortunate. Christians and Jews, of whom there were large numbers in Spain, had co-existed peacefully with the tolerant Moslems, but during the latter part of the Reconquest Christians were already becoming rabidly opposed to members of other faiths.

Persecution and expulsion of Jews had taken place even under the Visigoths; in the later stages of the Reconquest the practice took a different form. Ferdinand and Isabella were chronically short of funds with which to keep the war going and the Jews, as well as being among the most cultured people in Spain, were the wealthiest. If they would not abjure their faith and make generous donations to the coffers of the Catholic Kings as proof of their sincerity, they were burned. An official order expelling all practising Jews was issued in 1492.

Moslems, who had under the terms of Boabdil's surrender been allowed to stay, became victims of religious persecution only a few years later and many took up arms in revolt. In 1502 an order was issued compelling them, too, to accept baptism or leave the country; most of them chose the former course but another rebellion of *Moriscos* (Moorish Christians) in the mountains south of Granada some 65 years later ended in their being forcibly ejected from their villages. The Church-led Inquisition, established in 1480, tortured and put to death thousands of 'heretics', including Protestants, for over 200 years, even after the final expulsion of *Moriscos* in 1609.

Habsburgs and Empires

Ferdinand and Isabella's descendants maintained the same religious zeal while bringing Spain to the pinnacle of its power. They were succeeded by their grandson, Charles I of Spain, later the Holy Roman Emperor Charles V, as he is more usually known. His mother Juana (or Joan) had married the son of Austria's Emperor Maximilian and gone mad following her husband's death; when her son succeeded at the age of 16 (in 1516) he not only became King of Spain (where, having been brought up in Flanders, he was a total stranger) but also of much of what is now southern Italy. Three years later, when his Austrian grandfather died and he was elected Holy Roman Emperor, his extended realm included present-day Belgium and the Netherlands and part of France. In addition, of course, Spanish *conquistadores,* many from Extremadura, had by this time carved out a huge South American empire for Spain and taken possession of parts of North America as well.

Charles V was frequently at war: with France, to protect his European possessions; with the Protestants of Germany, where he failed to suppress the Reformation; with revolutionaries, notably the *communeros,* in Spain itself. His son and successor, Philip II, is best known for the defeat of his attempted sea-invasion of England, the Armada, but he also waged almost incessant war: against the Protestants of the Low Countries, among others; against the Portuguese, whom he invaded; and against the Muslim Turks, defeated by his half-brother Don Juan of Austria at the Battle of Lepanto in 1571.

Loss of Netherlands, French possessions

By the time Philip II died in 1598 the might of Spain was being eroded by debt, so costly had his wars and extravagant building projects proved, and his descendants were too weak to reverse the decline. During the 17th century Spain lost the Netherlands and, after the Thirty Years War, most of its French possessions. In spite of royal Franco-Spanish marriages (Elisabeth of Bourbon married Philip IV, his sister Anne of Austria married Louis XIII, and Philip IV's daughter, Maria Teresa, wed Louis XIV), there were further wars between Spain and France, stripping Spain of yet more of her territories.

The War of Succession

Charles II of Spain died without heir in 1700, having bequeathed his crown to Philip of Anjou, grandson of Louis XIV and Maria Teresa and ignored the counter-claim by the Holy Roman Empire candidate, the Archduke Charles. This sparked off the War of the Spanish Succession in which most of the countries of Europe allied themselves to fight the possibility of France and Spain becoming united. Spain lost more of her foreign possessions and forfeited others (including Gibraltar) under the Treaty of Utrecht which ended the war in 1713. Philip of Anjou ascended the Spanish throne as Philip V in the following year, bringing a host of strong French influences with him, and for the next 75 years Spain was relatively peaceful and competently governed.

The Peninsular War (War of Independence)

The next series of disasters was ushered in by the accession of the weak and decadent Charles IV, whose authority the Queen, Maria Luisa, and her lover Godoy, the chief Minister, had no trouble in usurping. There was more fighting against France, more territorial losses – mostly in the New World. In 1801 Godoy allowed the French to pass through Spain to attack Portugal; naturally they took parts of Spain as well. Godoy sought to buy peace with France after Napoleon had made himself Emperor in 1804 but by this time England had involved herself and the combined French and Spanish fleet was decimated by Admiral Lord Nelson at the Battle of Trafalgar in 1805.

Three years later Napoleon dismissed the King and placed his own brother, Joseph, on the Spanish throne. Now the people of Spain themselves rebelled, starting with the famous Madrid uprising on May 2, brutally put down on the following day by French troops; both dates are commemorated by Goya's magnificent *'Dos de Mayo'* and *'Tres de Mayo'* paintings in the Prado Museum in Madrid.

In the same year, at the invitation of the provincial government of Seville, later backed throughout Andalusía, England sent troops to the Peninsula to assist Spain in ridding herself of the French. Their commander, Sir Arthur Wellesley, later Duke of Wellington, was first concerned to make a secure base of Portugal (and particularly Lisbon); not until he had achieved this did he push into Spain, in July of 1809 (Battle of Talavera). By the following year he was again fighting off the French in Portugal and along the frontier; his major offensive in Spain started in January of 1812 at Ciudad Rodrigo, just outside the territory covered by this book. He took Badajoz in the same year, then Salamanca and Madrid, and had driven the French back across the Pyrenees by the autumn of 1813.

The Carlist Wars

Spain's South American colonies had taken advantage of the war to declare their independence; by the time the Bourbon King Ferdinand VII (son of Charles IV) had been restored to the throne the country was severely weakened. Ferdinand, unwisely, abolished all constitutional reforms and attempted to rule as an absolute monarch, crushing repeated liberal uprisings (the one at Cádiz was the most effective; Ferdinand was even imprisoned there for a short time).

When he died in 1833 leaving the Queen, Maria Christina, as regent for the infant heir, Isabella, short-lived governments of varying political persuasions failed to get to grips with the country's problems and there were numerous disturbances. These were further compounded by two bitter internal wars of succession, the Carlist Wars, between the supporters of Ferdinand's brother Carlos (hence 'Carlist') and supporters of Isabella (and of the principle that a woman could inherit). When Isabella finally came to the throne, political stability remained as elusive as before and the royal family was exiled in 1868. Amadeo of Savoy was invited to become king but his reign was challenged yet again by Carlos (the third Carlist War) and lasted only three years. A Republic was proclaimed and another king invited to the throne, this time the Pretender to Isabella's line, who became Alfonso XII.

Spanish-American War; Spanish Republic

During his 11-year reign (he died at 28), the regency of his widow, Maria Christina, and the first 20 years of the reign of his son, Alfonso

XIII, the only serious disturbance was the 1898 Spanish-American War, in which Spain lost Cuba, Puerto Rico and the Philippines. But after World War One, in which Spain remained neutral, trouble broke out in Spanish North Africa and a General, Miguel Primo de Rivera, backed by the King, took control. When his popularity waned and he went into exile his successor proved less effective; municipal elections in 1931 resulted in a huge victory for the Republicans and the King abdicated.

Civil unrest

Two years later, however, discontent was rife within the army, the right wing was becoming more militant, regions in the north (Asturias, Catalonia and the Basque Country) were agitating for reforms and autonomy and, in February of 1936, a Popular Front party, uniting all the left-wing elements, won power. The right-wing element walked out of the Cortes (Parliament) and the leader of its militant wing, José Antonio Primo de Rivera, son of the former dictator, was imprisoned; the Monarchist leader, José Calvo Sotelo, was assassinated; bitterly divided allegiances throughout the country made civil war inevitable.

The Civil War and afterwards

It was Spain's youngest general, Francisco Franco Bahamonde, then stationed in the Canary Islands, who made the radio announcement on July 18, 1936, that the Army was in revolt. Two days later he came back to Spain at the head of a large force to take command of operations in the south. There followed three years of appalling conflict in which the idealogical cause of the left, seen as battling bravely but fruitlessly against the military might of the Fascists, was championed by intellectuals all over the world.

Franco had in 1934 been called in to deal with an uprising of miners in Asturias and had done so swiftly and cruelly; his conduct in and immediately after the Civil War, which he won in April, 1939, was no less efficient and ruthless. Apart from giving token support to his fellow-dictators in Italy and Germany (both Mussolini and Hitler had obliged him in 1937, the latter by sending German bombers to carry out the first-ever raid on a civilian target, Guernica in the north), Franco kept Spain out of World War Two and in isolation for most of the decade that followed it, to lick her wounds and regain a modicum of stability. Not until 1953, when the United States persuaded Franco into allowing the establishment of US military bases there, did Spain's wall of isolation begin to crack. The country needed the economic aid that came with the bases, and in 1955 Spain became a member of the United Nations.

Economic improvement; restoration of monarchy

The next influx of economic aid came from tourism, which Franco and his hard-line, intensely moralistic, supporters saw as a mixed blessing, bringing as it did in its wake all sorts of liberal, not to say sinful, ideas and customs. But it was impossible to keep social changes at bay for ever, particularly as Spain also needed to attract foreign investment to build up industry, a process that started in the early 1970s.

Franco hung on to absolute power until his death in 1975, at the age of 82. He had already chosen as his successor the son of the Royal Pretender (and grandson of Alfonso XIII and his English Queen, Ena). To that end, he had had Prince Juan Carlos educated in Spain, under his own close personal supervision.

After the old man's death and to the surprise of a great many people, both inside and outside Spain, the new King proved himself to be not only committed to democracy but strong enough to steer his country towards it. Franco's opponents had already begun to make themselves heard towards the end of his 50-year dictatorship and, although there were political hiccoughs to begin with, Spain is now a stable constitutional monarchy. A soft-line Socialist government is in its third term of office, headed by a lawyer from Seville, Felipe González. The country's 17 autonomous regions have varying degrees of self-government; industry looks healthier and, with it, the economy. Spain now belongs to NATO and, since January 1, 1986, has been a member of the EEC.

Social changes

To those who knew the country in Franco's era, the social changes whose start even he could not stem have snowballed at incredible speed, not all of them, inevitably, for the better. There is more widespread prosperity, better social benefits. Young people are less shackled, have access to all sorts of entertainment that would previously have been denied or censored (and have in consequence become less blindly devout); women are increasingly liberated. On the other hand, the cities are plagued with the same problems as those everywhere: anarchic traffic, increased crime, drug-taking. As in most other countries, you need to get out into the rural areas to listen to the true heartbeat of Spain.

Architecture

Moorish

Rome's architectural legacy to southern Spain, most of it found in Extremadura and Andalusía, is of considerable interest, but the country's unique glory lies in what remains of the Moorish occupation: the brilliant palaces and mosques of Granada, Seville, Córdoba and elsewhere. Equally unique is the architecture of the *mudéjars* (Moslems), working for Christian masters, who continued to use their traditional art-forms until they were partly superseded by the arrival of the Gothic style from France, see page 209.

Mudéjar is the standard term for these arabesque art-forms applied to Christian buildings, whose basic shapes remained for a long time Romanesque, as adapted by the Christian Visigoths. *Mudéjar* work appears in early Gothic buildings, too, and even in Baroque ones; its distinguishing characteristic is the use of very simple materials such as brick and wood and plaster, skilfully worked into patterns to achieve rich and sophisticated effects – and, of course, the substitution of the keyhole arch for the rounded Romanesque one.

Other standard architectural terms used in the text include *artesonado* (marquetry work in the Moorish idiom, used particularly for ceilings, most of them either *alfraje,* resting on crossbeams, or coffred, consisting of sunken panels); *azulejo* (decorative ceramic tiling); *ajimez* (twin-arched, mostly applied to Moorish windows divided by a column); Alcázar and Alcazaba (Moorish citadel or palace) and Alameda (park or public garden). An art-form and architecture less often found is the *mozarabe,* or mozarabic, perpetrated by Christians under Moorish rule, who were called *mozarabes.*

Gothic and later

When it comes to describing Gothic, Baroque and later buildings, I have used several current Spanish words, chiefly to help people who might ask to see a particular feature: the *coro* (chancel, or choir, more often than not heavily enclosed, forming a building-within-a-building), *capilla mayor* (sacristy, where the high altar is), *retablo* (altarpiece); *sala capitular* (chapter house). And again, because you may have occasion to ask where it is (Tourist Information Offices are often situated in it), I have more often than not used the Spanish word *Ayuntimiento* for the Town Hall.

Background Reading

A number of books I have read while researching this one have given me especial pleasure and I have quoted freely from them where it seemed relevant. For those who might want to share my enjoyment, I list them below – with the warning that some are only obtainable second-hand, or from libraries:

'Handbook for Spain 1845', Richard Ford, 3 volumes, ed by Ian Robertson; Centaur Press 1966. Encyclopedic, quirky, often very funny.

'Gatherings from Spain', Richard Ford; Dent Everyman's Library. The abbreviated version.

'Companion Guide to the South of Spain', Alfonso Lowe; Collins. Agreeably idiosyncratic, in the manner of this excellent series.

'Cook's Handbook for Spain', A.F. Calvert; Thomas Cook, 1921. Early guide book by a noted Hispanophile, full of purple prose.
'Badeker's Spain and Portugal' – any early edition (mine is 1913). Full of sound, if out of date, Teutonic advice.
'A Stranger in Spain', H.V. Morton; Methuen. Journeyings by one of the most amiable and polished of 20th-century travel-writers.
'Wanderings in Spain', Augustus Hare, 1873. More journeyings, full of interesting sidelights on life in 19th-century Spain.
'The Bible in Spain', George Borrow, 1842; Century paperback edition, 1985. Chronicles of "the humble circulator" of the Gospels, rich in picaresque anecdotes.
'Dictionary of the Napoleonic Wars', David G. Chandler; Arms & Armour Press. A mine of information, not all of it on Spain; likewise his later 'Guide to the Battlefields of Europe', edited by David Chandler; Patrick Stephens, 1989.
'English Battles & Sieges in the Peninsula', Lt Gen Sir William Napier, KCB, (popular edition); John Murray; a treasure-house of soldierly prose.
'The Conquest of Granada', Washington Irving, 1910; Dent Everyman Library. History irresistibly romanticised, not to say occasionally fictionalised, and ironically funny.
'Spain', Sacheverell Sitwell; Batsford. Learned, relaxed and elegant.
'Spain', Jan Morris; Faber & Faber. One of this celebrated writer's best offerings.
'Silk Hats & No Breakfast', and 'Winter In Seville', both by Honor Tracy; Methuen. Acute observation, recounted with unfailing wit.
In addition, a wealth of comment and description from other past travellers has been gathered by David Mitchell into 'Here in Spain', published by Lookout Publications of Fuengirola (Malaga).

The Royal Palace, Madrid

Madrid: City and Southern Environs

The City of Madrid

Origins and Modernisation

Madrid (pop. c 3,200,000) is not only the highest of European capitals (over 650 metres, or about 2,000 feet) but also one of the newest: a fortress-post that gradually grew into a minor satellite of Toledo and found favour with Charles V because its climate suited his gout. "No situation can possibly be more odious to ordinary mortals," wrote Augustus Hare, but in fact the climate is not always vile, particularly in spring and autumn.

Charles's son, Philip II, established his court there in 1560 and for nearly 400 years the city kept much the same appearance and modest proportions acquired during its first century of existence; not until well after World War Two did it embark on the explosive expansion that has characterised the past three decades. Currently much effort is being put into bringing the resultant near-chaos under control in anticipation of 1992 when Madrid has been designated European Cultural Capital: monuments, squares, museums and theatres are being refurbished and new additions planned; there are ambitious plans to erase "urban traumas" (I quote from an official leaflet) by creating more green spaces, pedestrianising more streets, sending traffic underground and providing more parking.

Where to Stay

Meanwhile, the excellent Metro (underground) system makes it a manageable city for tourists who, provided they are reasonably near a Metro station, can reach most of the major sights easily wherever they are staying.

Obviously, most prefer to be near the centre, and at the top end of the range the Ritz is incomparably the best (and conveniently next door to the Prado Museum), followed by the Palace just across the same street, Paseo del Prado. A little further north of them is the more modest Alcalá, on the edge of the Retiro Park and with a good Basque restaurant. At the opposite (Plaza de España/Royal Palace) side of the city centre the modern Meliá Madrid on Princesa, near the Americas museum, is a five-star business hotel; not far from it, on the corner of Tutor and Calle Ventura Rodriguez, the Pullman Calatrava is also modern and more budget-priced. In the centre, near Plaza de Sta Ana, the old-established and atmospheric Victoria is good value. Restaurants I shall mention in their geographical context; where one is at mealtimes is a crucial factor in choosing. If you are there in winter, try to eat the delicious Madrid speciality, *cocido,* an elaborate casserole of various meats, sausage, chicken and vegetables.

Old Quarters

All distances in Spain are measured from Madrid's Puerta del Sol; it is the logical place to begin ('everybody must' said Ford, firmly). It is not much to look at, its central islands and fountains notwithstanding, but it is the historic centre of the city and a valuable orientation-point. Southeast of it, in the little streets between it and the Plaza de Sta Ana, are some of the most typical of Madrid's *tapa*-bars: Echegaray and its neighbouring streets are full of them. In one such street, S Jeronimo, you will also find one of Madrid's oldest restaurants, Lhardy's, founded in 1839 by a Swiss *patissier* and famous for its beautiful mirrors and chandeliers.

Plaza Mayor

Off the western end of the Puerta del Sol runs the Calle Mayor and from it three narrow alleys lead through archways into the Plaza

Mayor, Philip III's harmonious 17th-century square, modelled on the Place des Vosges in Paris, and one of the city's few traffic-free oases. At the time of writing, it was being given a face-lift and painted a glowing *sang-de-boeuf* pink, but work had not banished all the café tables and it is a good spot for resting, surveying the playing children and the strollers who provide the constant animation, and thinking of the more dramatic past scenes it has witnessed.

Autos-da-fe, or public confessions of heresy, were held here under the Inquisition; one such, in June of 1680, lasted from dawn until dusk. It has also witnessed public demonstrations and executions, ceremonials and spectacles – including the bullfight staged in 1623 for England's Charles I, then Prince of Wales, when he came to court the Infanta Maria. The north side of the square is dominated by a rather grander building than the others, with two little towers: it is called the *panaderia,* after the bakery that originally stood there, and its balconies were used as Royal Boxes for spectacles. At the more important of these the King, by tradition, presented "a collation in appropriate baskets" and elegant gifts to the grander spectators, which brought the cost of a spectacle to "more than 100,000 crowns," according to the writer Mme d'Aulnoy, whose account of 17th-century Spain was a best-seller for over 100 years. Nowadays, the commonest regular spectacle is the Sunday stamp- and coin-market.

Calle de Toledo

Opposite the *panaderia,* Calle de Toledo is one of the more attractive of Madrid's older streets, leading to the *barrio bajo,* or "lower" (in the geographical sense) quarter. Typical restaurants in this area include Botin and Las Cuevas de Luis Candelas in two of the tall, thin old houses that line Cuchilleros, and Los Galayos in Botoneras, all within a few paces of the Plaza Mayor. Halfway down Calle de Toledo is San Isidro, a dull 17th-century church that was raised to cathedral status in the last century.

Flea market, Boutiques

Beyond San Isidro a left fork leads downhill to where the Sunday morning flea-market, El Rastro, is held ("one of the largest rag-fairs in the world", says the 1913 Baedeker). Further downhill, the old fish-market by the Puerta de Toledo gate has been transformed into a shopping centre, full of antique shops and designer boutiques. Further downhill again, it crosses the Manzanares river by the Puente de Toledo, which Sacheverell Sitwell calls "one of the most fantastic and magnificent creations of decadent architecture". Unfortunately, it accentuates the puniness of the Manzanares, "which," says Augustus Hare, "can scarcely be called a river."

Three major churches

Coming back uphill, off Calle de Toledo to the west the Gran Via de San Francisco leads to the church of the same name, whose nave chapels were decorated by the young Goya. It was designed as a pantheon on the lines of Rome's but badly redecorated in the last century; it is being restored. A more interesting church is the Gothic Capilla del Obispo, on the pleasant Plaza del Marqués de Comillas (a Michelin-starred Basque restaurant, Gure-Etxea, is alongside it). Slightly further north, San Pedro has one of the only two *mudéjar* towers in Madrid.

Plaza de la Villa

Just downhill to the west of San Pedro, in Plaza de la Cruz Verde, is one of Madrid's many attractive fountains. From here you can climb the steps to picturesque Plazuela San Javier and thence via Plazuela del Cordón to Plaza de la Villa, with several historic buildings. The Lujanes Tower is a reconstruction of the one in which François I of France was imprisoned after Pavia (1525), one of the many battles he had with Charles V; only the door is original. Next to it is the city newspaper-library, opposite is the 17th-century City Hall, and alongside that is the Casa de Cisneros, with a handsome window overlooking Plazuela del Cordón.

Puerta del Sol to the Royal Palace

Convent of the Descalzes Reales

Two of the city's busiest shopping streets run northwest out of the Puerta del Sol, Preciados and Carmen, and just to the west of Preciados is the Convent of Descalzes Reales, open in the mornings and some afternoons. Built in the 16th century as a country house for Charles V and later turned into an aristocratic nunnery by his daughter Juana, part of it still houses an enclosed order and part is open to the public. It is extraordinarily interesting, but unfortunately, limited time is allowed for each guided tour and some guides try to cram too many facts into it, resulting in a machine-gun volley of commentary that even a Spaniard cannot fully take in.

The beautiful floors and beamed ceilings are original; there are Coello frescoes over the opulent staircase; a series of small chapels ("each cared for by a different nun") line the upstairs cloister. Room after room is hung with paintings good and bad – among the good being a Zurbarán St Francis, a Titian, a Breughel Adoration and, in the *salon del rey*, with a lovely *mudéjar* frieze, several portraits. Another room is hung with Rubens tapestries; one tiny chapel is full of jewel-boxes and another is crammed with reliquaries containing small portions of long-dead saints. a brief look from a window reveals a neat garden, planted with rows of vegetables; one longs to have more time to absorb everything more thoroughly.

Convent of the Incarnation

Less rich in treasures and thus easier to take in is the Convent of the Incarnation, a short walk away to the west behind a small, shady *plaza* off Calle de Bolsa and open in the mornings and most weekday afternoons. Founded in 1611, it has a charming cloister, a Baroque church and some good Spanish paintings. Its most astonishing sight, however, is the Reliquary Room, lined from floor to painted ceiling with shelves holding some 1,500 examples. Some are macabre jumbles of bones intertwined with artificial flowers and encased in glass boxes, others are elaborate kitsch, yet others are exquisite examples of the jeweller's art, never mind whether they are to your taste or not. Most venerated are one containing a phial of the blood of St Panteleon, believed to liquify once a year, and one encasing a fragment of the True Cross in a silver crucifix studded with tiny jewels.

Royal Palace (Palacio Real)

The convent is only a few steps from the Royal Palace, across the delightful gardens of the Plaza de Oriente with its splendid equestrian statue of Philip IV (based on drawings by Velázquez and cast in Florence), its back to the Opera House. The Palace is open daily, mornings and afternoons, including Mondays but not on public holidays or state occasions.

Guided tours of the State rooms, less rushed than the Descalzes Real tours, reveal Tiepolo frescoes, magnificent tapestries and plasterwork, silverware and porcelain, an extraordinary variety of chandeliers and an equally unusual collection of royal clocks (there are over 200 of them). Notable rooms include the State banqueting hall, Gasparini's 'Chinese' room with its high-relief ceiling, another Gasparini room, a small salon entirely lined with ceramic work, the Chapel and the Blue Room with its four Goya royal portraits. Other superb paintings include portraits by Van Loo, Winterhalter, Rubens and Van Dyck and canvases by Caravaggio, El Greco, Luca Giordano, Bosch, Mengs, Morales, Velázquez and Zurbarán.

South of the Palace is the still-unfinished new Cathedral of Our Lady of La Almudena.

Galician Restaurants

If you come back eastwards from the Palace, towards the Puerta del Sol, a network of charming little streets and squares to the north and south of Calle del Arenal include two that, between them, cross it: Bordadores and San Martín. Both are worth heading for if you feel like a different sort of culinary experience for, among their several restaurants, are two that specialise in Galician food: Pazo de Gondomar on San Martín and Casa Gallega on Bordadores.

Plaza de Espana Area

Calle de Bailén, to be freed eventually of its constant traffic, runs due north and south past the Royal Palace just at the point where the city starts to slope downhill to the Manzanares; there are fine views westwards towards the Casa de Campo park on the other side of the river. The north end of Bailén terminates in the Plaza de España, a green, gently sloping square with an interesting modern sculpture of Don Quixote and Sancho Panza at its centre, and a Tourist Information Office in the north corner (on Princesa).

Cerralbo Museum

In the western corner of the Plaza, entered from Calle de Ferraz, is the Cerralbo Museum, open until late Spanish lunchtime. Housed in a former private mansion and too often ignored (I had it almost to myself one May morning) it has a sumptuous collection of furniture, porcelain, pictures, tapestries, chandeliers, clocks and all manner of priceless *bric-à-brac* collected by generations of the same family. A beautiful El Greco of St Francis dominates the simple chapel; the wealth of other paintings include canvases by Tintoretto, Van Dyck, Zurbarán, Ribalta, Ribera and Herrera the Younger. There are carved ceilings and polished creaky floors, an enchanting two-tiered library, a reception salon with musicians' gallery, and more besides.

Round the corner from it, in Calle Ventura Rodriguez, the Restaurant/Bar Marejada has a huge selection of *tapas* which it serves in generous portions.

Egyptian Temple; Goya's St Anthony frescoes

Across Ferraz is the southern end of the big Parque del Oeste and, on a grassy plateau, the small 4th-century BC Egyptian Temple of Debod, presented to Spain to save it from disappearing beneath the waters of the Aswan Dam.

Above the treetops to the north you can see the cable-car that connects this park with the huge Casa de Campo (boating lake, zoo, sports facilities) across the river, and if you walk steeply downhill through the trees beneath the cable-car, past the rose-garden, and across the railway tracks at the bottom, you come to the twin chapels of San Antonio de la Flórida, one a modern copy of the other. In the dome of the older church (closed for restoration at the time of writing) are Goya's urbane frescoes of the miracle of St Anthony, in which the saint and the man he is raising from the dead are of secondary importance to the sophisticated, courtly crowd of onlookers. Goya himself is buried in the chapel.

Liria Palace; Museum of the Americas

From the north corner of the Plaza de España Calle de la Princesa runs towards the University City with two more noteworthy sights on its east side. The Liria Palace, screened by trees just opposite the Meliá Madrid hotel, is a post-war reconstruction of the 18th-century residence of the Dukes of Alba, ("of Berwik and Alba", a plaque in the wall reads), which was destroyed during the Civil War. Fortunately the treasures in the house were saved; they include important paintings and, although redecoration was in progress at the time of writing, prior applications by letter are rewarded by permission to visit on certain days.

Further up the avenue, and also closed for refurbishing at the time of writing, is the Museum of the Americas, with a rich collection of pre-Columbian art.

Northeast of the Puerta del Sol

Calle de Alcalá; Plaza del Rey

From the eastern corner of Plaza de Espana the Gran Via runs westwards to join Alcalá, bisecting central Madrid. Not so very long ago, Alcalá used to be a favourite place for sitting at pavement cafés and watching the world go by, but heavy traffic has put paid to that pleasure. At the Puerta del Sol end of Alcalá is the Fine Arts Museum (Real Academia de Bellas Artes de San Fernando), an imposing building, open all day every day except Saturday and Monday afternoons, containing some good Goyas and Zurbaráns, among others.

If you walk eastwards along Alcalá, just past its junction with the Gran Via, the narrow Calle Barquillo leads to the Plaza del Rey, and at the other end of this is the Casa de las Siete Chimeneas ('Seven Chimneys', rebuilt), the English Ambassador's residence in 1623 when his future King Charles I arrived without warning, against all the rules of etiquette, to pay court to Charles IV's sister, the Infanta Maria. Charles stayed there until a suitable protocol had been devised to cover the unusual situation, then moved to a suite of rooms in the Palace.

National Archaeological Museum

North again, by Plaza de Colón with its statue of the discoverer of America and its succession of waterfalls (Madrid is rich in fountains) is the National Archaeological Museum, open in the mornings. Beautifully laid out, it includes some wonderful early pieces, notably the massive, stone-carved Iberian mother-goddesses of the 4th century BC, the Dama de Baza and the Dama de Elche.

There are masses of other magnificent pieces: Iberian bronze votives from the 5th century BC, a beautiful little bronze bull from Teruel, 4th-century BC pewter, delicate 7th-century BC jewellery from Cáceres in Extremadura (the Aliseda treasure), unique Visigothic votive crowns and crucifixes, and even a full-scale reproduction of the prehistoric Altamira painted cave. It is a real treasure-house, and never anything like so crowded as the Prado.

Lazaró Galdiano Museum

Northwards, off Serrano, is an attractive grid of chic 19th-century streets full of shops, restaurants and *tapa*-bars and, further up Serrano, where it crosses Maria de Molina, the Lazaró Galdiano Museum. Outstanding in this once-private art collection are the enamels and ivories from Byzantine times to the 16th century; the medieval gold and silverwork, the Renaissance jewellery and *objets d'art,* the superb paintings and many other treasures.

Natural Science and Sorolla Museums

In the same area, close by it, are the Natural Science Museum (closed for alterations at the time of writing) and the Sorolla Museum, where sunlit seascapes by the turn-of-the-century Valencian painter are displayed in his former home and studio.

The Prado

The Prado Museum (open day-long except Mondays and some public holiday afternoons, free entrance on Wednesdays), has become so popular that, to have any hope of avoiding the crowds (which include boisterous school groups in term-time as well as tourist ones), you must be on the doorstep by opening time at 0900.

International collection

It is not, of course, purely a museum of Spanish paintings; it ranks high among the world's great art galleries. Monarch after monarch enriched the collection: Ferdinand and Isabella with Flemish paintings; Charles V and Philip II with Italian ones (both Titian and Tintoretto were invited to work in Spain, as was Tiepolo later). Philip IV bought a large part of the collection amassed by England's Charles I and sold after his execution; there are later Flemish canvases by Rubens and Van Dyck, Rembrandts, Poussins, Claude Lorrains and Watteaus. "It seems as if a year were too short to examine the contents," says Richard Ford.

Spanish paintings

For visitors, however, the Spanish paintings must be of paramount interest: the Coellos, Murillos, Zurbaráns, Canos, Morales and Riberas and many others, but especially the El Grecos, the matchless range of

Goyas (light-hearted tapestry cartoons, sombre studies of fear and poverty, horror-suffused Peninsular War scenes like the *'Dos de Mayo'* and *'Tres de Mayo'* the languorous *Majas,* among others) and the greatest works of the great Velázquez.

Royal portraits
I am particularly drawn by the portraits of Spanish kings and queens and their contemporaries, often spanning several decades in the same person's life. To take an extreme example: Mengs painted a lovely alert 13-year-old, Maria Luisa of Parma, just before her marriage to Charles IV in 1765 (to see it, ask to be shown to the Mengs room, which can be visited on request but is not part of the normal itinerary). Then come downstairs to the Goya portraits and look at the dreadful, ageing Messalina he so often caricatured some 35 years later: what did the king and Godoy, her lover, between them do to her?

Charles V and his son, the lugubrious Philip II are portrayed several times, the latter also at several stages of his life, and three of his wives are there (including the plain Mary Tudor, brilliantly painted by Antonio Moro). Portraits of his children include the sad Don Carlos, the subject of Schiller's tragedy and of the opera Verdi based on it, the enchanting Clara Eugenia Isabella, and Coello's study of the little Caterina Michaela, daughter of Elisabeth de Valois.

Velazquez portraits
The Velázquez royal portraits are fantastic, of course: there is Philip III astride a windblown grey and several of Philip IV, including the splendid equestrian one that was the model for the statue in the Plaza de Oriente. Philip IV's two wives are there: Isabella of Bourbon in rich brocade and Mariana of Austria with her mass of curls; Philip's children, the short-lived Don Balthazar, Isabella's son, proudly shouldering a gun and riding a horse, and Mariana's daughter Maria Margherita, the centrepiece of 'Las Meninas'.

Rigaud; Van Dyck
By no means all the interesting portraits are by the most famous Spanish artists, nor indeed are they all of Spanish royals: Rigaud's Louis XIV is there, as well as Van Dyck's Charles I; also countless ministers and members of the court. The list goes on and on, a year is indeed not enough even for the Prado's Spanish paintings.

Re-housing Prado treasures
Like many other Madrid museums, the Prado is in the throes of being remodelled. Not as extensively as had been hoped: at one time there were plans to re-house part of its vast collection in the Villahermosa Palace, across the street on Plaza Canovas de Castillo, but that palace has now been earmarked for the Thyssen collection, due to be

installed by 1992. Some works may go to the present Army Museum, now occupying all that is left of the former Buen Retiro Palace, just behind and to the north of the Prado, when its interesting collection of weaponry and military memorabilia is eventually re-housed in a projected new building near the Air Force Ministry. For the time being, however, the re-arrangement of the Prado will not be as full-scale as its directors would have wished.

The Prado area

Retiro Park

Behind the Prado, the church of S Jeronimo el Real is where the Royal Family worships, and to the south of them both is the Retiro Park, laid out in the 17th century when it was the Royal Palace grounds. Its cool, wooded corners and huge *estanque,* or lake, with Alfonso XII's statue reflected in it; its formal avenues and flowery plots are much frequented by *madrileños;* Augustus Hare admired "the costumes of the nurses... brilliant scarlet, orange, and purple, slashed with broad stripes of black velvet, and forming perfect rays of colour as they dart . . . after their children," and nursemaids, less gorgeously dressed, are still to be seen there today, along with mothers and grandmothers, supervising their beautifully turned-out charges.

Jardin Botanico

Even more delightful is the adjoining Jardin Botanico, founded by Ferdinand VI in 1755 and moved to its present site by Charles III in 1781. Its three terraces, divided into distinct plots by clipped box-hedges and shaded by trees, are beautifully kept and labelled; the collection of old roses is particularly good. There are also statues, benches, fountains, and a glazed exhibition building (also containing that Madrid rarity, public loos) with a pergola of vines running behind it.

Other major museums

National Ethnographical; Reina Sofia Art

To either side of Atocha Station, at the south end of the Jardin Botanico, are the National Ethnographical Museum (open mornings and afternoons) with exhibits from the Philippines, the Canaries and the former South American colonies; and the new Reina Sofia Art Centre. This is housed in an impressive old building around a central courtyard, where a museum of 20th-century Spanish art is planned, with Picasso's "Guernica" (presently housed in the Casón del Buen Retiro, near the Army Museum) as its centrepiece. The Centre (open from 1000-2100 except on Tuesdays) is currently used for temporary exhibitions but there are also lectures, and a cinema shows film classics (in English and French as well as Spanish) three times a day.

Observatory; Tapestry Factory
Near the Ethnological Museum is the Royal Observatory. At the southernmost tip of the Retiro Park, rather further to the southeast, close to Menendez Pelayo Metro station, the Royal Tapestry Factory (open weekday mornings), offers a display of Goya cartoons as well as the chance to watch tapestries being made by traditional methods.

Lope de Vega Museum; Cibeles Fountain
Northwards across Calle de Atocha, in a web of streets to the east of Plaza de Sta Ana, the evocative house of the great Spanish dramatist Lope de Vega in Calle de Cervantes is maintained as a museum (under restoration, at the time of writing, but worth hunting for on Tuesday and Thursday mornings when it re-opens). Working your way northwards, past the Prado, the Ritz and Palace hotels and the Villahermosa Palace, you come to Plaza de la Cibeles with perhaps Madrid's most beautiful fountain. Here too is the wildly ornate Palacio de Comunicaciones (main Post Office, but also housing telephones, fax and telex facilities, and even a Tourist Information desk), facing the equally imposing Bank of Spain building.

Museum of Decorative Arts
Calle Montalban runs between the south side of the Post Office and the portals of the Naval Museum (open mornings) up to the Retiro Park and, near this end, is another of Madrid's less-known gems: the National Museum of Decorative Arts, open mornings until late-Spanish lunchtime. This stunning collection of furniture, ceramics and porcelain and glassware, *artesonado* ceilings and other *mudéjar* features, leather and ironwork, kitchenware, dolls' houses and Christmas cribs and much more besides, gives a vivid impression of the development of Spain's decorative arts. Among the rooms arranged to reflect different styles are two kitchens, one a magnificently tiled example transported in its entirety from Valencia.

Local restaurants
If the sight of these has made you hungry, one of Madrid's grandest restaurants, Horcher, is round the corner in Calle de Alfonso XII with the more modest La Gamella opposite it. There are two eating-places on Montalban itself: El Comedor, immediately across from the museum, and the noisy, popular Bar Aguilera just down the street, with good *tapas.*

Waxworks; Carriages
Children may enjoy the Waxworks (Museo de Cera), opposite the Archaeological Museum, and the Carriage Museum, in the Campo de Moro gardens below the Royal Palace, both open mornings and

afternoons.

Local entertainment information

There are other museums, more specialised, that I have not mentioned; the leaflet 'Madrid Monumental', produced by the City tourism department, gives details of them as well as opening times (and valuable information on what is not currently open, thanks to refurbishing work). It also produces a booklet in English, 'Ciudad Viva' or 'Madrid by Night' with an exhaustive list of night-spots; 'Guidepost', a weekly publication, is a useful source of information about concerts, theatre, shows and spectacles. The theatre scene, in particular, will be enriched by 1992: there is already a new concert hall, the Teatro Real is being refurbished for opera, and a re-animated Zarzuela Theatre will present more popular (and modern) operettas and ballet; other plans, still taking shape, cover straight theatre and popular Spanish operetta, *zarzuela.*

Madrid: Southern Environs

Chinchón

Madrid is a province as well as a city, and at least two places in the southern part of that province add up to agreeable days out, or can be combined into a longer circuit to include Toledo. Chinchón (pop. c 4000) is a name you may have seen on bottles in Madrid bars, for it is famous for the powerful aniseed spirit that is distilled in the old castle, among other places. The little town, or rather one of its former aristocrats, has also given its name to the chinchona tree, from whose bark quinine is derived: a 17th-century Countess of Chinchón, wife of the Viceroy of Peru, who fell ill with malaria and was cured by a native remedy made from the bark. She brought it back to Europe in 1640 and it was eventually named after her. It is a charming town, 52 km (32 miles) south of Madrid, with a large Plaza Mayor, overlooked by balconied houses, where *corridas* take place in July (St James's Day, the 25th, when bulls are also run through the streets) and September.

Another good reason for visiting Chinchón is its lovely and luxurious Parador, installed in a former 17th-century convent.

Aranjuez

It is only 26 km (just over 16 miles) from Chinchón to the palaces of Aranjuez (pop. c 36,000), on the south bank of the Tagus. It is disfigured by the main Madrid-Andalusía highway (Chichón is a far pleasanter place to stay), but if you are without a car you can go to

Aranjuez on one of the old "strawberry train" *(Tren de la Fresa)* day-excursions from Madrid, run in spring, early summer and autumn. (The name comes from the fact that Aranjuez is renowned for its strawberries - and asparagus).

Royal Palaces

Despite the main road, the palace area is delightful, grown up from a 14th-century country house and attendant hamlet that were presented to Ferdinand and Isabella and, over the years, became one of Charles V's shooting-lodges. Philip II enlarged it and planted its gardens with English oaks and elms; Augustus Hare remarks that they were "perhaps, the only good which accrued to his native land from his marriage with our Mary (Tudor)".

Philip's palace went up in flames and the present buildings are an 18th-century pastiche of Louis XIV's Versailles, built by Spain's Bourbon kings nostalgic for all things French. Without a flurry of courtly activity the palatial buildings, now museums (buildings open mornings and afternoons, gardens until sunset, closed Tuesdays) can seem a trifle haunted, except when thronged with Spaniards at weekends, but they are lovingly maintained. The Royal Palace itself, frescoed and luxuriously furnished much as it was in the last century (the Porcelain Saloon is outstanding), abuts the formal Island Garden, formed by a canal and a bend in the Tagus, where fountains play on certain days.

Small palaces

To the east is the park-like Prince's Garden and the folly of a smaller palace, misleadingly called the *Casita del Labrador* or Workman's Cottage, a recognisable descendant of the Trianon. It, too, is opulently furnished and remarkable, like the Royal Palace in Madrid, for its inordinate number of clocks. Between the two, in another bend of the Tagus, is the beguiling *Casa de Marinos,* or Sailor's House, sheltering half a dozen splendid royal pleasure barges.

Peninsula War drama

Both palaces were the background for the terrible dramas that preceded the Peninsular War, for in March of 1808 Charles IV, his queen Maria Luisa and her lover, Godoy, were at Aranjuez with the entire court shortly after Godoy had enraged all Spain by granting Napoleon's armies the right of passage across the country to Portugal. Ferdinand, the heir to the throne, who detested Godoy and despised his parents, had taken advantage of the precarious political situation to muster support for himself; riots broke out, Godoy was hounded from the court, and the King was forced to abdicate in favour of his son.

(In the epilogue to this drama, some six weeks later, Napoleon summoned the King, Queen, Ferdinand and Godoy to meet him in Bayonne, across the French border, where he proclaimed his brother Joseph King of Spain. Joseph briefly held court at Aranjuez in 1812 before the imminent arrival of Wellington forced him to flee in disarray, with his own army attempting to plunder the convoy. "The procession was lugubrious and shocking," relates Gen Sir William Napier. ". . . crowds of weeping women and children and despairing men, courtiers of the highest rank, desperately struggling with savage soldiers for the animals on which they were endeavouring to save their families." Charles IV, Maria Luisa and Godoy never returned to Spain; Ferdinand, of course, was recalled after the Peninsular War to reign as Ferdinand VII.)

Windmills of La Mancha

Castilla-La Mancha

The 'Castilla' part of the region's modern name reflects its ancient one of New Castile which in turn reflects the fact that it was the first territory to be wrested by the infant kingdom of Castile, to the north, from the Moors. As far back as the reign of the united Castile and León's first king (Ferdinand I, 1037-1065), the Moslem ruler of the *taifa* of Toledo was more or less his vassal, and the city itself was ultimately conquered by Ferdinand's son, Alfonso VI in 1085 - of which more later.

Toledo Region

The province of Toledo, at the western edge of the autonomous region of Castilla-La Mancha, consists mainly of high table lands that are part of the central Meseta. They are not, however, quite so monotonous as those of La Mancha, being broken by rolling hills and watered by the Tagus and the Guadiana, which latter in Richard Ford's time was unwholesome in summer, "infected with fever and agues . . . moskitos and other light militia of air and earth."

In those days the population of the region congregated along these two great waterways and, to a certain extent, still does. But both have been disciplined and dammed over the past few decades to provide irrigation for the arid countryside and unhealthy swamps are a thing of the past – although pollution of a different, 20th-century kind affects both rivers.

En route to Toledo city; Illescas

Toledo (pop. c 54,500) can easily be combined with Aranjuez and Chinchón (see previous chapter) into a round trip of three or four days from Madrid, but if you are coming direct from the capital (along a road that is still being widened in parts to near-motorway standard) you will notice, as your road swings slightly to bypass the dull-looking industrial town of Illescas, an odd-looking signboard beside the turnoff to the city centre, depicting a gaunt-looking monk holding a pen and gazing heavenwards.

Poor Illescas: before it became wrapped about with industry and given a bypass it was a natural stop between Madrid and Toledo, for its convent church of La Caridad rejoices in no fewer than five paintings by El Greco. The most highly regarded is of S. Idelfonso taking down with a quill pen some words spoken to him by the Virgin, and Illescas is trying to tell you about its now-hidden treasures (which, as a matter of fact, make a good prelude to the feast of El Grecos awaiting you in Toledo itself).

The City of Toledo

History

"In a land where all is old, men marvel at the antiquity of Toledo", wrote A.F. Calvert in his Cook's Handbook, and of course it is almost a microcosm of Spanish history. It certainly existed long before the Romans took it early in the 2nd century BC and named it Toletum. When the Visigoths eventually succeeded them, some seven centuries later, and made it their capital as well as an archbishopric (it is still the senior archbishopric of Spain), they strengthened rather than demolished its walls and, to the expert eye, it is possible even now to spot both Roman and Visigothic work in the fortifications.

Visigothic legend

One of Toledo's many delightful legends concerns its loss to the

Moors by Rodrigo, last of the Visigothic kings. He is supposed to have seduced a damsel named Florinda, daughter of the governor of Ceuta on the North African coast and a lady-in-waiting at his court, and her father to have persuaded a Moslem force to cross the straits and help him take revenge. Rodrigo existed, and possibly Florinda too, but it was political dissention among the Visigoths, plus the active support of the Jewish population, who allied themselves at different times with both Christians and Moors, that led to the Moorish conquest of 711, not dishonoured maidenhood.

Moorish rule; Jewish influence
The Jews had established themselves in Toledo many centuries earlier: the oldest Sephardics are said to have come to Spain with the Phoenicians and the Greeks, and Toledo eventually became their spiritual capital. To begin with, both they and the Christians lived amicably enough under their mostly-tolerant Moorish masters, who remained in Toledo for nearly 400 years, but when the Moors started to tax Jews punitively they changed sides, appealed for help to the Christian kingdoms of the north, and paved the way for Toledo's fall to Alfonso VI of Castile and Leon in 1085.

By this time the Jewish population had contributed much to the enrichment of the city, both culturally and financially; it was an important centre of learning throughout the reigns of S Ferdinand (Ferdinand III), Alfonso the Wise and Pedro the Cruel. Oppression of the Jews began in the late 14th century and escalated, some 65 later, when the fanatical preacher of the Inquisition, S. Vicente Ferrer, instigated the massacre of the congregation of Sta Maria la Blanca, then a synagogue. ("This saint was a great mixture," writes Hare. "Cruel and vindictive beyond words in his persecution of heretics, he was saint-like in the practice of his own life.") Less than half a century later, in 1492, the Jews were finally expelled from all Spain by the Catholic Monarchs, Ferdinand and Isabella.

Sixteenth to Twentieth Centuries
Early in the 16th century Toledo was a stronghold of the *communeros,* led first by Juan de Padilla and then by his widow, Maria, who rose in brief and unsuccessful revolt against the new young Hapsburg monarch, Ferdinand and Isabella's son Charles. They were protesting against the influence wielded by the Flemish and Burgundian courtiers the king had brought with him from his homeland and especially against the taxes he was raising to fund his campaign for election as the Holy Roman Emperor Charles V. Maria de Padilla's heroic ten-month defence of the Alcázar before the Emperor's forces has taken its place among Toledo's most cherished legends; it was also one of the last episodes of its Golden Age, for after Charles's son Philip II moved the capital to Madrid in 1560, the city's

political importance steadily waned. In the present century, it suffered badly in 1936 during the Civil War.

Architectural styles

Toledo is one of the great treasure-houses of *mudéjar* art; their builders and craftsmen were equally patronised by both Jews and Christians and, apart from the cathedral, whose foundation-stone was laid in 1227 in the presence of Ferdinand III, 'the Saint', none of Toledo's monuments and mansions was built in any other style until the 15th century.

El Greco

The other Gothic churches belong to a later age, as indeed did its most famous inhabitant, El Greco: born in Crete, his real name was Domenico Theotocopoulos and, after some years in Italy, in the studios of Titian and Tintoretto (both of whom had worked in Spain), he too came to Spain, in 1577. He settled in Toledo soon afterwards and died there in 1614.

Where to stay

Where to stay is the first problem to resolve, for to try and absorb Toledo in the course of a day is to be avoided if at all possible. Its layout, piled as it is on a granite hill above a sharp bend in the Tagus, is a tangled maze of steep, twisting alleyways as narrow as Toledo blades; this, together with its abundance of riches, make it an extraordinarily confusing experience for day-trippers, especially in the summer when the heat is suffocating.

The Parador

In the hotter months, there is much to be said for the modern Parador, across the river and above the old *circunvalación* ring-road. Not only does it have a swimming pool but it also occupies more or less the same vantage-point from which El Greco painted his celebrated 'Views', one version in the Casa de El Greco in the city itself, another in New York's Metropolitan Museum. The harsh outlines of tawny roofs and towers rising from the rocky spur above the swirling river to dominate the inhospitable surrounding landscape have changed remarkably little since his time and are dramatic at all times of day, but particularly, perhaps, at sunset.

Other hotels; restaurants

In the cooler months, another option is the Hostál del Cardenál, a superb restaurant with a couple of dozen rooms, converted from an ancient mansion built up against the city walls. Yet another is the very agreeable Alfonso VI, at the top of the town close by the Alcázar; there is a garage close by in which to leave the car. Its restaurant is not to be recommended; instead, try some of the many that are scattered about the city and, as you wander in search of them, absorb the extraordinarily strong atmosphere of the place, which day-trippers must miss altogether.

Northern Approach

There is only one landward approach to the heart of Toledo and that is to the north, still well walled. The most usual entrance is alongside the 'new' Puerta de Bisagra, built towards the end of Charles V's reign, in 1550; the very useful Tourist Information Office is opposite it, outside the walls. The 'old', keyhole-arched, Puerta de Bisagra, dating back to the 9th century, is just west of it, at the start of a long, exposed stretch of Moorish walls and the Hostál del Cardenál is almost next to it.

Puerta de Alfonso VI

This old Islamic gateway is now known as the Puerta de Alfonso VI, recalling that the Castilian monarch used it when he entered Toledo as its conqueror in 1085. He had spent some time there previously, self-exiled and given sanctuary by its Moorish ruler, at a low point in his fight against his brother Sancho for the throne; relationships between Moors and Christians were often better than those between Christians and Christians, or Moors and Moors. Having carefully reconnoitred the city during his visit, he was now returning to possess it (his erstwhile host, it should be added, being by this time dead).

Santiago de Arrabal church

Alfonso's progress took him past what is now the church of Santiago de Arrabal, a lovely *mudéjar* building whose belfry was originally a minaret and where S Vicente Ferrer preached the hellfire and damnation credo of the Inquisition, past the (also *mudéjar*) Puerta del Sol gateway in the inner fortifications, and through the much more ancient Visigothic Puerta de Valmardon alongside it.

S Cristo de la Luz

Beyond this is a small garden and, on the other side of it, the tiny rectangular 10th-century former mosque known as S Cristo de la Luz, open mornings and afternoons. Here, according to another Toledo legend, either the King's horse or that of his companion, the Cid, stopped, bent its forelegs in obeisance and refused to move further. If indeed it was the Cid's horse, Babieca, it explains why the wall was immediately taken down, for Babieca could do no wrong; in the event a crucifix was found to be embedded in the wall, with a lighted flame burning in front of it, a miraculous relic of the Visigothic era. The mosque was re-named to commemorate the burning light and the first Christian Mass was said there. Inevitably, it was altered to give it a large apse and a presbytery, but the original Islamic part was mercifully untouched and beautiful double arches, one superimposed on another as in Córdoba, supported by Visigothic columns, rise to an elegant series of domes.

West to the river

Plaza Becquer
After S Cristo de la Luz, the direction one takes is largely a matter of chance and inclination. If you are staying for a couple of days or longer, make a point of wandering westwards, up into the maze of quiet, un-touristy streets around Plaza Becquer, where there is a concentration of charming, pink-brick convents.

S Roman church
A better-trodden route climbs southwards to Plaza S Vicente, where the Post Office is, and if you turn west here, past the Casa de Mesa (with one of the best *mudéjar* interiors in Toledo), you come to Plaza de Padilla. Just uphill of it is the church of S Roman, open mornings and afternoons, a fine mixture of *mudéjar* arches and early Christian frescoes (note especially a primitive Visigothic Last Judgement and, set into niches to either side of the inappropriately Baroque sanctuary and altar, some simple outlines of angels on a rust-coloured ground). A small Visigothic museum is installed in it, displaying jewellery (some of it Roman), architectural fragments from the Visigothic period, and copies of the beautiful Visigothic crowns in Madrid's Archaeological Museum.

S Juan de Los Reyes
Still working tortuously westwards, or possibly starting from the turreted Puerta del Cambrón gate, entrance to the ancient *aljama,* or Jewish quarter, you pass a former Visigothic palace just before coming to the Flamboyant (in Spain, called Isabelline) Gothic monastery church of S Juan de Los Reyes, founded by Ferdinand and Isabella in 1476 and open mornings and afternoons.

Around the outside of the apse rusting fetters were later hung, taken from Christian prisoners as they were progressively released from the Moors during the last stages of the Reconquest. The interior is richly decorated and the arms of Castile and Leon are much in evidence, as are the Kings' initials, F and Y (for Isabella). Among a wealth of other detailed carvings are the faces at the tops of the columns to either side of the altar: they are of the craftsmen who worked on the building. In the upper part of the cloister are some beguiling gargoyles, including one of a man playing a form of bagpipe.

Puente de San Martín
From the heights on which the monastery stands you can look down

at the river and slender 14th-century Puente de S Martin, with a gateway at either end of it. Another Toledo legend concerns the bridge-builder's wife who, unlike the heroines of many other such stories, did not conspire with the Devil and allow herself to be interred in the structure to strengthen it. On the contrary, when her husband confided to her that he had made a mistake in the planning and that the bridge would almost certainly collapse when the wooden scaffolding was removed, she sensibly set the scaffolding alight, which led everyone to believe that the fire had caused the damage.

Baths of Florinda

Between the bridge and the Puerta del Cambrón to the north are the ruins of the so-called baths of Florinda, where the young lady-in-waiting was supposed to have been bathing when King Roderick espied her from above. However, one look is enough to convince even the most romantic visitor that this is the ruin of an ancient bridgehead, an unlikely spot for a well brought-up girl to have chosen for bathing.

Jewish Quarter

Coming down from S Juan de los Reyes in the other direction, to the south, you plunge once more into the shadowy alleyways and minute squares of the former Jewish quarter, where the houses were deliberately built to look unprepossessing from the outside lest they betray often very opulent interiors. Yet another legend concerns this quarter and Alfonso VIII, husband of Richard Coeur-de-Lion's sister Eleanor. History seems to confirm that their marriage was singularly happy, and certainly Eleanor bore Alfonso 13 children before they died within a month of each other. But the legend (later dramatised by Lope de Vega) has it that Alfonso, who passed on his way to and from his triumph over the Moors at Las Navas de Tolosa in 1212, fell in love with a beautiful Jewess named Rachel and spent no fewer than seven years with her, hidden in the *aljama,* before resuming his fight against the infidel and his marital relations.

Sta Maria la Blanca

Returning to more tangible matters, the *aljama* contains three of Toledo's most famous sights. The 12-century Sta Maria la Blanca, open mornings and evenings, is one of only two remaining former synagogues (out of a total of ten) that were built in Toledo by *mudéjar* craftsmen. It had a triple apse added to it after the Reconquest and

Opposite: Madrid flea market (top)
Cibeles Fountain, Madrid (below)
Overleaf: Puente San Martín, Toledo (top)
Alcalá del Júcar, Castilla-La Mancha (below)

was damaged in the Peninsular War, after which the roof was rebuilt. At the time of writing the lower parts of the columns, which are topped by a delicate plasterwork pattern of pinecones, had been stripped of the white stucco coating that gives the building its name; when restoration is complete they will once more harmonise with the 24 pale horseshoe arches framing the five aisles, and the multi-lobed windows above them.

Sinagoga del Tránsito

South of this church, passing the only Jewish establishment in Toledo today, the Sinai Restaurant, the beautiful *mudéjar* Sinagoga del Tránsito (similar opening hours to Sta Maria la Blanca) is totally different. No arches here: this building feels almost secular, with silk-covered walls rising to elaborate stucco work, Hebrew texts and pierced *ajimez* windows, and one of the most beautiful *mudéjar* ceilings in Toledo; adjoining it is a Sephardic museum.

Casa de Greco Museum

The Tránsito was built in the 14th century by Pedro the Cruel's treasurer, one Samuel Levi, whom the king later accused of embezzling royal funds, and Levi's house, with a network of cellars beneath it in which the stolen treasures were supposedly hidden, stood close by. The site is now occupied by the Casa de Greco museum, a delightful house and garden well reproducing the early 17th-century style and open mornings and afternoons. A succession of small rooms lead off the central courtyard: one is a chapel with an octagonal ceiling, honeycomb-like pendentives and a lovely painting of S Bernadino; another contains one of several series El Greco did of the Twelve Apostles, and one of the three studies of the Repentant St Peter in Toledo; in another is one of his Views of the city.

Sto Tomé Church

Just north of El Greco's house is the Plaza del Conde de Fuensalida and the Sto Tomé church, with a fine *mudéjar* tower; it is open mornings and afternoons and chairs have thoughtfully been placed in the south aisle so that some of those who flock here can sit in comfort to gaze on El Greco's greatest painting (and others can more easily see over their heads). 'The Burial of the Count of Orgaz' is one of the first commissions the painter executed in Toledo (in about 1585) and is remarkable for its composition, deliberately split into two distinct

Previous page: Arcaded plaza, Zafra (top)
Roman Theatre, Mérida (below)
Opposite: Mezquita arches, Córdoba (top)
Torre del Oro, Seville (below)

halves to separate the heavenly happenings from the earthly ones. It is also intriguing by virtue of the countenances of the Spanish grandees gathered to witness the miraculous burial: every one of them is said to be a life portrait and Philip II is among them, as well as El Greco himself.

Fuensalida and Taller del Moro Palaces
A short way away along the square is the Fuensalida Palace, a finely-restored building where Charles V's queen died in 1537, and across the adjoining garden is the Taller del Moro, an old palace used by *mudéjar* workmen as a building yard. Here, according to tradition, one of the less tolerant Moslem governors of Toledo held a banquet for the city's leading Christians and had each guest's head cut off as he arrived.

Just round the corner from the Taller del Moro, back in Calle Sto Tomé, the Placido restaurant is a good choice in this area, and from it the Calle de la Trinidad leads past the church of S Salvador to the Cathedral.

The Cathedral:

It is hard to appreciate the Cathedral in its entirety from the outside, being hemmed about by buildings separated by alleyways, reducing the field of vision. The taller tower is 15th-century, the one capped by a dome is by El Greco's son in the 17th century; the three Gothic portals in the west front are contemporary with the earlier tower.

The Treasury
Sacheverell Sitwell, referring to the opening hours of the Cathedral treasury (they were not synchronised in his day; now both are open mornings and afternoons), complained that it was "always . . . too early or too late, for there is so much to see that one is tired long before it is time for the treasury to open." The loss was his, but today's problem is to find a moment when the treasury is not too crowded, something that can be judged by a quick glance to the left as you enter the Cathedral, for it is immediately beneath the tower.

It has a magnificent, gilded *mudéjar* ceiling, honeycomb-patterned, and contains both fine and historically interesting objects. Most arresting is a huge mostrance, its centrepiece made of the first gold brought from the Americas, presented by Isabella and later framed in a Gothic silver-gilt tabernacle set with precious stones and adorned with (they say) 5,000 miniature statues; it is processed through the streets on the Feast of Corpus Christi. Also on view is a Bible belonging to St Louis of France and given to his cousin St Ferdinand, Isabella's crown, and a Fra Angelico crucifix presented by Mussolini.

The Choir

The interior of the Cathedral itself is basically French Gothic and encrusted with decoration; the fine stained glass windows (many of them reproductions, thanks to the depredations of war) admit more light than in many Spanish cathedrals and enable you to study much of the detail. The pink marble columns round the outside of the *coro* are from the original mosque; within it, Rodrigo Alemán's wonderfully detailed carvings of scenes from the conquest of Granada are along the upper part of the choirstalls. Above them the carved screens are by Berruguete and Borgoña, and the misericords are enchanting.

Altarpiece

Across from the *coro* the vast gilded *retablo* around the high altar is breathtaking in its profusion of detail. Among the statues is one said to have been carved by Alfonso VIII and is of the miraculous shepherd-figure which appeared to guide his army through the mountains to vanquish the Moors at Las Navas de Tolosa in 1212; the other, opposite it, is of a Moor, Abu Walid. He was the principle guardian of the original mosque, whose safety had been guaranteed by Alfonso VI when he captured Toledo in 1085, but during his absence his queen and the Archbishop commandeered the mosque for Christian worship. Alfonso was furious and would have punished the Archbishop if Abu Walid had not interceded for him, and that is why a Moslem holy man stands among the Christian saints.

Royal tombs

Around the high altar are some fine royal tombs, and behind the *capilla mayor* is the theatrical Baroque *trasparente,* an elaborate Last Supper lit by a hole cut through the Cathedral roof. Just behind this, a little passage leads off the ambulatory into the *capilla de los Reyes Nuevos* (at the time of writing, closed for restoration) in which, among the "later kings" lies Catherine of Lancaster, daughter of John of Gaunt. Her marriage to Enrique III was arranged towards the end of the 14th century, during John of Gaunt's 'invasion' of Galicia to claim the Spanish throne through his wife, a daughter of Pedro the Cruel of Castile; the marriage of his daughter to the heir seems to have been an acceptable alternative and he renounced his own claim.

Sacristy and Chapter House

In the Sacristy, the many fine paintings include a wonderful 'Taking of Christ' by Goya, in which the cruel faces of the crowd surrounding the central figure are masterly; El Greco's *'Expolio'* (Christ stripped of his Raiment), one of his earliest Spanish paintings, and another of his series of portraits of the Apostles. Also exhibited are enamelled Romanesque reliquaries and a silver-clad Virgin and Child, and the crown, sword, spurs and pillow of Sancho IV. The Chapter House, lined with portraits of Toledan archbishops, two of them by Goya, boasts some staggering *mudéjar* work, notably ceilings, gilded and picked out in reds, blues and greens.

Mozarabic chapel
The mozarabic chapel, at the Cathedral's west end, is closed except when the ancient Visigoth Mass is said there every morning; H.V. Morton attended one such service and gives a detailed account of it in 'A Stranger in Spain'. It has a strange history: at the end of Toledo's reconquest a furious dispute broke out over which liturgy should be used, the Roman or the *mozarabe,* and it was decided to settle the matter by a combat between two knights which the *mozarabe* champion won. However, the Roman faction refused to accept this outcome and it was decided to place copies of both rituals on a bonfire, to see which burned first. The Roman one was blown off the pyre before the flames could reach it, Hare recounts, but the *mozarabe* one survived unharmed; thus Visigothic rites continue to be practised in Toledo.

Local restaurants and specialities

There is a concentration of very acceptable restaurants near the north side of the Cathedral, where Calle Hombre de Palo becomes the city's main shopping street, Calle de Commercio: El Cobertizo, Casa Aurelio, Mesón Aurelio and La Tarasca, and another to the south of it, this one called simply Aurelio. And in Plaza Magdalena, just downhill of the Alcázar and the Alfonso VI hotel, two bars called Capri and Ledena offer delicious *tapas,* the latter specialising in skewered beef, the former in more varied dishes including a Toledo speciality, *carcamusas,* based on chopped up *morcilla* (black pudding).

Another gastronomic speciality of Toledo is game, cooked in a variety of ways; a third is marzipan, by tradition first confected at the time Alfonso VI was laying siege to the city and the inhabitants were short of almost everything except almonds, sugar and bread. Charles V, who was inordinately fond of his food, had a strong partiality for Toledan marzipan.

Toledo steel
The non-gastronomic speciality, of course, is fine-worked Damascene ware: steel, incised into patterns which are filled with gold and silver wire and baked, turning the steel black.

Other major monuments

The Alcázar
The Alcázar, which vies with the Cathedral to dominate the skyline of Toledo, has so often been destroyed and rebuilt that it lacks the almost tangible atmosphere of the other monuments; even the great stair-

case which Charles V declared made him "feel truly Emperor", faithful restoration though it is, fails to overawe. Its most recent drama occurred during the dreadful Civil War siege of 1936 when beleaguered families sheltered in its cellars and the commandant, Colonel Moscardo, was told that his son would be shot if he did not surrender. He refused; his son died.

Museo de Sta Cruz

To the north of it, near the Plaza de Zocodover, the animated social centre of Toledo, is the Museo de Sta Cruz behind a beautiful Plateresque facade and open all day long. It was founded in the 17th century by Cardinal Mendoza as a home for orphans and is built in cruciform shape with a dome at the crossing; two storeys high, it has a Renaissance *artesonado* ceiling to the lower one and *mudéjar* one above. It houses fine pieces of furniture, hangings and other furnishings from all over the province and also no fewer than 20-odd El Grecos, including another 'Repentant St Peter' and a 'Holy Family'. Among the other fine paintings and sculptures is a Goya 'Crucifixion'; historical exhibits include the burial-book of Sto Tomé church, open at the page recording El Greco's death, and a document signed by Charles V pardoning the *communero* rebels.

Hospital de Tavera

Before leaving Toledo, or before venturing into the city centre, spare time for the Hospital de Tavera, built in the 16th century by Cardinal Tavera as a poorhouse and open mornings and afternoons; it lies north of the New Bisagra Gate and the Tourist Office, across a shady park. Still the property of the Dukes of Lerma, it has a beautiful double-storeyed patio and a chapel containing an El Greco canvas of the Baptism of Christ that was not quite finished at his death. There are more El Grecos in the superb library, including a beautiful 'Holy Family' and the third, perhaps finest, 'St Peter Repentant'; a Titian of Charles V and many other treasures. In another small room hangs a truly gruesome canvas, said to have been painted from life, of two elderly, bearded men, one of them suckling a child; it is called 'La Mujer Barbuda' ('The Bearded Woman').

Alcántara Bridge; S Servando Castle

A few remains of Roman Toletum, notably the circus, lie a short distance away to the west; to the southeast are the last of the great monuments: the wonderful 13th-century Alcántara Bridge across the Tagus, damaged and repaired innumerable times, with a *mudéjar* tower at either end, and above it the restored 14th-century S Servando castle.

Guadamur castle

Another very fine castle, Guadamur, lies a few miles to the southwest;

it is privately owned and only rarely open to the public but makes a splendid sight from the minor road that runs past it, its 15th-century curtain walls, squat tower and fat turrets rising from the summit of a low hill.

Toledo to Ocaña

The greater part of Castilla-La Mancha lies east and south of Toledo and belies the area's popular image of unrelieved monotony. Even if you take one of the two somewhat dreary main highways to the south and east (N301 via Albacete for Levante or NIV via Valdepeñas and Bailén for Andalusía) you will find variety on even the flattest plains as the moving sun changes the angle and intensity of the light and the occasional cloud casts astonishingly-hued shadows on vineyards and fields of grain. But by looping east and south first, and then northwards again, avoiding main roads as far as possible, you discover just how much the landscapes alter. Moreover, as the name 'Castilla' (derived from the older one of New Castile) implies, there is also a succession of splendid castles punctuating and lending drama to the terrain.

Ocaña

Coming east from Toledo or south from Madrid, Ocaña (almost equidistant at under 64 km, or 40 miles from both) is somewhat forlorn these days but it has a charming, arcaded, 18th-century Plaza Mayor that merits a pause, as well as several fine churches, a splendid fountain and a 16th-century aqueduct. During the Peninsular War it was the scene of a terrible débacle when a large Spanish army under an incompetent commander was routed by a much smaller French force under the great Soult, who then sacked it.

Cuenca Region

Ocaña to Cuenca City

East of Ocaña, and into the province of Cuenca, instead of sticking to the N400, consider two brief detours. Southwards, the N111 has a turnoff to the left to Uclés and the huge monastery known as the Escorial of La Mancha, extensively restored after its sacking by the French during the Peninsular War and combining Baroque features with the finer Plateresque style that succeeded it.

Roman Segobriga

Back on the N111, you come next to a turnoff for Saelices, near which the remains of the Roman city of Segobriga are slowly being excavated; you can see the amphitheatre, several houses, and a small museum housing some of the finds.

Huete

A minor road brings you back to the N400 in 16 km (10 miles) at Carrascosa del Campo, whose church has an exceptionally fine portal, and from here you can make the second, rather greater detour (it is about 100 km, or just over 60 miles, longer than the direct route to Cuenca). First comes the little town of Huete, with a delightful arcaded Plaza Mayor, remains of walls and of a Moorish castle; its history goes back to Roman times and it was an important Muslim stronghold that was ceded to Castile as part of the dowry of a Moorish princess who married the Christian king, Alfonso VI, conqueror of Toledo, two years before he died.

Buendia

Northwards again are the lakes called the Mar de Castilla and the attractive village of Buendia standing on a promontory above the water; a popular summer retreat for the city dwellers of Madrid and Guadalajara. A pretty minor road borders the lake as far as Sacedon and the Entrepeñas dam, and the N320 brings you back to join the N400 just short of Cuenca.

The City of Cuenca

This old town (pop c. 42,000), teetering on its rocky spur above the confluence of the Júcar and Huécar rivers, both deep in ravines below it, looks undramatic as you approach it from almost any direction, masked as it is by the sprawling modern town. However, apart from one or two pensions (the charming little Posada de San José among them) in the old town, all the hotels and most good restaurants are in the lower part: the Torremangana and the Alfonso are the best of them.

Origins

Backed by the Serranía de Cuenca and the easternmost outpost of La Mancha, Cuenca's origins are Moorish. In 1106 it was ceded, like Huete (see above), to Alfonso VI, but it became irked by Castilian rule some 70 years later and had to be reconquered belligerently after all. Much of what you see in the old town today dates from the time of the 16th-century *conquistadores:* American gold paid for those tall, thin houses, many only one room deep. Hojeda, who sailed with Columbus and later explored Guiana, was born there, and so was one of the viceroys of Peru, and it is said that the last Mexican Aztec prince ended his life there.

Old Town

It is a mistake to try to venture up by car: the streets are steep and narrow and parking limited. Explore on foot, climbing higher and higher, ducking under archways where houses are built over alleyways, admiring fine wooden balconies and the carved beam-ends that support them, monumental doorways and armorial carvings, and coming finally to almost the only level spot in town, the odd-shaped plaza in front of the Cathedral, screened from the south by the arcades supporting the Ayuntimiento.

The Cathedral

The Cathedral's west front was rebuilt in the 17th century and collapsed again at the beginning of this one; the result is unworthy of the interior, the proportions of whose nave and transept bear kinship to some of the finest early French Gothic churches. The apse is 15th century, and Moorish-influenced; the intrusive features date from the 17th-century restoration and later, among then the *coro* and high altar. The wrought-iron screens and some of the side-chapels are worth examining, particularly the tombs, likewise the cloister and the portal alongside it. The treasury has some fine pieces, notably a beautiful Byzantine diptych and two paintings by El Greco.

Bishop's Palace; Museums

Beside the Cathedral a little street leads downhill past the Bishop's Palace and the Archaeological Museum, open mornings and afternoons and charmingly laid out in a pretty building around a courtyard; it contains interesting Roman finds from Valeria, Segobriga and elsewhere in the province. Beyond it the excellent Museum of Abstract Art (open late mornings, and afternoons) reflects the fascination Cuenca has exerted during this century over Spanish artists as well as tourists; in the 1913 Baedeker, for instance, it rated less than half a page in small type, mostly about the Cathedral.

Hanging houses

Alongside the museum is an atmospheric restaurant, Meson Casas Colgadas, and then the street dives beneath an arch and leads down to a dismayingly bouncy footbridge suspended across the Júcar gorge. From here you can look up to the back of the restaurant, in one of the medieval Casas Colgadas, or Hanging Houses, half-cantilevered out from the clifftop, and then down to little vegetable plots tucked alongside the river at the foot of the gorge.

S Pedro Church; Júcar ravine

Coming back uphill, past the Cathedral, is the charming 17th-century octagonal church of S Pedro and beyond it is the archway that once gave sole access to the city. Down to the west of S Pedro, a stepped alleyway ends in a dramatic view of the Júcar ravine; below you are a Franciscan hermitage and a convent.

"Excursions near Cuenca . . . are full of attraction for the geologist and angler" wrote Richard Ford; for collectors of oddities, too, he might have added, since he goes on to describe one lake supposedly linked below ground with another miles away ("some cattle drowned in one having reappeared in the other"). Of a third lake he tells us that "a Don Buesso, according to legend, threw in twenty-four of his mistresses stark naked, one of whom pulled him in after her". More prosaically, the wild empty countryside and geological oddities of the Serranía de Cuenca are both intriguing and rewarding. Among the oddities are the curious cavernous depressions, called Las Torcas, to the south, caused by the movement of underground rivers to which Ford was doubtless referring.

Júcar Gorge

But perhaps the more northerly route, the CU921 along the Júcar gorge, is the most dramatic. At first it is wide enough for there to be space for picknickers, bathers and fishermen; then a turning to the right leads to another major oddity, the so-called Ciudad Encantada, a wild chaos of rocks and boulders isolated from their limestone mass and eroded into weird and monstrous shapes.

Gargante rocks; La Toba lake

The Júcar gorge itself gets increasingly majestic as you go further into the Serranía, gradually becoming squeezed between the rock faces known as the Garganta, so strangly shaped that in places they look like man-made ramparts. A tactfully-designed and sited hydroelectric plant at Villalba de la Sierra is fed from a small dam at Uña and there is a bigger artificial lake at La Toba; even at this short distance from its source the greeny-blue Júcar is no mere stream and the trout fishing is excellent.

South-east of Júcar Gorge

Tragacete to Cañete

Just short of Tragacete, a popular centre for fishermen, a right turn off CU921 takes you through countryside that at this altitude (over 3,000 feet) is fresh and green even in high summer, and you rejoin a main road (the N420) at Cañete, where a ruined 15th-century hilltop castle is still connected by a massive curtain wall to the half-walled village below.

Rincón de Valencia; Ademuz; Utiel

From here, if you turn north, there is more dramatic scenery in the area known as the Rincón de Valencia: coppery-red cliffs layered like piles of ginger pancakes and occasionally broken by vertical rib-formations. If you turn south on the N330 you go through the ancient village of

Ademuz (hotel) and eventually reach Utiel and the main road to Valencia.

La Pena del Escrito: cave paintings

If, instead, you turn right at Cañete and follow the N 420 back towards Cuenca, you can turn left at Carboneras de Guadazón, left again at Cardenete, and arrive after 40 km (25 miles) at the prehistoric cave of la Pena del Escrito, with well-defined prehistoric paintings of hunters and hunted. A succession of minor roads from Cardenete will bring you back to Utiel and the main Valencia road.

Cuenca city to Alarcón

Roman Valeria

Quitting Cuenca for the last time, to the south, there are two alternative roads. The pleasant secondary N320 leads to Motilla de Palancar, running within 14 km (under 10 miles) of the remains of Roman Valeria.

Alarcón reservoir

The more major N420, which describes a huge southwards loop just short of Cuenca, roughly parallels for some 20 km (12 miles) the course of the Júcar, flowing far below you at the foot of its chasm of a gorge. The Júcar opens into the northern tip of the huge Alarcón reservoir and at its southern end is Alarcón itself (also easily reachable from the Valencia area).

Alarcón Castle

For miles in all directions you can see the topmost part of the castle outlined against the sky; only when you get close to it do you realise that it stands on a spur of the Júcar river gorge like a galleon atop a petrified wave.

The castle originally belonged to the Pacheco-Villenas, and its curtain walling runs steeply down the hill and half encloses the village behind it. A toylike mini-castle and watchtowers on the hills around it, all originally linked by curtain walling, must have made this place well-nigh impregnable and, indeed, its history as a fortified site goes back to earliest times.

One of the sons of the Visigothic King Alaric took it from the Romans, but the present fortifications date from the Moorish occupation in the eighth century. It later became one of the strongholds of Ibn-Hafsun, veteran of many rebellions against the Caliphate of Córdoba, and before it finally fell to Castile in the late 12th century the commander of the besieging forces had literally to scale the walls in person, with swords wedged into the masonry as footholds.

It came into the possession of the powerful Villenas in the 15th century and the then Marqués was lucky to keep it, because in the fight for the throne of Castile he unwisely sided against Isabella the Catholic and with her rival, Juana la Beltraneja; even though he later betrayed Juana, Isabella was not one to forget this sort of misjudgement. Alarcón castle is thus something of a microcosm of Spanish history, and both village and castle have been brought gently into the 20th century by the castle's conversion into one of the nicest of the Paradors I have stayed in, its 11 bedrooms opening off a tiny courtyard shaded by a huge fig-tree and looking out, on the other side, over the Júcar gorge.

Alarcón village

There is also a small *hostál* in the village, once a sizeable fortified township, which today consists of little more than two streets and a couple of plazas. It is all being gradually and sympathetically restored and the new buildings are in harmony with the original style. One of its five churches was being given a new roof at the time of writing; another had already been restored (but not returned to worship); another has a beautiful neo-classical Renaissance porch and portal and yet another a portal in the delicately-chiselled Plateresque style. There are some handsome mansions and a lovely little colonnaded Renaissance *Ayuntimiento* in the quiet main square.

Tour to Belmonte

If you stay at Alarcón for a couple of nights there is a pleasant tour of some 160 km (100 miles) south to Sisante and thence by the C311 to S Clemente, a delightful village with a 16th-century Plaza Mayor, and on to Belmonte, another of the great romantic castles of La Mancha. It is a magnificent sight, its massive outlines dominating a hilltop and its curtain-walls spilling down to the old town below.

Belmonte town

Arched gateways give access to Belmonte's drowsy, stone-flanked streets and lead to a fine Colegiata church. The town (pop c. 2,800) is held in as much esteem by Spaniards as is the castle, for it was the birthplace of the great 16th-century humanist, Luis de León, who taught at Salamanca University and was imprisoned by the Inquisition for his liberal thinking.

Belmonte Castle

The hexagonal 15th-century castle, open mornings and afternoons, enclosed by a perfectly harmonious ensemble of turrets and stepped merlons and crenellations, has witnessed more than a few political intrigues – and has been used as a film-set, for shooting parts of 'El Cid'. Like Alarcón, it was owned by the Pacheco-Villena family and it was here that the then Marqués decided to change sides in the struggle for the Castilian throne and betray Isabella's rival, Juana la Beltraneja; as a result, the poor lady was forced to escape through a gate that still bears her name.

The courtyard interior was transformed in the last century by the exiled Empress Eugenia de Montijo, wife of Napoleon III and friend of Queen Victoria, but the castle interior, only partly restored, is still much as it originally was. There are marvellous wooden *mudéjar* ceilings, including strange, pagoda-shaped ones in the master bedrooms, beautiful stone-carved tracery in some of the deep window embrasures, fine chimneypieces and superb views from the rooftops.

Albacete Region

Leaving Alarcón to resume this clockwise circuit of Castilla-La Mancha, take the N111 via Motilla del Palancar to Miglianilla and then turn south on AB820 to Alcalá del Júcar over the border in the province of Albacete.

Alcalá del Júcar
Backed by the gentle Sierra de la Caballa, Alcala del Júcar appears at first to lie on a flattish plain; as you approach, however, you realise that over the centuries the Júcar river has cut a precipitous gorge through it and the township (pop c. 1,800) is piled up against one side of this, a handsome castle and a church at its summit. Below them, many of the houses (and those of Jorquera, just west of it) are cut into the rockface which is not solid hillside but a sharp, isolated spur around whose foot the river describes a hairpin bend. Some householders have tunnelled clear through the spur, so that their back windows open over a sheer drop to the river on the other side, giving them excellent ventilation.

A few houses are open to visitors at weekends and, although the incumbents are blatant about their status as tourist attractions, having installed bars and folksy displays of olive presses and souvenirs, there is nothing remotely fake about the houses or the site, which are quite unique. There is good parking (and public conveniences) down by the river, and plenty of cafés and small *hostáls;* to get to the summit of the town, you must walk.

Side-trip into Valencia; Alpera

The Júcar has another surprise along its downstream course if you turn northeast for Casas de Ves, and then due east along AB852 through tiny, depopulated Cantoblanco and its more prosperous-looking neighbouring *pueblos* of El Viso and Balsa de Ves. You come first to Los Hervideros, with thermal springs and an attractive, rambling spa hotel (the Balneario Hervideros de Cofrentes) in a wooded valley, and then to Cofrentes.

Cofrentes

Here a hydro-electric station tapping the waters of the Júcar has been rather unfortunately sited within view of yet another castle on a spur above the river, virtually unrestored, its deep reddish stone glowing vividly in the afternoon sun.

Requeña

If you turn north at Cofrentes along the N330 you reach Requeña, at the heart of the important Requeña-Utiel wine-growing area; its hotels are not to be recommended but its old quarter is pleasant enough, with two good Gothic churches, the shuttered remains of a castle known, for some inexplicable reason, as the Mesón del Cid, and a really excellent and reasonably-priced restaurant called the Mesón del Vino, part of which is an equally excellent *tapa* bar.

Alpera

If, instead of turning north, you head south from Cofrentes, you pass Ayora and its castle and, 11 kms (7 miles) further on, see a turnoff to the right for the charming village of Alpera.

Prehistoric cave

The functionaries of Alpera's Town Hall are charged with the care of the prehistoric cave of La Vieja, some 13 km (8 miles) away, a shallow shelter in the side of the hill rather than a cave, sitting just above a farmhouse on a hillside and one of the most easily accessible of prehistoric sites in the area. It is screened by a protective grille, but once you are over the surrounding railings you can see it very well even if the key-holder at the Town Hall is unavailable. The famous figure of a warrior in Red Indian-style headgear is hard to decipher but many of the animals are beautifully delineated.

Almansa to Albacete City

Almansa Castle

Twenty-two kilometres (about 14 miles) from Alpera to the south and east is Almansa (pop c. 20,500), unprepossessing but for its castle, perched on top of a solitary limestone protrusion that soars above the town. Its origins are Moorish but it was largely rebuilt in the 15th century; it has been partly restored and makes a striking sight.

War of Spanish Succession

Almansa's other claim to fame is its association with one of the few battles in the War of the Spanish Succession actually to take place on Spanish soil. This strange war, in which half the nations of Europe allied to take up arms for fear of France and Spain becoming united through the accession of Louis XIV's grandson (the Bourbon Philip V) to the Spanish throne, was mostly fought outside the peninsula - in France, and in Flanders and Italy, where Spain lost her possessions as a result. It was also the war that gained Gibraltar for Britain and the dukedom of Marlborough for John Churchill.

Battle of Almansa 1707

The battle of Almansa, which was fought early in 1707, was particularly strange, for on that occasion the Franco-Spanish army was commanded by an exiled English Catholic, the Duke of Berwick, illegitimate son of James II of England and nephew to Marlborough, while the Allied force was under an exiled French Protestant who had been created Earl of Galway.

Galway's army, marching to capture Madrid, was depleted because half of it had been sent to occupy Aragón and Catalonia; Berwick's defensive force, on the other hand, had just been reinforced by an extra 8,000 Frenchmen. By the time they met, just south of Almansa, the Allies numbered about 15,000 while Berwick's French and Spaniards were over twice as numerous, Galway, inevitably, was disastrously defeated; Berwick went on to become a Marshall of France and his title now belongs to the Dukes of Alba.

Chinchilla de Monte Aragon

The main N430 road from Almansa to Albacete is fairly unremarkable until you get to Chinchilla de Monte Aragón, just short of Albacete, an ancient hillside town with the almost *de rigueur* 15th-century castle. It has the slightly apologetic air of one who has come down in the world (it was, along with Belmonte and Alarcón, part of the Pacheco-Villena family possessions and, briefly in the last century, the provincial capital), but is very charming: many a fine old house lines its narrow streets and the Plaza Mayor has an arcade supported by wooden pillars and an ornate, 18th-century Town Hall.

The City of Albacete

By no stretch of the imagination could the present provincial capital of Albacete (pop c. 117,000) be termed touristically important, though it does boast a handsome and efficient modern Parador on its southern outskirts, and the museum houses some interesting pre-historic and Roman finds from various sites throughout the province.

Daggers and cutlery

Thanks to its age-old tradition of making daggers and sprung clasp-knives, it is also a good place in which to shop for such things as well as other cutlery – a view that Richard Ford did not share. "Albacete is called the Sheffield of Spain . . . but everything is by comparison", he sniffed. "The coarse cutlery . . . at whose make and material an English artisan sneers, perfectly answers native wants . . . to 'chip bread and kill a man' and our readers are advised to have . . . little to do with them." These derogations obviously passed unnoticed among the craftsmen, for Augustus Hare remarks, some decades later, that Albacete cutlery was always sold at the railway station by "picturesque men . . .hung all round with knives with inlaid handles."

Saffron

Albacete is also interesting in being one of Spain's two principal saffron-producing centres (the other is Cuenca), and if you are in the area in season you should look out for the purple-hued saffron crocus fields, originally cultivated by the Arabs who imported bulbs from the East, and if possible watch the workers delicately removing the golden stamens from the flowers with fine brushes. (Powdered saffron is often mixed with a slightly similar, cheaper Eastern spice called curcuma, or with turmeric; only when you can recognise the stamens can you be sure it is unadulterated *crocus sativus*).

Albacete to Alcaraz

You are now on the threshold of La Mancha proper: that vast, high plain of unbroken vistas punctuated by windmills and lines of windbreaking trees; of cornfields and vineyards; of little hot towns jealously guarding their historical and architectural treasures; of Don Quixote and of castles.

Alcaraz

Alcaraz (pop c. 1,800) lies about 82 km (just over 50 miles) southwest of Albacete, on the edge of its sierra: an elegant little town grouped beneath an early 16th-century castle ruin, with a charming Plaza Mayor surrounded by finely proportioned Renaissance buildings. It was the birthplace of the Renaissance architect Vandelvira, in fact, though most of his work was done in Andalusía.

Cuidad Real Region

Alcaraz to Manzanares

Ruidera Lakes

From Alcaraz the C415 Valdepeñas road goes west via Villanueva de la Fuente and Villanueva de los Infantes. Between them, at Villahermosa, a side-road (CR640) leads north in some 40 km (25 miles) towards the string of little lakes from which rise the headwaters of the Guadiana, called the Lagunas de Ruidera. A landscaped national park, Ruidera is popular with campers, fishermen and water-sports enthusiasts and has several small inns; it was there that Don Quixote gave battle to the puppets.

Campo de Montiel

On the way there, the road from Villahermosa crosses the Campo de Montiel, also associated with Don Quixote, where in 1369 Enrique de Trastamara killed his half-brother, Pedro the Cruel, and thus won the throne of Castile as Enrique II. Earlier battles between the two had brought the Black Prince into Spain as Pedro's ally; he was rewarded (though not in a form that could be used to feed his army) with the great ruby that is now set into Britain's Imperial State Crown. His brothers and companions-at-arms, John of Gaunt and Edmund of Langley, ended by marrying two of Pedro's daughters.

Manzanares

There is a good road from Ruidera west to Manzanares (pop c. 17,500), an old but not particularly interesting town (one of George Borrow's best anecdotes concerns a blind seer who occupies herself in making prophecies about travellers arriving on the Madrid coach). It is, however an alternative to Almagro, slightly further west, as a centre for exploring this part of La Mancha. It has a friendly Parador, built in the early thirties, with a shady garden; if it is hot enough for swimming the modern El Cruce hotel down the road has a large pool.

Manzanares to Cuidad Real City

Birthplace of Don Quixote

Southeast of Manzanares, a turnoff at the typical small town of La Solana leads to S Carlos del Valle, with a pretty Plaza Mayor; to the northeast Argamasilla de Alba, equally handy for the Ruidera lakes, claims to be the birthplace of Don Quixote. Cervantes may in fact have conceived, if not actually started writing, his epic in the rebuilt half-subterranean former prison known as the Cueva de Medrano.

Valdepeñas; Las Virtudes

Valdepeñas (pop c. 25,000), to the south, is a sprawling colour-washed town famous for its wines: the countryside around is an ocean of vineyards, and *bodegas* (wine stores) that can be visited literally pepper the outskirts of the town. Beyond it, again to the south along the main NIV road and close to Sta Cruz de Mudela, Las Virtudes has a rectangular plaza claimed to be the oldest bullfighting arena in Spain.

La Calzada de Calatrava

A minor road leads west from Sta Cruz to La Calzada de Calatrava, just outside of which, on the Puertollano road, the hills begin to loom ahead of you and two castles stand watch over the pass that in former times marked the frontier between Christian Castile and Moslem Andalusia. Salvatierra is to the east and totally ruined; the seond, on the other side of the road and seeming to grow out of the rocky pinnacle on which it stands, is Calatrava La Nueva, founded in the 13th century by Spain's first military order, the Knights of Calatrava. It is one of the most romantic ruins imaginable, mercifully not over-restored, its arches outlined in red sandstone and brick. It has an echoing, early Gothic monastery church whose interior, lit by an empty rose window, rises to red stone cross-vaulting supporting a brick roof. The views northward from it, over La Mancha, are incomparable.

Almagro

Turning back northwards through La Calzada again and crossing the Jabalón, the little town of Almagro (pop c. 8,300) is one of the gems of La Mancha. Its faintly oval Plaza Mayor has a garden at one end and its other three sides are lined with old stone columns supporting massive oaks beams. Above these, the glazed walls of galleries present an unbroken band of panes whose frames are painted a uniform shade of muted green; above again are uneven pantiled roofs.

At the centre of the south portico is a 16th-century theatre, beautifully restored and still used for festive performances. Charming lamp-brackets, pebble-mosaic underfoot and an air of being cherished add to the delightful impression; even the litter bins are adorned with the emblem of the Knights of Calatrava who once owned the town.

Along the attractive alleyways leading away from the square are distinguished mansions with sculptured doorways; the old Covento de Calatrava (Convento de la Asunción) has a lovely cloister and the former S Francisco convent has been converted into a beautiful Parador.

Diego de Almagro, the conqueror of Chile, came from this little town; today it is almost as famous for its lace, made in many of the little villages in the vicinity, and for its pickled aubergines.

The city of Ciudad Real

Ciudad Real, the provincial capital (pop c. 51,000), is pleasant enough and has several hotels if the Almagro Parador is full. One keyhole-arched gateway, the Puerta de Toledo, remains from its medieval walls, linked by the Calle de Toledo to the arcaded main square by way of some handsome buildings. Its best church is the elegant Gothic S Pedro, close to the main plaza.

North-east of Ciudad Real

Calatrava la Nueva; Daimiel

Just north of Ciudad Real, overlooking the Guadiana, are the ruins of the original seat of the Knights of Calatrava: Calatrava la Vieja, nowhere near so interesting as Calatrava la Nueva. West of it is a scatter of small lakes and marshes, part of them a national park where migrating waterfowl pause to rest (open daily except Mondays), and just south of this the wine town of Daimiel (pop c. 16,300) lies wrapped around a pleasant Plaza Mayor.

Calatrava Plain

Anyone hunting for windmills to tilt at in this part of La Mancha, the Calatrava Plain, will be disappointed: electricity and telegraph poles march to every horizon, but not sails. There are other details to break the uniformity of the vine clothed landscape, however: innumerable wells, a few still with their bucket-studded wheels that were worked by blindfolded mules plodding round in circles, and huge, traditional pottery wine jars, no longer used for storage, doing duty as gateposts or signposts to private properties.

Dry as it is – you can detect for miles the passage of goats or donkeys by the miniature dust storms they raise – and flat as it is, the plain is by no means monotonous: the changing light draws a whole spectrum of different colours from it, highlighting the greenness of the vines and the redness of the soil, reflecting the silvery sheen of olive trees.

Puerto Lapice: Don Quixote's inn

From Daimiel it is 35 km (about 22 miles) to Puerto Lapice, on N420 at its junction with the Madrid road; this is supposedly where Don Quixote was dubbed a knight by the innkeeper. However, the Venta del Quijote does itself a disservice by trading so blatantly upon this connection, which may well put many people off. In fact it is an interesting (though modernised) relic of the days of Ford and Borrow, when Spanish country inns were crude in the extreme and chiefly designed to shelter itinerant livestock. "The accommodation for the **beast** is excellent," says Ford; ". . . as regards **man**, it is just the reverse." "The rooms were many and large," says Borrow (of another 'typical' *posada*) "floored with either brick or stone, generally with an alcove at the end, in which stood a wretched flock bed," The better class of travellers betook himself to the upper part of the building, of which Ford observes that "it is not upstairs that he eats, but where **he** is eaten . . . the walls are frequently stained with the marks of nocturnal combats" (with hungry insects).

The inn at Puerto Lapice is of course no longer a "school for the slaves of comforts" (Ford), where travellers learned how many essential services they could manage to do without, but with its courtyard and balconied upper storey it recalls its predecessors - and serves good, regional food.

Herencia; Alcázar de San Juan

On the N420 east from Puerto Lapice, Herencia is the original home of Manchegan cheese, now manufactured all over the area, and 11 km (about 7 miles) further east is Alcázar de S Juan (pop c. 25,500). A sprawling, whitewashed wine centre that takes its name from the Order of the Knights of St John, whose stronghold it was, it has a restored red brick tower whose foundations rest on part of a Roman castle (mosaics have been found nearby). It was later part of a Moorish castle and can be visited by applying to the Ayuntimiento; also worth visiting is the fine Romanesque church of Sta Maria, next door. The Don Quijote hotel is very acceptable and there are several good restaurants.

Quixote's windmills; Dulcinea's village

Just south of town is one of the best and most evocative views of windmills, four of them, outlined against the sky on the crest of a low hill and from a distance quite easily interpreted in a poor light as being potentially menacing. The actual windmills at which Don Quixote is supposed to have charged, now rebuilt, are above Campo de Criptana, to the west of Alcázar de S Juan, and if you then head due northwest you will come to the evocative village of El Toboso, home of Dulcinea, the princess of Don Quixote's chivalric reveries. The house proclaimed to be that of her prototype, a rustic lass called Ana Zarco de Morales, was once the village olive oil refinery and has been turned into a little folk museum; in the Town Hall are early editions of Cervantes' epic, including foreign translations donated by famous owners. One was Mussolini's.

El Toboso to Consuegra

A minor road west from El Toboso brings you to the main N301; here you can turn south towards Albacete and see more windmills (and a ruined castle) at Mota del Cuervo, or turn north towards Madrid to Quintana de Ordén, another important cheese-making town. If you are heading towards Toledo from here, or from Alcázar de S Juan, there is one more village to claim your attention: Consuegra, overlooked by yet more fine windmills and a ruined 12th-century castle, and today known for its attractive pottery.

Figueroa Castle, Salvatierra de los Barros, near Zafra

Extremadura

The Land and its History

One of the least populated and least visited regions of Spain, Extremadura is nevertheless one of the most beautiful to those who relish scenery on a grand scale. It was the heartland of Roman Lusitania (which included most of present-day Portugal), bisected by the Via Plata which ran from the Mediterranean to the Bay of Biscay, and was the artery by which Rome's authority filtered through its westernmost Iberian dominion. It scarcely figures in the more spectacular annals of the Reconquest, despite the fact that it gave birth to at least two of the chivalrous Orders of the time, notably Alcántara, and that its nobility were thus fighting Islam all over Spain.

World explorers

But the very harshness of Extremadura stimulated its later sons to exploits further afield: Pizarro and Cortés, *conquistadores* respectively of Peru and Mexico; Balboa, who crossed the Panamanian isthmus to the Pacific; Valdivía, founder of Santiago de Chile, were all Extremeños and so were thousands of their followers – "urged", says Ford nastily, "by an adequate stimulant, avarice for instance."

Artists

On the other hand, two of Spain's best known religious painters, Morales, who specialised in nobly-browed madonnas and saints in the 16th century, and Zurbarán in the following one, were also Extremeños – whom Ford described more kindly, when referring to those of his own time, as "kind-hearted . . . remarkably civil and courteous, especially to the passing stranger . . . a mixture between the gay swaggering Andalusian and the serious proud Castilian." The same holds true today.

Cork oaks

Cork oaks are a predominant feature of the rolling Extremeñan countryside and, now that cork is enjoying a revival, their bark makes a useful contribution to the local economy while their acorns continue to feed the foraging flocks of pinky-brown Extremeñan pigs.

Merino sheep

The region has for centuries also been home to other species of livestock. In the years following the Reconquest the large scale sheep farmers of the Sierra de Gredos took to driving their flocks into the plains of Extremadura for winter pasture; a practice that continues, to a lesser extent, to this day. To forestall arguments with local landowners, an informal regulatory system, the *Mesta,* administered by members of both communities, was set up to allow free passage for the flocks without utterly ravaging Extremeñan crops; needless to say, the crops suffered nonetheless. Although these merino sheep were more prized for their wool than for their meat, mutton is still an important staple of the Extremeñan cuisine.

Extremeñan pigs

Extremadura's chief gastronomic claims to fame, however, derive from pigs; the diet that the cork oak, chestnut and beech forests provide for the ubiquitous Extremeñan swine produces succulent *jamons, chorizos, tocinos* and other charcuterie that are prized throughout Spain. (In former times, apparently, the most delicious hams came from pigs nourished almost exclusively on the vipers that proliferated in the pigs' enclosures, but enquiries about viper-fed swine nowadays are met with blank incomprehension).

Montánchez, between Cáceres and Mérida, is particularly famous for its pork products, which Charles V made a regular part of his copious daily diet, but you get lovely charcuterie all over the province.

Game and wine

Although the Guadiana no longer oozes into vast swamplands where wild fowl breed, there is still plenty of game in the region – partridge, pheasant, hare and the like – and from the light, dry soil come some surprisingly good wines.

The Road from Madrid

The main highway from Madrid to Extremadura, the NV, is a fast dual carriageway almost to the western edge of the province of Castilla-La Mancha. At Maqueda, 77 km (nearly 50 miles) from the capital, where a huge rectangular hilltop castle (recently partly restored) overlooks the little town and its attractive *mudéjar* church tower, it is joined by the road from Toledo, 40 km (25 miles) away. Once into Extremadura, it continues to be a reasonably fast road, going through Navalmoral de la Mata, past the nuclear power station at Almaraz and over the dramatic Puerto de Miravete pass before it reaches Trujillo. It is only recommended, however, to those who are already familiar with the scores of places that merit attention between Madrid and the Extremadura heartland.

Peninsula War battle

About nine km (just over five miles) short of Talavera de la Reina, the main highway crosses the Alberche, near its junction with the Tagus, by a new bridge that parallels a ruined 15th-century one. For anyone stirred by military history, this is haunted country: here in July of 1809 the exhausted, under-provisioned army of Sir Arthur Wellesley (later Duke of Wellington), making its first foray into Spain to assist in ridding the country of Napoleon's army, battled for two days with the forces of Joseph Bonaparte, Napoleon's brother, who had been placed on the Spanish throne. Wellesley finally drove the French back towards Toledo but then faced a new hazard: another French force was approaching from the north to threaten his rear and he decided to retreat towards Portugal.

Talavera de la Reina

But Talavera de la Reina (pop c. 64,000) is more than just the name of Britain's first major Peninsular War victory on Spanish soil (and the one that earned Wellesley a viscountcy); it also gives its name to the beautiful blue and yellow ceramic ware that has been made there since the 15th century. Coming in from Madrid, the gleaming dome of the Ermita del Virgen del Prado, rising alongside the bullring, is difficult to miss; its *azulejo* tile decorations, both outside and within, span almost every period of Talavera design. And the bullring itself is famous throughout Spain as the place where the great bullfighter Joselito was killed.

Defy the one-way traffic system, aimed at getting people round Talavera and away from it as fast as possible, and there is more fine architecture and tiling to be seen in the heart of town which is still, as in Ford's day, "full of nice bits for the sketch book." *Azulejos* decorate several housefronts and the benches in the shady little plaza in front of the church of Sta Maria Mayor, which has a beautiful rose window displaying strong Arabesque influences. In the streets between this plaza and the Plaza Mayor are traces of Moorish walls and the church of Santiago is typical of the best Toledan *mudéjar.*

The Arco de S Pedro is a Roman archway converted into a chapel; there is a small museum of old Talavera pottery and, of course, countless shops selling the modern variety, all of it adding up to a very agreeable few hours' visit.

Oropesa

Thirty-three km (just over 20 miles) west of Talavera is Oropesa (pop c. 3,000), topping a low hill; the heavily castellated, crenellated and turreted outlines of its castle visible for miles. In the former palace that adjoins it is one of the earliest of the State-owned Paradors and still one of the pleasantest. The Counts of Oropesa, one of whom was a Viceroy of Peru noted for his reform of the draconian Indian laws, were given to supporting the losing side in affairs nearer home. In the quarrel over the throne of Castile, the family espoused the cause of Enrique IV's supposedly illegitimate daughter, La Beltraneja, against that of his sister Isabella, which ensured their social ostracism for many a decade, and they later sided with the *communeros* in their revolt against Isabella's grandson, Charles V.

But their palace now makes a splendid halting place on the way to Extremadura and the partly-walled village is full of interest, too. Old women sit in doorways in front of the seigneurial mansions that line its streets, working away at the traditional embroidery whose designs, followed or adapted since the 16th century, are faintly geometric and for the most part incorporated into table linen, handkerchiefs and blouses. You can buy it in Oropesa's little shops and at the Parador, but the real heart of this cottage industry is a mile or two further west, at Lagartera.

Puente de l'Arzobispo

Oropesa is at a crossroads where decisions must be made: whether to turn north and enter Extremadura by way of the Sierra de Gredos, to turn south and go via Guadalupe, or to continue by the main road. A roundabout route that combines the first two options is the most satisfactory, setting off in a southerly direction first, to Puente de l'Arzobispo. This is another pottery town, less appealing to the casual buyer than Talavera, but still preserving the 14th-century bridge over which Wellesley and his weary English army, forced after all to retreat after the victory over the French at Talavera, made its way back towards Portugal.

Caceres Region

Guadalupe

Heading south from Puente del Arzobispo, a side-road to the left off the TO702 soon after you cross the Tagus leads to the remains of the Roman city of Vascos, about 11 km (seven miles) away and now on the edge of the Azutan dam. Continuing southwards again, the TO702 winds through lovely hills to Guadalupe and its famous monastery, cradled in the sierras just 86 km (about 54 miles) from the Oropesa Parador.

In spring and early summer the roadsides are ablaze with wild flowers; later in the summer small fields of tobacco chequer the country to either side of the road; behind them the lower slopes of the rock-crested sierras are planted with pine and eucalyptus. Hereabouts, mules are still used for ploughing and other agricultural work, and for carrying loads; it is an intensely rural area.

The town

There are wonderful views from the Puerto de S Vicente pass, 40 km (25 miles) short of Guadalupe and then, as you come over the final hill, of the massively-walled monastery itself, dominating the little town (pop c. 2,800). Refreshingly free of the nastier forms of commercialism that flourish in most major pilgrimage-places, the "narrow wynds of Guadalupe" (Ford) are neatly cobbled and edged by little old houses whose upper storeys project over the pavements, supported by pillars or carved beam-ends. Flowers spill from between balcony railings, old pantiles make patterns between whitewashed walls and the sky, tourist shops are relatively inoffensive and the place has an aura of contentment.

Our Lady of Guadalupe

Like many other venerated statues of the Virgin in Spain, that of Our Lady of Guadalupe was discovered (in 1330) by a peasant, having been buried for centuries during the Moslem occupation. ("What with the finding of statues and the seeing of visions," Honor Tracy observes in 'Winter in Seville', "the services of shepherds, cowherds and goatherds to the Church in Spain have been well nigh incalculable.") In this case the discoverer was a cowherd and the statue was immediately identified as being the work of St Luke.

Building of the monastery

A hermitage was built on the spot, to be replaced ten years later by a chapel raised by Alfonso XI of Castile, who also commanded the monastery to be built after his victory over the Moors on the banks of the

Salado, just south of Cádiz. In gratitude for this triumph, he also dedicated part of his battle spoils to the Virgin of Guadalupe, and thus began the royal connection with her. (The bridge at Puente del Arzobispo was built in 1337-8 by the Archbishop of Toledo to make access to her shrine easier from the north.)

Spread of the cult

Since the Virgin was Extremadura's most powerful protectress, she was especially venerated by Extremeñan explorers and *conquistadores.* Columbus, whose crew numbered many men from Extremadura, named an island for her and came bearing a huge candle to give her thanks for saving his ship in a storm; the later conquerors of the New World customarily showered both devotions and wealth upon her. Don John of Austria, half-brother of Philip II, presented her with a lamp captured from a Turkish ship at the Battle of Lepanto in 1571; it still hangs in the sacristy. Forty years earlier, an Indian in Mexico claimed to have seen her in a vision, after which her cult became as powerful there as it was in Spain and spread to South America as well; Latin Americans are invariably among her daily visitors.

Eclipse of the monastery

The monastery's pre-eminence began to be eclipsed by that of the Virgin of Zaragoza towards the end of the 18th century, and in 1809 the French sacked it and their general, Victor, carried off cartloads of treasure but "left the image behind", says Ford, "because although carved by St Luke, it would not have fetched five francs on the Pont Neuf at Paris." Soon after that the buildings were all but abandoned and were beginning to fall into ruin when Ford visited them.

The 1913 Baedeker mentions that it had once been among the richest monasteries in Spain but gives only a brief description of the church and cloister, which by then had been re-occupied by the Franciscans. By 1928 it had revived sufficiently for Alfonso XIII to present the effigy with a new crown and to pronounce her one of Spain's official Virgin Queens (Spaniards tend to regard Our Lady of Montserrat, Our Lady of Zaragoza, Our Lady of Guadalupe and other miracle-working Virgins as though they were unrelated to one another and almost in competition.)

Parador and Hospice

Since then, Guadalupe has been the object of increasing attention and considerable restoration. The pleasant Parador is a conversion of a couple of 15th-century pilgrim hospices and named for the painter Zurbarán; there is also a hospice (the Hospedería del Real Monasterio) within the monastery itself, off the Gothic cloister, where you can lodge and eat simply but adequately.

Church and Monastery

From the sloping, triangular Plaza Mayor, a few yards down the street from the Parador, a flight of steps leads to the adjacent doors of church and monastery, bronze-covered and set in an ochre stone Flamboyant Gothic façade that looks cramped between the austere defensive towers that flank it.

The cloister

The guided tours (mornings and afternoons, every day) tend to take visitors along a narrow monastic corridor and into the beautiful 15th-century *mudéjar* cloister first, where orange trees and roses and hydrangeas burgeon between box hedges. The two storeys of brick-built horseshoe arches, delicately picked out in rose colour-wash, look inward to a Moorish ablution fountain sheltered by a three-tiered pavilion patterned with green and white tiles. In one corner of the cloister is an ancient *lavabo* and the former refectory, now housing a collection of embroidered vestments and altar-cloths.

The chapter house

The chapter house, opening off its own little cloister, has a painted Arabesque ceiling springing from fan-vaults and houses illuminated manuscripts and a variety of other treasures: Philip II's ivory crucifix, a Flemish triptych, a lovely little Goya and a series of small paintings by the Extremeñan master, Zurbarán.

Church choir

From there you move into the *coro* of the church, which is, unusually, on a balcony above the nave and contains Churrigueresque carved choirstalls, a curious, triangular 14th-century wooden candelabrum, and some marvellous old organs as well as a modern one. From there, looking eastward down the nave and through the superb early 16th-century wrought-iron screen that divides it, you have your first view of the distant, illuminated statue of the Virgin, high above the altar.

The sacristy; reliquary room

The church is open all day long and you can examine the tombs and other features at will, so the guide scurries his party along to the sacristy, a beautifully proportioned room decorated in high Baroque where hang the famous series of huge Zurbarán paintings: some of St Jerome, some of former priors of the monastery. Next, you are ushered into the octagonal *relicario,* glittering with more precious objects (a large oblong reliquary of the mid 15th century, with alternate panels of *repousse* silver and enamel work, is noteworthy).

The jewel room

Up a flight of red jasper stairs is the *joyero,* where a monk takes over from the secular guide and often infuses the proceedings with more warmth. The *joyero,* or jewel room, contains the collection of crowns, headdresses and regalia that have at one time or another been presented to the Virgin. Some, interspersed with disappointing paintings by Luca Giordano and a few polychrome wooden statues of saints, are already on display, and if the monk is feeling benign he may bring out others for the watchers to exclaim over as well.

The shrine

When he feels the time is right, the monk solemnly opens the door to the *camarín,* a tiny Baroque chamber immediately behind the statue above the high altar. Its centrepiece at first appears to be nothing more interesting than a series of modern gilt and enamel panels set into the wall, each depicting a scene from the Virgin's life. But with a theatrical flourish, the monk touches one side of the ensemble and it pivots to bring the statue itself into view from the reverse side. It is no more than three feet high and obviously very old: the face, possibly of oak, is dark and faintly mottled but appealingly carved, and this is all you can see of it apart from one age-blackened hand emerging from the jewelled robes - in which the Child Jesus is all but submerged. Everyone reverently kisses not her actual robe but a silvery disc suspended on a ribbon below it, and then everyone files piously out after depositing an offering into a conveniently-placed receptacle.

Guadalupe to Plasencia

There are hermitages and a couple of former royal palaces tucked into the hills around Guadalupe, and the little wine town of Cañamero to the southwest, on the most direct route to Mérida, but I would head north along the CC713, winding through more lovely, hilly countryside and crossing the huge Valdecañas dam.

Jarandilla de la Vera

In 80 km (50 miles) it briefly joins the main NV near Navalmoral de la Mata where a turnoff to the right leads to Jarandilla de la Vera, 34 km (just over 20 miles) further north, across the Tagus in the Sierra de Gredos foothills. The castle in which Charles V stayed before he moved to Yuste is now a Parador and a convenient place from which to visit the spot in which the Holy Roman Emperor spent the final months of his life.

Charles V's abdication

Grandson of Ferdinand and Isabella and son of their recently dead, half-crazed daughter, Charles was only 55 when he summoned his son (later Philip II) away from England and Mary Tudor's court to Brussels and, in 1555, ceremonially abdicated in his favour. But

Charles was already toothless, racked with gout and other ailments, and suffused with melancholia inherited from his mother. He had chosen Yuste earlier as his place of retirement, and he set sail for Laredo, near Santander, had himself borne on a litter to Jarandilla, and occupied the castle while his apartments at the monastery were being built.

Yuste: monastery and imperial apartments

He chose well: the spot is green and enchanting and the little monastery surprisingly pretty for so gloomy a man to have chosen, with red-tiled roofs and a lovely garden. It was sacked during the Peninsular War but faithfully restored and one cannot visit much of the monastery itself apart from the church crypt in which Charles's body lay for 16 years before being moved to the Escorial.

Of equal interest are the austere imperial apartments, hung with black in memory of his unfortunate mother, where he lived for 18 months, "half like a monk and half like a retired country gentleman," says Ford.

Charles V's retirement and death

Occasionally he clambered aboard a pony for a sedate ride when his gout allowed it (which was not often, since he could not resist the rich foods that compounded his suffering); sometimes he negotiated the specially constructed ramp from his patio to the garden, to enjoy the flowers. When not at prayer, his attention was divided between the mechanics of clocks and watches (which seem to have been an obsession with all Spanishs royals) and the company of a small boy called Jerome. When he died in September of 1558, a private letter to Philip II was found among his papers in which the emperor admitted the paternity of this child – who grew up to become the dashing Don John of Austria.

Tobacco fields

Leaving Yuste and taking the C501 westwards, the hills are terraced into tiny fields, many planted with tobacco, and the huge sheds in which it is dried are a feature of every village.

Plasencia

Fifty-five km (35 miles) away, the outskirts of Plasencia (pop c. 32,000) are predictably modern and ugly but the city, founded by Alfonso VIII of Castile in 1190 on a Roman site that rides a ridge above the Jerte, more than repays the effort of penetrating them. It is ringed with much-restored walls and semi-circular turrets that look more decorative than fearsome, and crowned by the pinnacles of its Cathedral.

The Cathedral

The Cathedral is an odd building in a mixture of styles. Particularly interesting are its choirstalls (ask to visit the *coro*), some of whose brilliantly carved 16th-century seat-backs and misericords juxtapose conventional Biblical scenes with a strange assortment of everyday ones, some perfectly proper, like the bullfight and the barber's shop, others frankly Rabelaisian. They are by Rodrigo Alemán, whose work on the choirstalls of Toledo, 25 years earlier, is staid by contrast.

The old town

The old part of town, around the cathedral, boasts some beautiful old mansions, including the Casa de Déan, now the law courts, the Palacio de Mirabel and the Palacio de las Bovedas, abutting Sto Domingo church. In the arcaded Plaza Mayor the 16th-century Ayuntimiento has a fanciful clock on its roof; other attractive squares are Plaza S Vicente Ferrer and Plaza S Nicolás.

Plasencia to Cáceres

Alcántara Dam

The main road south from Plasencia, N630, eventually crosses the huge Alcántara dam, beneath which a ruined Roman bridge is submerged; from the depths of one of the smaller lakes off it an ancient hexagonal tower, once part of a castle, protrudes forlornly.

Coria

Turn right just before the Roman bridge and you come in 32 km (20 miles) to Coria, the former Roman Corium, overlooking the Alagón river at the heart of the tobacco country. Its bridge and some of its walls and archways stand on Roman foundations and its 15th-century cathedral has a later, Baroque tower. In 1812 it was the headquarters of one of Wellington's commanders at the start of the campaign that finally drove Napoleon's armies from Spanish soil.

Alcántara's Roman bridge

If you go north from Coria and turn left at Moraleja the CC214, running along the Alagón valley close to the Portuguese border, brings you in 72 kn (45 miles) to the western tip of the Alcántara dam and Alcántara itself (pop c. 2,500). The name is from the Arabic, El Kantara, meaning "bridge", and the great six-arched drystone construction, the world's tallest surviving Roman bridge, built in 105 AD on the orders of Emperor Trajan across a bleak stretch of the Tagus gorge, is indeed "worth going 100 L. to see" (Ford). It has been seriously damaged twice, once in 1213 by the Moors, after which Charles V had it repaired, and once almost 600 years later when General Mayne demolished one of its arches to prevent Napoleon's forces from crossing. Subsequently the British threw a rope suspension bridge across the breach and this continued in use long after the Peninsular War ended – until 1836, in fact.

The bridge was thoroughly restored in 1860; the triumphal arch at the halfway point and the little temple on the left bank are both originally Roman but the tomb of the architect, Caius Julius Lacer, who was buried nearby, has vanished.

Alcántara town

The little town of Alcántara, plundered by the French in 1809 and in Ford's day still "a ruined abode of misery", was the headquarters of one of the most famous of the medieval chivalric orders formed to combat Islam in the name of Christ. The Knights of Alcántara took this name after successfully repelling the Moors from the town's citadel in 1218. The castle is now a ruin, but the 13th-century Sta Maria church has some interesting tombs of former Grand Masters of the Order, and a series of *retablo* paintings by Morales. Restoration is in progress on the later church and convent of S Benito. Alcántara was the birthplace of one of Spain's most revered saints, the 16th-century mystic S Pedro de Alcántara, confessor for a time to Sta Teresa of Ávila. He spent most of his life in Extremadura and is buried only just outside its boundaries, at Arenas de S Pedro in the Sierra de Gredos.

Brozas; Arroyo de la Luz

At a spot almost on the Portuguese border, to the northwest of town, a battle took place in 1580 that gained Portugal for Philip II of Spain and his heirs for a period of 60 years. Moving south, the C523 curves past Brozas, a neglected but evocative little township with a splendid towered 16th-century church and several fine mansions, built by the newly-rich families of its *conquistador* sons, and continues in 64 km (40 miles) via Arroyo de la Luz. Just north of the village is the little white pilgrimage chapel of Nuestra Señora de la Luz, where a well-attended local *romería,* or religious festival, takes place in October; the newly-restored Gothic church of the Asunción in Arroyo de la Luz itself has a many-panelled *retablo* painted by Morales in the 1560s, representing some of his finest work.

The City of Cáceres

Accommodation; Parking

Cáceres (pop c. 72,000), the provincial capital, has the usual collar of dull, modern development ringing it but it is a good place for a stopover thanks to a fair choice of hotels. The Hotel Extremadura, on the outskirts, has the advantage of a swimming pool; the Alcántara, across the street, lacks this amenity but is otherwise comparable. Driving into the city centre, head for Plaza del General Mola, where the

Town Hall and Tourist Office are; it offers the best hope of parking and old Cáceres is no place to try and explore by car.

Old city

A gem of a late medieval city, lovingly preserved and restored, its walls rising from Roman foundations (one of the gates, the Arco del Cristo in the southeast, is almost completely Roman), Cáceres has an extraordinarily secretive atmosphere. It is a city to wander in after the working population has gone home and left it half-deserted, letting its otherworldly aura wash over you. In spring, storks stand stiffly on their untidy nests far above the harmonious, honey-coloured ensemble of encircling walls and 15th and 16th-century seigneurial mansions in rough stone encrusted with armorial reliefs and separated by tiny streets and odd-shaped plazas.

Plazas and palaces

A narrow alley leads from the broad Arco de Estrella archway, at the top of a flight of steps out of Plaza del General Mola, into Plaza Sta Maria, hemmed about with superb façades (the Archbishop's and Mayoralgo palaces, especially), facing in towards the 16th-century church. The magisterial Palacio de los Golfinos de Abajo (Lower Golfines Palace) is just off the plaza, with its twin Moorish *ajimez* windows and its intricately carved later frieze of contorted griffons. In the northern angle of the city walls, the Casa de Toledo-Montezuma, now housing a bank, was built by one of the Saavedra family, descended from a member of Cortés' band of *conquistadores* who married an Aztec princess, Montezuma's daughter.

Apart from coats-of-arms, galleries, massive stone balconies and windows (some carved out of the corners of houses as though scooped from blocks of fudge), there is little external decoration on these sturdy walls but many a monumental gateway is sometimes left open, affording glimpses of patios where a Roman column or two may stand among the later ones, and of loggias embellished with *mudéjar* patterned brickwork or inset Roman *stelae.* The Upper Golfines Palace and the mansion across from it are particularly worth penetrating if possible.

Medieval towers

Towers are attached to houses everywhere, many of them decapitated in 1477 by order of Isabella the Catholic, whose disciplinary hand was quick to fall upon anyone considered to be growing too proud and powerful. One that escaped is that of S Mateo church; next to it, the only secular tower still standing is the Torre de las Cigueñas, above a well-scrubbed barracks.

Casas de las Veletas

Near it, the Casa de las Veletas is built over an 11th-century Moorish cistern designed for the former *alcázar.* A balustrade at roof level, created by balancing green and white pottery jars alternately on top of one another, gives it an unusually jaunty air, compounded by a series of polychrome ceramic gargoyles looking down from it. Inside is the small Provincial Museum (open mornings and most afternoons, closed Sundays) with Roman and earlier objects, some interesting regional folk costumes, and the original cistern, its roof upheld by five rows of horseshoe arches and still fed with rainwater by those gargoyles above.

Trujillo

Parador

Trujillo (pop c. 9,500) is only 49 km (just over 30 miles) to the east and until fairly recently you would have been best advised to make a day's outing of it from Cáceres, since its hotel resources were limited to the modest, if adequate, Las Cigueñas hotel out on the Mérida road. Now, however, it also has a fine Parador converted from an old convent in the centre of town so it is equally logical to make that your base instead of Cáceres.

Trujillo's conquistadors

Between the two cities the largely empty landscapes, looking to city-dwellers from abroad exhilaratingly untamed, must have seemed bleak beyond words to the ambitious young men of the 15th and 16th centuries, and you realise that to escape them probably seemed worth any risk and hardship. Certainly Trujillo gave birth to many a *conquistador,* among them Orellana, who explored the Amazon from Peru, and the Herculean warrior Paredes. Most famous of them all was Francisco Pizarro, the bastard son of a soldier, who started his career as a swineherd. He and his three brothers, only the oldest of them legitimate, all left to seek fame and fortune in the Indies.

Francisco Pizarro

It was Francisco Pizarro who led the tiny band of men that overwhelmed the Incas of Peru. He ruled the country brutally in the name of Spain until he was murdered in his palace in Lima in 1541; just retribution, perhaps, for his own horrible murder of the Inca Emperor Atahualpa eight years earlier. A rather gruesome-looking corpse, almost certainly not Pizarro's, lies enshrined in a glass coffin in Lima Cathedral; I was told that at one point the *conquistador's* tomb was vandalised and that a more seemly-looking corpse had been installed in it later. At any rate, the so-called tomb of Pizarro in Trujillo's Sta Maria church is certainly not his.

Plaza Mayor

On the approach, the city looks like a crumbling ruin, half-encircled by biscuity ramparts and the haphazard modern town, its skyline enlivened by shaggy storks' nests. As you penetrate towards the centre, the streets first close in on you as though to repel invaders and then suddenly erupt into the lovely, eccentrically shaped and many-levelled Plaza Mayor, one of the most delightful sights in all Southern Spain. In the middle of this superb setting is the wonderfully patinated (modern) bronze equestrian statue of the tough old warrior himself, plumes flying from his helmet, feet thrusting into his stirrups, one hand reining harshly at his charger's head and the other brandishing a sword. A row of medieval houses rests on stone arches at the top of the broad, shallow flight of stone steps behind the statue.

Pizarro's Palace

Opposite the sculpture and downhill is the huge, pinkish-ochre Marqués de la Conquista's Palace, also known as Pizarro's Palace, with an immense coat-of-arms wrapped around one corner above a window, some more conventional windows covered by lovely grilles, and a row of primitive statues edging the roof. Francisco Pizarro himself never lived there: it was built by his older brother Hernando, who kept a prudently low profile in Peru but became later involved in a lawsuit that had him languishing for many years in a Spanish jail. He married his own niece, the daughter of Francisco by an Inca princess, and emerged from prison at a ripe old age to build this noble pile, doubtless with the proceeds of Peruvian spoils. His descendants, who still own it, took the title of Marquésas de la Conquista.

Other palaces; restaurants

More splendid arcaded stone houses stud the square, including the Piedras Albas and San Carlos palaces, the latter now housing an enclosed order of nuns who nevertheless permit you to visit its round, two-storied inner courtyard. Just off the plaza, by way of an atmospheric alleyway and the fine former Town Hall, is the Orellana-Pizarro Palace, with a gloriously carved upper gallery.

One of three very acceptable restaurants on the Plaza Mayor makes a strategic vantage point from which to survey some of these splendours and to notice more of their detail; one odd feature of many coats-of-arms is a pair of pigs staring up into the branches of a tree, perhaps recalling Francisco Pizarro's time as a swineherd.

S Martín church; Parador

S Martín church, at the top of the square, is paved with funerary tablets and has a prized 18th-century organ. Higher uphill to the east of it is the former Convent of Sta Clara, now housing the Parador, and a web of small streets edged by houses only marginally more plebeian than those in the square.

The Alfiler

Above the Plaza Mayor to the north and west rise square stone towers; one, the Alfiler, crowned with a decayed beehive-shaped structure and haphazardly studded with *azulejo* tiles, is a *mudéjar* belfry. Beyond and above are the restored 12th-century Moorish curtain walls of the castle, their crenellations floodlit at night.

Sta Maria church

Sta Maria church is on a circuitous uphill route to the castle, passing first beneath the Santiago Arch, one of the city's original gates, linking a secular tower with the 13th-century belfry of Santiago church. Inside Sta Maria, in the raised *coro,* are the carved stone kiosks in which the Catholic monarchs, Ferdinand and Isabella, sat to hear Mass when their travels brought them to Trujillo. Many of the city's great men are buried in this church, even if Pizarro himself is not, and the fine *retablo* paintings are said to be by Gallego. From the restored *mudéjar* belfry and from the splendid castle gateway uphill of it, the views are tremendous and include intimate glimpses of life in storks' nests.

Trujillo to Arroyomolinos

South from Trujillo, the main road (NV) takes you to Mérida in 88 km (55 miles); it is joined at Miajadas by the direct road from Guadalupe. A more attractive and no longer road south from Trujillo is the CC800 via Montánchez, which eventually joins the main Cáceres-Mérida road. This latter is less busy than the Trujillo road, recently improved; its first stretch, through cork oak groves and rolling meadowland, is punctuated by two superb 15th-century castles between the road and the Salor dam, followed soon after by a ruined one.

Montánchez

The turnoff to Montánchez comes some 16 km (10 miles) after it. Ford called it the "capital of the bacon district... (where)... the Duque de Arcos used to shut up the pigs in places abounding in vipers, on which they fattened." Although little more than a village, you can see Montánchez for miles in all directions, crowning a low sierra that seems to rise out of the plain for no other purpose than to support it. It is a dusty place of flaking old houses and a noble castle ruin, somehow epitomising the harsher qualities of life in Extremadura, but plump hams hang in shop windows – not all of them home-cured nowadays – and ham is prominently featured in the *tapa* bars.

Arroyomolinos

Just south of it, but not on the Mérida road, the village of

Arroyomolinos was where Wellington sent General Hill to surprise and rout General Girard's French army in 1811; the action, conducted at dead of night and in filthy weather, ended Girard's career in disgrace.

Badajoz Region

Medellín: birthplace of Cortés

If you decide to take the main road (NV) from Trujillo to Mérida, the most interesting detour (under 10 miles) is to Medellín, birthplace of the conqueror of Mexico, Hernán Cortés, its hilltop castle overlooking the Guadiana. Once a prosperous township, it was almost totally destroyed by the French general, Victor, when he trounced a Spanish army under Cuesta there in 1809. The castle and the 17th-century bridge acrosss the river are all that remain of its past riches; it is perhaps tempting to feel sympathy with Cortés' desire to get away.

In fact, Cortés came of a fairly well-to-do family, unlike many *conquistadores,* and began his quest for fame in Cuba. Most people's image of him, and probably all the *conquistadores,* is of a greedy ruffian, ruthlessly destroying primitive civilisations for personal gain; Ford calls Cortés "reckless, devoid alike of mercy, justice or good faith," and goes on to accuse him of "avarice, cruelty, bloodshed, bigotry . . ." But H V Morton, that most kindly of 20th-century travellers, drawing on the memoirs of Cortés' contemporary, Bernál Diaz del Castillo, presents him in a better light, balancing the picture by pointing out that the Mexican Aztecs, in particular, practised a savage and bloodthirsty form of religion quite contrary to the reported nobility of their Emperor, Montezuma. At all events, Cortés was the first of the *conquistadores* who meant to settle in the New World rather than merely plunder it, ritually burning his boats soon after he landed in Mexico. His conquests brought him little satisfaction, however; when he died back in Spain in 1547, he was all but forgotten.

Mérida

History

Mérida (pop c. 42,000), once the capital of Roman Lusitania, lying across the Via de Plata and, according to Ausonius in the fourth century, the ninth most important city in the Roman Empire, is archaeologically one of the most interesting towns in both Extremadura and all Spain. Founded in about 25 BC as Augusta Emerita, it throve and prospered and, unlike many a Roman city, managed to retain much of its legacy – though its classical structures, according to Baedeker in 1913, were "mostly in poor preservation". Ford tells us that the Goths "used Emerita kindly", repairing in 686 the magnificent Roman bridge and allowing it to remain largely Roman. "Such was its solid magnificence," Ford continues, "and so unlike Oriental filigree, that Musa and the Moors who came to attack it exclaimed 'All the world must have been called together to build such a city'."

The Moors used the town kindly, too, and its decline only started when it was reconquered by Alfonso IX of León in 1228. Thereafter, despite half-hearted efforts by Philip II and later conservationists under Charles III, it crumbled from neglect; only in the last century have its merits been appreciated and excavation and restoration work, some of it perhaps over-enthusiastic, been put in hand.

Mérida town; Parador
The town itself, white and searingly hot in high summer, and too full of shoddy modern buildings, is not at first very appealing, but it grows on you. This is especially true if you stay at the Parador: a low, whitewashed former convent wrapped about an enchanting patio, once the cloister, in which pots of greenery sit between Roman columns. An awning is pulled across it each morning to keep out the sun and the air stays cool. H V Morton succumbed to sunstroke while staying in the Mérida Parador and was nursed by a kindly chambermaid who brought him food he did not want and thus had surreptitiously to dispose of. It was mostly soup, presenting few problems, but "my luck still held when she brought me a steak," he recounts, "for there happened to pass beneath the window at the right moment what turned out to be the most astonished dog in Spain."

Hotels; restaurants
Alternative, more modest, hotels are the Emperatriz in Plaza de España and the Nova Roma in Calle Suárez Somonte, between the centre of town and the Roman theatre. The best restaurant is Nicolás, alongside the market, but at midday it is possible to mitigate high summer heat by taking a picnic out to the nearby reservoir.

Roman reservoir
Just north of town, this little reservoir, the Lago de Proserpina, was originally dammed by the Romans. You can still see the Roman stonework of the dam wall, though the water is no longer taken into the city along the Roman aqueduct; the citizens of Mérida now enjoy their Roman legacy by using the lake as their summer bathing-place.

Los Milagros acqueduct
The Proserpina dam is of course among the least of Mérida's Roman treasures. The Los Milagros acqueduct that brought its waters into

town is among the major ones: ten of its lofty arches are still virtually complete and, together with broken ones, march in symmetry northwards across the railways tracks and the trickling Albarregas, parallel with the Cáceres road. Storks favour the top of Los Milagros, whose monumental stone piers are striped with layers of red brick-work, perhaps as cushioning against earthquakes. Ford, who seldom waxed unconditionally lyrical, reflected that "perhaps these arches never, even when perfect, were so touchingly picturesque as now; the Vandal has destroyed their proportions, but time has healed the scars with lichens, and tinted the weather-beaten fragments."

Roman bridge

The bridge across the Albarregas rests on Roman foundations still, but is nothing like so fine as the 64-arched one bestriding two arms of the Guadiana and the islet between them on the other (west) side of Mérida. This is the Roman bridge the Visigoths repaired, and the world's longest; it has been patched up several times. Just upstream of it are the remnants of another Roman structure, designed to protect the piers from flash floods, and on the banks between them gypsies can often be seen camping; a gypsy fair is held here in October as well as a more cultural summer festival.

The Alcázar

The tactfully-restored Moorish Alcázar at the town end of the bridge is a direct descendant of the Roman palace that once stood on the site; the Visigoths took it over in their turn and the enormous cistern, reached from the courtyard by steps beneath a great carved beam, is one of their legacies. There is a small museum in the courtyard of the Alcázar, supplementing the exhibits in the museum proper (of which more later), but if you look about you you soon realise that all Mérida is potentially a Roman museum.

Casa del Conde de los Corbos

Walking from the Alcázar eastwards through a network of back streets one evening some 12 years ago, I saw a building site with Roman fragments among the rubble. On my most recent visit, a mint-new reconstruction was arising there, with casts of two huge circular stone panels set above the pediment (the originals are in the museum). Again, the Casa del Conde de los Corbos, when I first saw it, was built into the Roman temple of Diana and had its original Corinthian pillars across the facade. It had been thus for at least 70 years, since the 1913 Baedeker mentions it; now a restoration exercise is going on whose complecity must be taxing the archaeologists to the utmost.

The temple's front portico has been cleared of later masonry, the columns freed and drastically restored, and behind them the best features of the later mansion are being left *in situ.* These include a double storeyed patio with arabesque arches and a bit of wall with a fine medieval carved window-surround featuring a windswept *conquistador*-figure. At the rear, the temple base, with (so far) only column-bases studding it, has been exposed by sweeping away a neighbouring house or two; no doubt new columns will eventually rise upon it.

Sta Eulalia shrine

The shrine of Sta Eulalia, near the station at the north edge of town, is made up of stones from an earlier shrine to the god Mars. Sta Eulalia is Mérida's patroness: she was a child-martyr during the reign of Diocletian, a time when Christians went to extraordinary lengths to get themselves put to death, in the hope of becoming saints. In her case, she vilified the Roman gods and creeds and then spat in the face of a magistrate who was trying to curb her vituperations. She was roasted alive and her shrine, supposedly occupying the spot on which she was martyred, is known as 'El Hornito', the little oven. The young girls of Mérida would traditionally offer her locks of their hair at one time but this may no longer be so; a street called Calle John Lennon seems to indicate new allegiances.

Roman amphitheatre

The two most important Roman monuments lie close together at the western side of the town: the Roman amphitheatre and the theatre, both open all day long. The amphitheatre, severely restored, could hold some 15,000 spectators and was designed so that it could be flooded for water-combats as well as used dry for gladiatorial tournaments and chariot races.

Roman theatre; villa remains

The theatre is as complete as any I have seen, barring that of Aspendos in Turkey, to which it is closely related. Public buildings like this were, of course, built to standardised patterns from plans sent throughout the Empire by some central architects' department in Rome, but how closely the plans were followed depended upon the skills and whims of the local builders.

Mérida's theatre is more delicately proportioned than that of Aspendos and its tall stage wall, with its engaging central curve, built during Hadrian's reign in the second century, is particularly graceful. Two registers of pale grey marble columns with Corinthian capitals frame a series of niches, some of which still shelter parts of statues set against the honey-coloured stone background, and are linked by pieced-together remnants of white marble frieze. The rebuilt seats are divided into seven sections and beneath them the *vomitoria,* or access passages, are in perfect condition. Nearby are the remains of a villa with fine mosaic paving of a trio treading grapes, and all around are pretty gardens.

Museum of Roman Art

The stylish new museum, now called the National Museum of Roman Art (open mornings and afternoons) is opposite the entrance to the Roman theatre (the Tourist Office is between them) and has been built of small bricks to resemble a vast, vaulted Roman building with tall arches that down one side of the building are uninterrupted through three storeys and, on the other, are broken by walkways. There is a crypt below, where guided tours take you to see part of the excavations of the Roman town; in the building itself are well organised displays of a rich variety of finds.

Town centre

The Plaza de España, in the town centre, is rather an architectural hotch-potch (in terms of new buildings Mérida does not live up to her past) but it is big and animated. The main street, the pedestrianised Calle Sta Eulalia, leads out of it and is also somewhat jumbled architecturally. To the northwest of Plaza de España, on the way to the Parador, is the Arco de Santiago, a Roman arch bereft of its facing.

Nearby towns

Among the little towns worth visiting to the east and southeast of Mérida, apart from Medellín (mentioned earlier in this chapter) are Villanueva de la Serena, birthplace of Pedro de Valdivía, who founded Santiago de Chile, and Alange, with a ruined Moorish hilltop castle, one of Extremadura's few spas and patronised since Roman times.

The City of Badajoz

Routes from Mérida

To the west, Badajoz is an easy day's outing: under 70 kms (44 miles) whether you go by the main road that crosses the great Roman bridge or by the secondary road to the north of the Guadiana (via Montijo, whence came the family of Napoleon's III's wife Eugenia). It is best to go by the northerly road because it brings you into Badajoz (pop c. 114,500) across the river by the handsome late 16th-century bridge, designed by Juan de Herrera, which is the city's best feature and from which you can get a good view of the fortifications. Even so, it is merely a glimpse, thanks to the huge amount of new development that engulfs what is now the biggest and most prosperous town in Extremadura.

Early history

Badajoz only became important in the 11th century after the Caliphate of Córdoba disintegrated and it split into an independent *taifa,* or kingdom. It was made the provincial capital in place of Mérida after its reconquest in 1229, but not until Portugal began to win autonomy in the late 14th century did Badajoz acquire the dubious distinction of a key frontier post. Thus its history is full of battles and it claims several adventurer sons, notably Hernando de Soto, who crossed Florida and explored the Mississippi, as well as two major painters, Morales and Ayala.

Peninsular War sieges

Another son of Badajoz was Manuel Godoy, favourite of Charles IV and lover of his wife, Maria Luisa; it was this virtual ruler of Spain who opened its gates to Napoleon and, ironically, thereby caused Badajoz to be the scene of some of the ugliest episodes of the resultant Peninsular War. The French, abetted by a treacherous Spanish commander, took it in the spring of 1811 and two British sieges proved abortive. The third and bloodiest, in April 1812 with Wellington in command, succeeded - at fearful cost in terms of lives, and not only those of soldiers, for the British army proceeded to sack the town and decimate the inhabitants and Wellington was unable to get them under control for three days.

Civil War massacre; opinions of the town

It was the scene of another massacre during the Civil War, not a pretty history, and not really a pretty city, either. George Borrow, who had travelled by ship to Lisbon to spend the years from 1835-40 in Spain on behalf of the Bible Society, first entered Spain at Badajoz and commented that it "did not prepossess one much in favour of the country which I had just entered." Nearly a century later, V S Pritchett, passing through Badajoz in the course of a walking tour ('Marching Spain', published by Hogarth Press) met Borrow's successors and remarked that "for the Bible sellers, Spain can have changed little since the days of Borrow . . . Don Francisco told stories that made the blood boil."

Alcázaba and Museum

Neither, probably would recognise Badajoz today except for a few narrow streets and little plazas in the old part near the market and beneath the remains of the Moorish Alcázaba. A building within its precincts, housing the Archaeological Museum, is probably the most architecturally interesting in town.

Mérida to Zafra

Two main routes

It is, in fact, quite practical to see Badajoz in an hour or so and go on south by devious ways towards Zafra afterwards. The direct Mérida-

Zafra road, the N630 (total distance 63 km, or just over 40 miles) arrows its way through mile upon mile of vineyards interspersed with a few cork oak, olive and fruit plantations and the only place of interest apart from Almendralejo, full of wineries, are a few castle-crowned villages off the road to the west: Villaba de los Barros, Feria, and Salvatierra de los Barros. The other main road, N432 from Badajoz to Zafra, is relieved - for battlefield enthusiasts - only by La Albuera, where an extraordinarily confused and murderous battle was fought in May of 1811 during the early part of the struggle for Badajoz.

A roundabout route; Olivenza

It is thus of far greater interest to go by the roundabout way, first to Olivenza, about 25 km (15 miles) southwest of Badajoz on the pretty C436 minor road that skirts the Portuguese border. Olivenza (pop c. 32,000) was a Portuguese town from the late 13th century until 1801, when it surrendered to Godoy's Spanish troops in a forlorn attempt to defuse the inevitable war with the French. It thus keeps a measure of Portuguese character: the portal of the town library is pure Portuguese Manueline with its motifs of twisted ropes and knots and spheres, suggesting the Portuguese discoverers, and the nave of La Magdalena church is probably by the Arruda brothers, who designed Lisbon's magnificent Hieronymite Monastery façade. It is a pleasant little town, its layers of whitewashed houses crowned by the fat keep of an early 14th-century castle built by King Denis of Portugal. There are other good churches, including Sta Maria and the Misericordia, with beautiful old *azulejos,* a palm-surrounded main square and atmospheric little streets.

Alconchel to Salvatierra de los Barros

South of Olivenza is Alconchel, overlooked by a splendidly restored castle sitting on a conical hill, and here you can turn east to wind towards Zafra through pretty, hilly country via Barracotta (where de Soto's family originally came from) and picturesque Salvatierra de Los Barros.

Jerez de los Caballeros: history

Or you can continue on the same road, through the border town of Villanueva del Fresno and Oliva de la Frontera to Jerez de los Caballeros (pop c. 10,000), which on this approach appears to have been skewered to its hilltop by five towers. The "caballeros" of this Jerez were the Knights Templar, who won the hilltop site from the Moors in 1229, fortified it and somehow left their imprint upon it forever, even though it was handed over to the Knight of Santiago when the Templars, having grown too powerful and arrogant, were disbanded in disgrace in the early 14th century.

Jerez de los Caballeros: the town
Vasco Nuñez de Balboa, who first crossed the Panama isthmus, Darien, and "stared at the Pacific" (Keats' sonnet, of course, credits the wrong man) was born here; the cork industry and the curing of excellent hams have kept it prosperous. Cobbled streets lined with white houses twist up and down two steep hills between the Templars' castle on one and the church of S Bartolmé on the other. This has the tallest of two wildly Baroque towers, with layers of moulding picked out in red and white, inset with glass and *azulejos* and studded with blue pinnacles. Inside, its more conventionally Baroque organ loft is striking. On the south side of town is a medieval gate and, below the castle, a shady belvedere.

From here to Zafra it is just 40 km (25 miles) by the direct road, through Burguillos del Cerro with another Templars' castle.

Zafra and Llerena

An Iberian settlement before the Romans came and subsequently the Moorish Zafar, Zafra (pop c. 13,000) slid gently into decay during the following centuries, assisted by the depredations of Napoleon's armies. Ford describes it as "full of buildings begun in better times and on a grand scale" and Honor Tracy, in 'Silk Hats and No Breakfast', remarks that it was "sadly in need of paint and repair." That is exactly what it has had in recent decades, transforming it into a perfect stage set.

Zafra Parador
The reversal of its fortunes started in 1968 when a Parador was installed into the 15th-century palace of the Figueroas, later Counts and finally Dukes of Feria. Lorenzo de Figueroa had converted it from the former Alcázar and from without it still looks faintly Moorish: a pile of sherry-coloured stone spiked by tall, circular, merlon-crowned towers. Inside, in complete contrast, the patio is pure Renaissance. Look at it even if you cannot stay – in which case, the Huerta Honda is an excellent alternative.

Dukes of Feria
The Dukes of Feria were powerful in Extremadura. One of them was a patron of Cortés, after whom the Parador is named; a later one accompanied Philip II to England when he went to wed Mary Tudor. He became the Spanish Ambassador in London and married Jane Dormer, one of the Queen's ladies-in-waiting. After the accession of Elizabeth, however, the English-born Catholic Duchess of Feria came to live at Zafra, where she survived to a ripe old age and befriended many exiled English Catholics. She and her husband are buried in the Convent of Sta Clara (though Jane's heart was sent, at her request, to England);

the cupola-ed chapel of Sta Marina, next door to the Parador, contains the tomb of her cousin Margaret Harrington ('Doña Margarite Harinton'), who accompanied the Duchess to Spain.

Zafra's Plaza Mayor; churches

There is a nice shady park on the edge of Zafra and, in the other direction, the Calle Mayor leads to the beautifully restored 18th-century Plaza Mayor, surrounded by graceful, whitewashed, arcaded buildings, some with wrought-iron balconies, others with decorative balustrades edging their roofs, yet others with slender, paired *ajimez* windows. Through an archway is the smaller and older but equally charming Plaza Chica and, radiating away from this precinct in a spider web of little streets, are two good churches, the Colegiata and the Candelaria, and any number of fine houses.

Llerena

Southeast of Zafra by 35 km (just over 21 miles) along N432, Llerena is a little country town with an astonishing monumental Plaza Mayor, unlike any other you have seen in Extremadura, overlooked by the huge Baroque belfry of N S de Granada (*granada* means pomegranate, and a stone carving of one features in the tympanum of the main door).

St Mark's bull

Ford tells us of a curious practice in Llerena: on the eve of St Mark the priest would choose a bull from the herd, christen it after the Apostle, and take it to Mass, after which it became tame for 24 hours and an object of reverence among the citizens as it wandered the streets. "If (it) stopped before any house, the inhabitants were suspected of heresy or Judaism," he continues. "It will easily be guessed what a powerful engine in the hands of the priest this . . . must have been, and how effectually it secured the payment of church rates and **voluntary** offerings."

Routes into Andalusía

You can come back to Zafra from Llerena via Fuente de Cantos, birthplace of Zurbarán, or you can turn south there on the main road to Seville. Better still, you can spend another night in Zafra and set off south for Andalusía across the Sierra Morena, following the N435 via Fregenal de la Sierra. This is almost as theatrical on first sight as Jerez de los Caballeros, with huge 13th-century castle walls at its summit that enclose a couple of attractive churches; it was the birthplace of the first librarian of Philip II's Escorial Palace, Ariás Montano.

Typical Andalusían hill town, Alcalá de los Gazules

Western Andalusía

Background to Andalusía

Andalusía, the huge underbelly of Spain, has so individual a character that it is more like a country in its own right than a part of one, fenced off as it is from the rest of the nation by the peaks of the Sierra Morena and washed by both Atlantic and Mediterranean. Even within its own boundaries it has two distinct geographical variations. One is the great Guadalquivir basin, over 350 miles long and immensely broad, running parallel with the Sierra Morena to the north, where the land is fertile and the climate hot and humid in summer, wet in winter. By contrast, the mountains of Ronda and Granada that in the south separate the lowlands from the Mediterranean, have a climate that is almost Alpine, particularly up in the Sierra Nevada that enclose Andalusía to the east.

History

Romans and Moslems

Historically it was a Roman province after the passing of the first Phoenician and Greek colonists, and the fall of Carthage, and was called Baetica from the Roman name for the Guadalquivir, Baetis. A short-lived Vandal invasion at the beginning of the fifth century probably gave it its present name, an adaptation of Vandalusia, which the Moslems later varied to 'Al Andalus' and applied to all their Spanish territory. From shortly after their first invasion in 711, with the arrival of the Ummayyad ruler Abderrahman I in the middle of the eighth century, until the 11th century – throughout Europe's Dark Ages, in fact – Andalusía in general and Córdoba in particular was a brilliant centre of civilisation, learning and wealth. It stayed under Moorish occupation longer than any other part of Spain – until 1492 in the case of the kingdom of Granada – and it is this long Moorish heritage, much of it still more or less intact, that gives it its special character.

Early economy

Then as now its natural wealth derived both from the mineral deposits in the Sierra Morena and from its agriculture. With the collapse of Moslem rule and the eventual expulsion from Spain in 1609 of most of the remaining Moslem-descended population, agriculture suffered: it had been the *Moriscos,* or Christianised Moors, who kept alive their forefathers' farming techniques. Trade declined as a result, and Richard Ford described vast areas as being *dehesas y despoblados* (depopulated wastes) as late as 1845. Now, of course, it has been greatly revived and its industries are also making an increasing contribution to Andalusian wealth, notably in the form of tourism.

First tourists

Modern tourism in Spain started in Andalusía, in fact, after the end of the Peninsular War: Spaniards were favourably disposed towards the British and soldiers' tales of the sunny south caught the imagination of fashionable London. Sherry started to be drunk again in society and a few adventurous souls, like Byron, Benjamin Disraeli, and Lady Holland, ventured to Spain and recorded their experiences. In 1817 Mozart's 'Don Giovanni' had its London première; the following year Rossini's 'Barber of Seville' was staged there. People plunged into Washington Irving's 'Tales of the Allhambra' and 'The Conquest of Granada', published in 1832 and 1829 respectively, and a new interest was awakened in Iberian travel.

Richard Ford's Handbook

Richard Ford's 1845 'Handbook for Spain', published by John Murray, greatly stimulated the flow of travellers. A wealthy and scholarly man in his mid-thirties and already widely travelled, he went to Spain in the autumn of 1830 and stayed for three years, managing to cover an astonishing amount of ground by public transport or on horseback and to gather the mass of material from which he eventually compiled the monumental 'Hand-Book'. After the enjoyable discursive preliminaries, this opens with Andalusía, which he says ". . . in local position, climate, fertility, objects of interest and facility of access, must take precedence of all (other provinces) in Spain."

Access and appeal

Access was an important contributory factor. Even for those prone to seasickness, it was probably far less wearing to make the six-day voyage from England to Cádiz than it was (say) to travel overland to Italy, so the rich middle classes started coming to Andalusía. What kept them coming, ease of access apart, was the climate, the unique beauty of its Moorish architecture, and the character and peculiar culture of the people. English visitors were beguiled and captivated by Andalusían arches, the Andalusían mixture of dignity and gaiety, the flamboyance of Andalusían dress and *fiestas,* Andalusían *flamenco* and gipsy music, and these are still the popular tourist images of Spain – notwithstanding the fact that Andalusía is hardly typical of Spain as a whole and that tourism has diluted much of its quality.

Fifteenth-century hooligans

It is, of course, a truism to say that the quality of the tourists themselves has become diluted. In a dissertation upon Spanish manners, Ford remarks that "the value of an Englishman's good faith has sunk deeply in the (Spanish) mind . . . thus a Spaniard . . . considers the word of an Englishman to be . . . a sufficient security; and hitherto . . . no self-expatriated swindler has tarnished the honourable reputation of this country." The self-expatriated villains who nowadays live it up on the Costa del Crime has rather out-dated that observation, but it is worth pointing out what Ford ignored: that British hooligans in Spain are not an entirely 20th-century phenomenon. In 1486, Washington Irving relates, the forces of Ferdinand and Isabella were supplemented by "catholic knights" from other lands, among them "Lord Scales, Earl of Rivers, related to the Queen of England, wife of Henry VII", who had "distinguished himself, in the preceding year, at the Battle of Bosworth Field." The Earl, apparently "retaining a passion for warlike scenes . . . brought with him a hundred archers . . . also two hundred yeoman . . . men robust of frame and of prodigious strength . . . huge feeders and deep carousers (who) must fain eat and drink after the manner of their own country. They were often noisy and unruly, also, in their wassail; and their quarter of the camp was prone to be a scene of loud revel and sudden brawl."

Edible specialities

No doubt the Earl and his entourage of huge feeders partook of various Andalusían specialities that their successors enjoy today, such as *gazpacho,* the iced vegetable soup that is nowadays almost as national a dish as *paella.* But there are other local soups to look for, some made with almonds, such as *sopa de ajo con uvas* (garlic soup with grapes). There are also various fish soups that may not be classically Andalusían but, by their combination of ingredients (the use of orange juice, or sherry) have a strongly regional character. With so much fine olive oil, the Andalusían cook is, not surprisingly, unsurpassed at frying, and the *fritura mixta de pescados* (assorted fish, crisply fried), to be found all round the coast, is one of the prime pleasures of the Andalusían table. They have a way with eggs, too *(huevos a la flamenco)* and some original salads (*piriñaca,* made with onions and grilled and peeled sweet red and green peppers). Meat is less ubiquitous than fish, vegetables and fruit, but Andalusían cuisine includes the classic *riñones al Jerez* (kidneys in sherry sauce) and a similar dish based on veal.

Wines

In matters of wine, sherry (from Jerez) takes precedence, followed by the lighter amontillado from Montilla and manzanilla from Sanlúcar de Barrameda ("it strengthens the stomach, without heating or inebriating like sherry," wrote Ford of manzanilla). Andalusía is also the home of Spanish brandy, but produces no memorable table wines; the popular drink nowadays is *sangría,* an ice-cold mixture of red wine, soda water and sometimes a dash of brandy, to which slices of fruit are added.

Approaches to Western Andalusía

Andalusía is so vast and varied that it seems convenient to divide it into two sections: one lying to the west of Córdoba and Málaga; the other, Málaga and Córdoba eastwards. But the chief gateway to Western Andalusía is still Málaga itself, even for the traveller not bound for the populous playgrounds of the Costa del Sol, thanks to frequent and relatively cheap air services and the ease of hiring a car. Only those who have brought their own cars to Spain by the Plymouth-Santander ferry can choose alternatives: the direct NIV main highway south from Madrid, for instance, which meets the Andalusían border at that most dramatic of Sierra Morena passes, the Desfiladero de Despenaperros. But this brings you first to Eastern Andalusía: for Seville and the west, a more logical approach is through Extremadura and over the Sierra Morena by way of Aracena.

Seville and Huelva Regions

The route from Málaga

Those who are coming from Málaga or the Costa de Sol will quickly catch up with this approach: the distance involved by the direct main road is a shade over 200 km (126 miles) and there are only three place of note along it.

Antequera

The market town of Antequera (pop c. 35,000) involves only a slight detour and a very rewarding one, well deserving an overnight stop; if, for instance, your schedule gets you there in the late afternoon, it has an excellent Parador. It also has some charming old houses along its busy shopping streets and some striking *mudéjar* church architecture. Outstanding is the octagonal Baroque-*mudéjar* belfry of S Sebastian which, together with the tower of S Augustín, dominates the skyline. Both are best appreciated from the graceful archway that gives into the half-ruined hilltop Alcázaba, within whose precincts is the church of Sta Maria, built in 1503 and recently restored. Restrained Baroque in style, it has beautiful *mudéjar* ceilings and a finely carved dome above the apse, lit by *ajimez* windows. On the hillside below the church, excavations are in progress on a Roman site.

Prehistoric Dolmens

The town's most famous sights are on the outskirts, discouraging most people from bothering about its delightful centre. They are the remarkable prehistoric dolmens going back to about 2,500 BC and open mornings and afternoons. One, the Cueva de Menga, is enormous, with a row of monolithic columns dividing it; the Cueva de Viera is close by it and a third dolmen, the Romeral, is further east.

Estepa

Forty-nine km (about 30 miles) beyond Antequera, the road sweeps past Estepa, crowned by a theatrical-looking castle, its curtain walling punctuated by towers and enclosing several churches. It has a long history going back to Iberian times when it put up a fierce resistance to the Romans.

Osuna

Another 23 km (just under 15 miles) and you pass Osuna (pop c. 16,000), whose less majestic-looking castle should not put you off pausing there. Within the castle precinct (you can drive right up to it) is the 16th-century Colegiata church of S Juan Bautista with a series of cloisters, patios and crypts containing the tombs of the Dukes of Osuna; nearby is the 16th-century former university, with a harmonious patio. Downhill of it is the attractive Plaza de España with a lovely, stone-arched market off to one side and some elegant streets with not a tourist shop in sight. From there, the city of Seville is only 89 km (about 55 miles) distant by an easy road.

The route from Extremadura

Coming south to Seville from Extremadura is a much more leisurely affair. The roads from both Zafra and Jerez de los Caballeros converge at Fregenal de la Sierra, after which you climb through increasingly green country thick with forests of cork oak, pine and deciduous trees towards Jabugo, famous for its hams.

Aracena

Just short of Jabugo there is a left turn for Aracena (pop c. 6,400), a flowery Andalusian hill town of white houses with pantiled roofs around a pleasant market square, much favoured for its coolness by weekenders from Seville; as a result it has numerous inns and restaurants. At the top of the town is a half-ruined castle, originally Moorish but partly rebuilt by the Knights Templar in the 13th century; fortunately they failed to demolish the minaret of the mosque, which now does duty as the tower of their church of N S de Dolores. The views up there are lyrical over miles of splendid walking-country.

Virgen de los Angeles Shrine

Even better are the views from the shrine of the Virgen de los Angeles, on a hillside above whitewashed Alájar, some 13 km (eight miles) west of Aracena; in a cave nearby, Philip II is said to have come to visit the humanist-scholar Ariás Montano, who had been Spain's envoy to the Council of Trent and then Philip's first librarian at the Escorial before retiring to Aracena.

Caves: Gruta de las Maravillas

Another cave, or series of caves, is a more heavily-promoted tourist attraction: the Gruta de las Maravillas, open day-long, running through a rock-fault in the hill beneath the castle and half-full of water that reflects on its surface the stalactites and other 'marvels' above.

Riotinto mines

There is a lovely winding secondary road southwards through the sierra to Riotinto, where the 'coloured river' (tinted by copper and iron pyrites) rises at the heart of one of the world's oldest mining areas, worked by the Romans and possibly by the Phoenicians before them. Here you can turn east through the twin mining town of Nerva, passing countless harsh red gashes generations of miners have torn in the green hillsides, to rejoin the main N 630 road into Seville, a distance of 185 km (about 115 miles) from Fregenal.

Roman Italica: Emperors' birthplace

Before reaching the city itself, the ruins of Italica sprawl almost alongside the road, Scipio Africanus founded it in 206 BC, on the site of an Iberian settlement, to house the veterans of his wars against Carthage; Julius Caesar visited it in 45 BC and it claims to be the birthplace of the three great Spanish Roman Emperors, Trajan, Hadrian and Theodosius. The Visigoths half-abandoned it when the Guadalquivir retreated from it, carting off tons of its stone and marble to build Seville; the Moors continued the practice and the earthquake of 1755 put the finishing touch to it. No longer roamed by the "vast bands of black pigs, which live in its vaulted passages" that Augustus Hare observed, but instead peopled with copies of some of the statues found there (the originals are in Seville's Archaeological Museum) the ruins are nevertheless often hard to decipher, apart from those of the amphitheatre, the mosaic floors in several villas, and a theatre that is gradually being excavated.

Santiponce: baroque church
In Santiponce, slightly nearer the city, the disaffected 13th-century monastery of S Isidoro is hemmed about by factories and warehouses. Marooned within it is a small Baroque church with a painting by Montañes of St Jerome and the alabaster tomb of the founder, Alfonso Guzmán 'the good', first Duke of Medina Sidonia and ancestor of the commander of the Armada. With him lie his wife, his son, and a lady called Doña Urraca Osorio, who was burned at the stake for spurning the advances of the amorous Pedro the Cruel. Her servant died with her and is also buried there and in this company lay the body of Cortés, who had expired nearby in 1547; it was on its way to burial in Mexico.

The City of Seville

Hotels and parking
Seville (pop c. 654,000) is among the most daunting of cities for motorists, with a confusing and inadequately signposted one-way system that rules out the off-chance search for an hotel by car, except possibly during the afternoon *siesta* when traffic is lighter. Best to book ahead and choose an hotel with a garage or parking: this is no place in which to leave it, or anything valuable, unguarded. The beautifully-refurbished Alfonso XIII heads the list, but is expensive; the Inglaterra in Plaza Nueva, the Becquer on Reyes Catolicos, and the Fernando III on S José are all equally central, relatively easy to locate and more reasonably priced. Without a car to worry about, the Murillo in the atmospheric Sta Cruz quarter would be a good alternative.

Giralda Tower
This problem solved, you cannot do otherwise than gravitate towards the Cathedral, the outline of the Giralda tower, soaring above it, acting as a guiding beacon. The edge of the fountain in the Plaza de la Virgen de los Reyes (flanked by the handsome façade of the Archbishop's Palace), where the drivers of horse-drawn carriages await passengers, makes an excellent vantage-point from which to contemplate the ensemble of the Cathedral and the glorious Giralda Tower alongside it.

Originally a minaret - a duplicate, by the same architect, of the Koutoubia in Marrakech - its delicately patterned Moorish brickwork and chiselled *ajimez* windows were capped in the late 16th century by a Renaissance bell-chamber and lantern, together with a revolving figure of Faith at the summit, and the blend is surprisingly harmonious.

A broad, gently sloping ramp (open mornings and afternoons, except Sunday and holiday afternoons) leads to the top where, says Augustus Hare, "nothing could be more enchanting than to spend a morning . . . (overlooking) . . . the whole city, the soft bends of the Guadalquivir, and the sunny green plains."

It is said to stand on Roman foundations, for the Romans had a river port there before the Visigoths started quarrying Italica to make Seville their chief city in the fifth century.

Seville Cathedral

Origins
Alongside the Giralda was the first great mosque, begun in 1171, twelve years before the Giralda, by which time the Emirate of Córdoba had disintegrated and Seville was an independent *taifa* of the Almohades. When St Ferdinand (Ferdinand III of Castile) conquered it in 1248 the mosque was simply rededicated and used as a Christian church, but in 1401 the chapter resolved to pull it down and build a cathedral so immense that posterity would say "that those who dared to devise such a work must have been mad." The result is not just the largest Gothic church in Christendom but also the third largest church in Europe after St Peter's in Rome and St Paul's in London. Oddly, though, despite the fact that its architects were French, and despite the welter of external flying buttresses and pinnacles, its interior still faintly recalls a mosque.

Cathedral Patio
This impression is strengthened if you enter the Cathedral (open mornings and afternoons) by the traditional way, on the north side, through the keyhole-shaped Moorish Puerta del Perdón with its bronze doors. This brings you into the Patio de los Naranjos, the orange-tree planted courtyard of the original mosque, complete with its ablution-fountain, and from there into the cathedral itself.

Biblioteca Columbina
One side of the patio is flanked by the Sagrario, or parish church, the other by the Biblioteca Columbina. This houses a quantity of precious manuscripts, the nucleus of which was donated by Fernando, son of Columbus, and it includes Columbus's own small and carefully

annotated library. The Biblioteca has been closed to all but scholars for many years and is currently being restored and partly rebuilt; when this major work is completed the public will also be allowed to visit it. Until then, the Patio de los Naranjos is closed and you enter the Cathedral by a door at the east end.

Cathedral nave
George Borrow, who spent a good deal of time in Seville, commented that the interior abounded "in solemn darkness and gloomy pomp, the principal requisite of a cathedral," and certainly its sheer immensity is awesome. Through the dimness loom the gigantic pillars of the nave: four rows of them support ceiling vaulting that is almost out of sight. As so often in Spain, the bulky *coro* blocks the centre of this vastness in which even sizeable groups of tourists are dwarfed and the usually strident voices of their guides are reduced to the chirrupings of crickets.

The surrounding chapels gleam across the distances between them: Seville was one of the principal ports for ships to and from the New World and much of its wealth rubbed off here. (Not until the 18th century did the city start to decline, due partly to the silting up of the Guadalquivir, partly to the loss of American colonies.)

Royal tombs
Beneath the fine Renaissance dome of the *capilla real,* behind the *capilla mayor* and the high altar, lies the Christian conqueror of Seville, Ferdinand III (the Saint), his silver-gilt sarcophagus watched over by a sumptuously-dressed madonna, the Virgen de los Reyes, said to have been given to St Ferdinand by his younger first cousin, St Louis of France. Also entombed in this chapel are Beatrice of Swabia, St Ferdinand's queen, and their son Alfonso the Wise of Castile. St Ferdinand had strong English associations: his mother was descended from the daughter of Henry II and Eleanor of Aquitaine and his own daughter, another Eleanor, married England's Edward I. And in the miniature royal pantheon below this chapel lie the relics of another Castilian king whose offspring wed English princes: Pedro the Cruel, whose daughters married the Black Prince's brothers.

Chancel and altarpiece
The *capilla mayor* has a heavily gilded *retablo* whose richness of detail is only partially masked by the delicate grilles that screen it, and rows of pews allow you to sit while you take it all in.

The choir
Behind you as you sit is the *coro,* with masterly 15th/16th-century carved choirstalls, currently closed for restoration. During the weeks of Corpus Christi, the Immaculate Conception and the Assumption,

the pews are removed and young choristers dressed like miniature 17th-century courtiers perform the stately *seises* dance, said to have originated in the celebrations held at the time of Seville's reconquest.

Columbus's memorial

There is a wealth of important paintings to see, many by native artists like Murillo, Pacheco and Valdés Leal, and by Zurbarán who spent most of his working life here although born in Extremadura. There is also one more important monument: Columbus's colossal memorial, a 19th-century work opposite the south door, representing the discoverer's coffin being supported by four bronze figures symbolising the Kingdoms of Castile, León, Aragón and Navarre. They are several times life-size, but even so do not look too huge for this Cathedral.

The Trade Exchange

In the square outside the Cathedral's south door is the former Casa Lonja, or trade exchange, a handsome 16th-century building in which are kept the so-called 'Indies Archives'. In its cool, quiet galleries (open mornings only) are thousands of documents relating to the discovery and administration of Spain's colonies in the New World, and on display are photostats of historic letters and documents signed by Amerigo Vespucci, Columbus himself, Cortés, Pizarro, Magellan – and even Cervantes, who wanted to emigrate to America.

As must have been the case in the archives of Ancient Rome, there are plans and drawings for buildings to be erected in the colonies, some of which will instantly be recognised by people who have travelled in South America.

The Alcázar

Beyond the Lonja is the Tourist Office, and just east of it the Alcázar, open mornings and afternoons every day, which is not a Moorish palace at all, though one was built here in 1181 on the site of a Visigothic one that had in turn replaced a Roman *praetorium*. The Alcázar of Seville was built in the *mudéjar* style for the 14th-century Castilian king most closely associated with Seville, Pedro the Cruel. Known in Seville as Pedro the Wise, he was an odd character: he had been brought to Seville when his mother felt he was threatened by the older twin sons of his father, Alfonso XI, by his mistress, Leonora Guzmán.

King Pedro's marriages

While quite young he met and became passionately attached to an aristocratic beauty called Maria de Padilla, whom he married morganatically. His mother and chief minister were scandalised and forced him into an official marriage with the French princess Blanche of Bourbon, but after three days he deserted her and returned to Maria, who bore him the daughters who later married John of Gaunt and Edmund of Langley. Poor Blanche was imprisoned for many years and finally executed at Medina Sidonia.

Pedro's murders

Pedro, whose amatory pursuits were legendary, also perpetrated at least two nasty murders in Seville. The Moorish king of Granada was disposed of for the sake of a casket of jewels, one of them the ruby Pedro later presented to the Black Prince that now adorns England's Imperial State Crown. The other victim was his bastard half-brother, Fadrique, whom he conveniently accused of having seduced Blanche of Bourbon while escorting her to Spain; this was avenged six years later by Fadrique's twin, Enrique de Trastamara (second of the sons born to Leonora Guzmán), who stabbed Pedro and siezed his throne.

Architecture of the Alcázar

Later Christian kings used Pedro's palace as their residence in Seville and made often inappropriate alterations and additions to it; it is thus an astonishing mixture of styles and includes a chapel installed by Isabella the Catholic, several rooms added by Charles V (who married Isabella of Portugal here). Other kings who remodelled it to a greater or lesser degree included Philip IV in the 17th century, and Philip V and Ferdinand VI in the 18th. But it retains its beautiful *mudéjar* façade and vistas of delicately scolloped arches upheld by thin columns framing exquisite patios; there are superb *artesonado* ceilings and doors and *azulejo* friezes and lacy plasterwork. The imposition of later upper storeys upon these airy structures is unfortunate but some of the later rooms, notably Isabella's oratory and Charles V's saloon, are very fine and there is a notable collection of tapestries in the other Charles V rooms.

The Alcázar gardens

The gardens, laid out by Charles V, are charming; there are pools full of fat goldfish, fountains and orange trees, hedges and arches of greenery, the vault-shaded 'bath' of Maria de Padilla, with a hole in the roof through which Pedro the Cruel could look at her, and Charles V's own 'bath' and charming domed pavilion.

Parks and Plazas

Murillo and Ribera gardens

Gardens indeed are a feature of Seville: the ones of the Alcázar are complemented by the neighbouring Murillo and Ribera gardens, on the northern edge of which, in Plaza Cano y Cueto, is the excellent and popular Modesto restaurant and *tapa* bar. Across Avenida S Fernando at the southern end of the Ribera gardens the large, sober 18th-century building with frivolous pinnacles that now houses the university was one once the tobacco factory at which the prototype of Bizet's Carmen worked and whom Ford describes thus: "Very few . . . are good looking, yet these *cigarreras* are among the lions of Seville, and, like the *grisettes* of Paris, form a class of themselves. They are reputed to be more impertinent than chaste."

Maria Luisa Park; Plaza de España

Behind that the Delicias gardens merge into the lovely Maria Luisa Park, but in Borrow's time the Delicias, with its tall trees and "long, shady walks" covered the whole area; the more formal park was not created until the 19th century and was re-designed in 1929 to accommodate an international exhibition. Sitwell thought the Maria Luisa Park "the most beautiful . . . in Europe" and the adjoining Plaza de España, its semi-circle of buildings fronted by flowers, fountains and a moat crossed by ceramic-tiled bridges, must certainly be the most successful attempt at making municipal offices look light-hearted. Nor are these the only gardens: in every square and spare corner of the city and on every balcony someone has planted flowers or shrubs and palm trees.

The Barrio - Jewish quarter

A narrow alleyway alongside the Alcázar leads into the Barrio de Sta Cruz, the old Jewish quarter of Seville, whose streets in Borrow's time (although he joyfully rented lodgings there) were "badly paved and full of misery and beggary." Now its tiny alleyways are scrupulously whitewashed, setting off to perfection the intricate window-grilles and balconies and cascading flowers, and affording glimpses of enchanting patios: the Andalusía of the tourist posters.

Barrio restaurants

Yet the Barrio manages to stop short of parodying its own prettiness and there are good, honest restaurants: Laurel, opposite the Hospicio de Venerables for instance and, nearby, the La Albahace, occupying a typical old house in the Plaza Sta Cruz. Murillo lived and died in the Barrio; Washington Irving, as well as Borrow, lodged there, the 'Barber of Seville' and 'Don Giovanni' were set there. Echoes of the Don seem to pervade it still; even today, despite the canned music in too many bars, you can come across someone fingering the strings of a guitar, or meet a group of youngsters singing for the sheer pleasure of it.

North to the Macarena Gate

King Pedro's duel

But the Barrio has not the monopoly of Seville's attractive streets, nor of its fine mansions. Start an anti-clockwise walk about the rest of the city by heading north and, in a tiny plaza halfway along Calle Cabeza del Rey Don Pedro, you will see a small stone head of Pedro the Cruel set into a niche in a wall. It comes to be there because the king had an argument that led to a duel on that spot, late one night, and his opponent was killed. Believing the affair to have been unobserved the king offered, when it was discovered that the dead youth was one of the aristocratic Guzmáns, to nail his killer's head to the wall if he could be identified. In fact there had been a witness to the duel and Pedro bought his silence, but in order to satisfy the Guzmáns' honour, he had this portrait head of himself sent to them in a crate, with instructions not to open it until his own death.

The 'House of Pilate'; Don Juan's prototype
Slightly to the east of this odd memorial is the even odder Casa de Pilatos, built in the 15th century by a returned Crusader in so-called 'imitation' of Pilate's house in Jerusalem. Open mornings and afternoons, it is a remarkable combination of the *mudéjar* and Renaissance styles with gorgeous lustre *azulejos,* delicate plasterwork, a great domed staircase and several symbols relating to the condemnation of Christ, such as a hand-washing basin, the 'pillar of the scourging' and 'the' table on which the 30 pieces of silver were laid.

A little further north again is the quarter in which lived the prototype Don Juan: Don Miguel de Manara, who by tradition repented of his wickedness and founded the Hospital de la Caridad (see below).

Palacio de las Duenas; Sta Paula
In this quarter is the huge Palacio de las Duenas, privately owned and rarely open to the public but very beautiful; due east of it, past S Marco, is Sta Paula, with some of the finest *azulejos* in all Seville.

Basilica de la Macarena
If you go more or less due north from Sta Paula you come to the old Córdoba gate, at the end of a stretch of the 12th-century Almohad city walls. Walk alongside them westwards and at the end is the Macarena gate and two more churches, side by side. One is the Basilica de la Macarena, containing one of Seville's most famous Virgins, a leading figure in the city's Holy Week processions: the sorrowful La Esperanza, glistening with glass tears. She is especially revered by the poor and by bullfighters, who pray to her before going into the ring.

South to the river

Convent of Sta Clara
Keep working clockwise, westwards, and you come to the convent of

S Clemente, one of St Ferdinand's first foundations, though partly rebuilt in the 18th century; turn south here and halfway down Calle de Sta Clara is the beautiful Convent of Sta Clara, with a romantic little courtyard, to which the noble and virtuous Doña Maria Coronel retreated to escape the attentions of Pedro the Cruel, even disfiguring her face in her efforts to repel him. Alongside it is the golden brick Torre de Don Fadrique, all that remains of a mid 13th-century palace, its lower windows Romanesque and its upper ones Gothic.

Alameda de Hercules; Arts museum

Nearby is the long, shady Alameda de Hercules with a couple of Roman columns at each end of it and a lively Sunday flea market. Just west of it, S Lorenzo is on the northern edge of the commercial and social heart of Seville, where the plazas of La Gavidia, Concordia and del Duque lead out of one another to La Campana. Away to the west of this plaza, along Alfonso XII or its parallel street, Monsalves, where Richard Ford spent his last winter in Spain, is the Museo de Bellas Artes, housed as it was in Ford's time in a former friary. Its well laid out collection includes some unusual primitives and works by such Seville artists as Murillo, Pacheco, Herrera, Valdés Leal and Zurbarán, and Velázquez.

From La Campana to the Ayuntimiento

Leading south from La Campana is the pedestrianised main shopping street, Sierpes, and in the equally narrow parallel street, Cuna, is the Lebrija Palace with some marvellous mosaics from Italica in its patio. The old university church, well restored, is just behind it, and an alleyway off Sierpes leads to the tiny gilded Baroque chapel of S José. Southwards yet again, the handsome Ayuntimiento makes an island between two squares. Plaza Nueva and Plaza S Francisco (with a restaurant of the same name in one of its old houses), and at this point turn west towards the river.

Markets; restaurants

Close to the Puente Isabel II (still often called the Puente de Triana) is the old Arenal fish market with a useful car park below it, and across the river is the equally long-established general market. This quarter, Triana, used to be the gypsy quarter ("inhabited by the dregs of the populace," writes Borrow); now it is becoming noticeably gentrified. It has several popular riverside cafés and restaurants (Rio Grande is among the better ones) offering fine views across the water; its late 13th-century Sta Ana church, set slightly back from the riverside, is the oldest in Seville.

The Bullring; the Golden Tower

Walk downstream along the left bank and you come to the bullring, despite its age (the oldest in Spain) a frivolous-looking confection in white picked out with ochre and roofed in pantiles; it sets you thinking again of Bizet's 'Carmen', for which it was of course a setting. Now you are approaching the fat, Moorish Torre del Oro, built by the Almohades in 1220 and bristling with pointed merlons. Its name comes from the golden *azulejos* that used to cover its entire upper part and in former times the port of Seville could be closed off by hauling a chain across to a similar tower on the Triana bank.

Hospital de la Caridad

Just before the Torre del Oro and slightly back from the river is the 17th-century Hospital de la Caridad, the old men's home (open in the mornings) founded by the reformed rake Don Miguel, with a deep red-painted double storeyed patio from which you can see into the long, well-scrubbed dormitories. In the chapel is a series of fine, if dimly-lit Murillos on the walls (in the little antechamber giving on to the chapel are displayed photographs of other Murillos 'abducted' during the Peninsular War and now housed elsewhere).

The chapel also contains two lugubrious Valdés Leal canvases in which skeletons and other dead emblems figure strongly; Murillo, who executed the lovely *azulejo* panels on the street facade, remarked that the Valdés Leals made him want to hold his nose.

S Telmo; Easter Fair

Back by the river and past the Torre del Oro, the next landmark is the S Telmo Bridge, near which Magellan started his voyage of discovery. The twin outlines of the Baroque S Telmo Palace and the now resplendent Hotel Alfonso XIII partly screen this view of the former tobacco factory; on the other side of it, the former Quemadero (crematorium, where the victims of the Inquisition were burned) has been overlaid with gardens. It is now called the Prado de S Sebastián and is the venue for the brilliant post-Easter *feria,* where beautifully-mounted *caballeros,* their ruffle-swathed *senoritas* sitting effortlessly up behind them, weave between swanky carriages and rows of decorated kiosks, or *casetas,* consuming *tapas* and drinking wine, singing and dancing far into the night.

Seville's future plans; Archaeological Museum

Now the circuit of Seville is almost complete – until April 1992, when the ambitiously-conceived Universal Exposition opens on its island site on the northeast edge of the city. Until then, and until the new marina-development at Gelves, just downstream, is fully operational, all that remains is to take a stroll or a carriage-ride south through the Maria Luisa Park to the Archaeological Museum, to see its very fine collection of treasures, notably Roman finds from the ruins of Italica.

Carmona

Roman necropolis

More relics of Roman rule in Andalusía are to be found at the Roman necropolis of Carmona (pop c. 22,000), 33 km (just over 20 miles) to the east. It lies outside the city's Seville gate, which has the remains of a Moorish Alcázar piled above it and an odd-looking church with an imitation Giralda tower just outside it, at the top of the modern town.

A strange place, dating back to the first century BC, the necropolis is riddled with rock-cut underground tombs reached by stairs or shafts, some simply pits to receive the ashes of the poor, some respectable family tombs with vaulted ceilings and niches for the urns in which the remains of the departed were sealed. Others are larger and divided into several chambers; one has a primitive carving of a baby elephant between two vaults and a fountain in the courtyard outside. The biggest has traces of frescoes in rooms that surrounded an open patio with a pool, and column-bases that originally supported the arcade.

History of Carmona

Carmona's history goes back long past the Roman era, however; it is probably older than Seville or Italica and very picturesque, crowning a low hilltop that overlooks the Guadalquivir basin for miles around. Julius Caesar fortified it; the Visigoths succeeded the Romans and the invading Abbasids, in the early eighth century, took it from them. In 763 the Ummayyad ruler Abderrahman I, battling to establish his Caliphate of Córdoba, retreated within its walls for two months to regroup for another onslaught against the Abbasids, which he won. Ferdinand the Saint captured it in 1247, the year before he conquered Seville, and later Castilian kings used the Moorish castle as a second summer residence, especially Pedro the Cruel who made it, according to Ford, "what Edward III did of Windsor . . . Here he kept his jewels, money, mistresses and children." The castle is now a fine Parador and still feels much like a fortress; only the creature comforts keep the illusion at bay.

Carmona town

Below the Parador is the Córdoba gate, dating from the second century and not inappropriately refaced during the Renaissance; past it a beguiling network of old streets slopes gently towards the equally ancient Seville gate, which was given a double horseshoe arch by the Moors, on the western side of town. The pretty main square, Plaza S Fernando, has several good buildings around it, among them a 16th-century Ayuntimiento with a Roman mosaic in its courtyard and another 16th-century mansion with *ajimez* windows banded in red and white. The most attractive church is late Gothic Sta Maria, built on the site of the former mosque whose patio, of brick arches surrounding a miniature orange grove, it has adopted.

East of Carmona: a round trip

If you spend a couple of nights at Carmona you can make a tour of some of the typically Andalusian townships to the east of it, starting with Ecija (pop c. 34,500) as early as possible, because it is reputedly the hottest place in the entire Guadalquivir depression.

Ecija

On a hazy summer's day this ancient town, probably founded by the Greeks, can look from a distance like a froth of veiling pinned in place by its *azulejo*-decorated Baroque belfries. But the attractive Plaza Mayor is mercifully arcaded and palm and orange trees shade its *azulejo*-faced benches and at the café-bar Gasolina in one corner of the Plaza you can sit over *tapas* and take in its heterogeneous array of old houses, some with *ajimez* windows to the upper storeys, and unexpected patches of frescoes vying for attention.

The church of Sta Barbara, recently restored, has Roman columns in the nave and a curious semi-cylindrical tower topped with merlons, and the streets radiating from the plaza are full of other churches, some half-ruined, whose Baroque belfries are enhanced by the multi-coloured *azulejos* set into them.

Ecija's Palacio de Peñaflor

There are masses of fine houses, some with intricately-crafted brick-work portals, others with carved stone gateways (the Police Station among them), all enclosing tiled patios exploding with potted plants. Among them, not far from the Plaza Mayor, are a couple of splendid mansions. The Palacio de Peñaflor is outstanding: a long, slightly elliptical building with huge arched windows at ground-floor level, a long balcony carried on fine wrought-iron supports above, and above this a broad, curving roof-cornice decorated with *trompe l'oeuil* frescoes. Across from it, two fierce stone characters wielding clubs guard the door of another palatial house whose top floor is a stone loggia with carved reliefs along it.

Princess Subh and Almansor

Less obvious sights include an early Christian sarcophagus in the Sta Cruz church and an Arabic plaque set into its tower that chronicles the donation of a fountain to Ecija in 977. The donor was Princess Subh, Basque born, who became the concubine of Abderrahman III's son Al-Haqem and, despite his predilection for boys (she is said to have worn male clothing), bore him an heir. While the child was still an infant an administrator was appointed to his mother's household who found his way to her bed: he was the Yemeni warrior Almansor. In the year of Al-Haqem's death – the year before the presentation of the fountain – he assumed the regency for the 11-year-old boy and eventually climbed to absolute power over the shoulders of mother and son. His death in 1002 marked the beginning of the end for the Ummayyad Caliphate of Córdoba; of Princess Subh, first rung in Almansor's career-ladder, this plaque is the sole record.

Marchena: the town
From Ecija, it is just over 39 km (under 25 miles) south-westwards by the N333 to Marchena (pop c. 16,000), which is perhaps the most appealing of all the small towns hereabouts. Most of its houses are immaculately painted, with pot-plants trailing from behind graceful window-grilles and, occasionally, coats of arms set into their façades. A restored Moorish tower houses the Tourist Office and a small archaeological museum.

Marchena: the Palace
At the summit of town, within Moorish walls, once stood the Palace of the Marqués of Cadiz, Rodrigo Ponce de Léon, who rode out from there to score one of the first Christian victories in the long struggle to oust the Moors from Granada. Rodrigo Ponce de Léon is seldom out of the pages of Washington Irving's account of the campaign, where he is portrayed as embodying all the knightly virtues; sadly, all that remains today of his castle precincts are an Arabesque gateway and a colonnade leading to the church of Sta Maria, its pierced belfry set with *azulejos.* The views, however, are marvellous.

Guadalquivir landscape
The landscape of the Guadalquivir basin, flattish though it is, is not without interest: here and there you see huge old farmsteads, like self-contained hamlets, sometimes walled and even including private chapels; in times of trouble, of which there were many during the latter stages of the Reconquest, an entire farming community and its live-stock could retreat into them. Fields of wheat alternate with sunflower plantations and olive groves and there are clumps of umbrella-pine and eucalyptus.

Three routes back to Carmona
Morón de la Frontera is 18 km (11 miles) to the southwest: the finest view of its huge, half-ruined castle is just before you come into town, from the north. From here you can come back to Carmona, 45 km away (27-odd miles) along a delightfully rural secondary road, via El Arahal, or head westwards first, along almost equally rural C342, and take in Utrera on the way. Another option, if you have missed it previously, is to extend this circuit by only some 39 km (under 40 miles) and include a visit to Osuna after leaving Ecija.

Carmona to Huelva

Castilleja de la Cuesta

Starting again from Carmona but in the other direction, southwestwards, the minor C432 takes you past the castle of Alcalá de Guadaira, skirting Seville's eastern outskirts, but it is still necessary to go almost into the city to get across the Guadalquivir. Once across, the *autopista* is quick but much duller than the old main road, N431. This takes you first through Castilleja de la Cuesta, half-buried in the suburbs of Seville, where Cortés, the conqueror of Mexico, died almost forgotten in 1547; there are a few memorabilia in an Arab-style 18th-century house erected on the spot.

Umbrete; Sanlúcar la Mayor

Beyond Castilleja, between the old main road and the *autopista,* and *azulejos* on the dome of Umbrete church glitter in the sun and there are more *azulejos* on the imposing *mudéjar* tower at Sanlúcar la Mayor, once a Roman town, which also boasts a ruined Moorish fortress.

Niebla

About 44 km (27 miles) further west, the road crosses the still-reddish Rio Tinto by a bridge whose foundations are Roman. Above it are the walls of Niebla, remarkably intact and breached by a Moorish gate that seems to promise a fantastic medieval city. In fact this small town, which goes back to Iberian times, is somewhat decaying, with an air of having been bypassed by time, but despite - or perhaps because of - this, it has great charm.

Niebla's Alcázar, church, dolmen

There are grand old mansions framing dusty gaps were others once stood, and the remains of a Moorish Alcázar whose cannons, the first in Spain, held off the besieging forces of Alfonso the Wise of Castile for nearly a year in 1261-2. Of particular note is the little white church of Sta Maria de la Granada, with a Moorish doorway and ablution-fountain and some lovely old *azulejos.* Nearby, and in private ownership, the prehistoric dolmen known as the Cueva del Zancarrón de Soto has wall paintings and can sometimes be visited: ask at Niebla's Ayuntimiento.

Moguer

There is another church dedicated to Sta Maria de la Granada (*granada* means pomegranate) in Moguer, just off the road as it nears Huelva and once an important port on the Rio Tinto estuary.

More interesting, though, is the Sta Clara convent on the village outskirts, founded in the mid-14th century and well preserved. Its pale brick buildings with their *mudéjar* features include a lovely church with carved and painted choirstalls; many of Columbus's sailors, natives of Moguer, and Columbus himself worshipped there. It also enshrines the tombs of the founders, which are not the least handsome feature of this attractive church. The sister of Isabella the Catholic was once Mother Superior of the adjoining convent, now a museum. Nearby, the unassuming Bar Sta Clara serves copious and delicious *tapas*.

Huelva city

Huelva (pop c. 128,000), sprawled across the tongue of land that separates the Rio Tinto and Rio Odiel estuaries, is a big, busy and prosperous port whose evidences of great antiquity were shivered into ruins by the earthquake that destroyed Lisbon in 1755, Only a handful of churches, notably S Pedro, La Concepción between the market and the main shopping streets, and S Francisco at one end of the main square, antedate that catastrophe, as do the remnants of an aqueduct on the northern outskirts. But it is an agreeable town and its museum, immediately across from the luxurious Luz Huelva hotel, has an interesting archaeological section with finds from the Phoenician and Roman mining town of Tharsis, away to the northwest beyond S Bartolomé de la Torre.

La Rábida to Ayamonte

La Rábida

Huelva's beaches are at Punta Umbria across the Odiel estuary, but it is the road that crosses the Rio Tinto, to the east, that draws most tourists. Past the ponderously symbolic American-built memorial to Columbus that guards the bridge is the white-walled convent of La Rábida, badly shaken in the 1755 earthquake but carefully restored. Here the navigator arrived in 1484, holding his small son by the hand, seeking refuge after "the wisest kings and councils had rejected as visionary (his) scheme of the discovery of the New World," as Ford puts it. As luck would have it the prior at the time, Juan Perez de Marchena, was not only farsighted enough to recognise the feasibility of Columbus's vision of a world that was round but also influential enough (he had been Queen Isabella's confessor) to be able to re-open negotiations on his behalf.

Columbus museum

Before this happened, however, Columbus spent six years at La Rábida, expanding his studies and improving on his plans, conferring with the monks and with members of the local, ship-building Pinzón family, two of whom eventually accompanied him on that first voyage, commanding the 'Santa Maria's' sister ships, the 'Nina' and the

'Pinta'. A small, bare cell is pointed out as the one in which Columbus lodged and worked during those years, and another room has been turned into a museum, with models of the three ships and caskets of earth from each of America's former Spanish possessions.

Palos de la Frontera

Up river from La Rábida, but separated now from the estuary by alluvial fields, is the little town of Palos, in Columbus's time a thriving port and one from which he eventually set sail at daybreak on August 3, 1492. In the church of S Jorge he and his crews heard Mass before going aboard; across the road is a well from which the ships are said to have been watered, and a few rusty iron rings to which they might have moored (there are plans to reconstruct the 'quay' in time for the 1992 quincentenary). One of these rings might also have secured the ship of Hernán Cortés, who sailed back to Palos from Mexico in 1528 and may even have berthed alongside Pizarro, who at about the same time was embarking upon his own voyage of conquest to Peru.

Two routes to Ayamonte

A little further westwards, past the ruined castle of Cartaya and across the Rio Piedras, two roads lead to Ayamonte, on the Portuguese frontier. One is direct; the other, more interesting, hugs the coast and goes through Las Antillas and the fishing village and summer resort of Isla Cristina.

Ayamonte

Ayamonte (pop c. 16,200), an attractively whitewashed town, is a pleasant place in which to sit at a café or at the modern Parador in the evening and watch the sun sink over the Guadiana river with Portugal on the other side. A somewhat primitive ferry currently carries cars and passengers across the estuary but by the end of 1990 the much talked of bridge, five km (about 3 miles) further upstream, should be relieving the inevitable summer traffic jams at the ferry.

South-east from La Rábida

The coast road

Going south-east from La Rábida, a secondary road hugs the coast, which is virtually one broad ribbon of sand all the way from Huelva's twin estuaries to that of the Guadalquivir. Pinewoods have been planted to stabilise the sand-dunes and among them new resorts are springing up.

Mazagón is the first and the most mature and has a peaceful modern Parador named for Columbus some six km (four miles) beyond it. Next come Torre del Oro and Torre la Higuera which runs into the newer, bigger and brasher resort of Matalascañas, 48 km (30 miles) from the town of Huelva.

Nature reserves
Here the coast road ends, for this is the western edge of the Coto de Donana nature reserve, a vast roadless marshland of rush-covered flats and salty lagoons, crossed only by a network of drainage canals and the course of the Guadalquivir, upon whose invisible surface the occasional ship, seen from a distance, looks like a mirage.

Coto de Doñana; Coto del Rey
The Coto de Doñana and the adjacent Coto del Rey were formerly shooting preserves; Ford, who had scathing things to say about the unsportsman-like manner in which the Spaniards of his day pursued this sport, nevertheless went out frequently with Francisco, the royal gamekeeper, and admits that "no man who is fond of shooting will fail spending a week either at the Coto del Rey or that of Doña Ana" – of which Doñana is a corruption.

Palacio de Doña Ana
The former shooting box of the Medina Sidonias still stands there, still bearing the grandiose name of Palacio de Doña Ana, about which Ford warned his readers not to be deceived, for in reality it was just four bare walls. "A prudent man will always send on a *galera* laden with everything from a cook to a mattress; take especially good wine, for fuel and game alone are to be had." Nowadays there is no game to be had, either, and shooting is done exclusively with cameras: the Coto is the preserve of professional and amateur zoologists and ornithologists.

Game and bird life
As well as a plethora of bird life, it shelters many sorts of small game, including boar, wild cat, lynx, and at one time even a few camels released there after the shooting of the film 'Lawrence of Arabia'. Myriads of insects there are, too, from midges to scorpions. Strictly protected, permission to get into it can be obtained from the Park offices in El Rocío (see below).

El Rocío: Whitsun Festival

Turning away from the sea and heading north along the boundary of the Coto you come in 16 km (10 miles) to El Rocío. Most of the year a pretty but near-deserted ghost village, like an abandoned Western film set, it comes to life at Whitsuntide as the focal point of one of the most attractive pilgrimages in Spain, the *romeria* to the miraculous Virgin of El Rocío, enshrined in the whitewashed village church.

Virgin of El Rocío

The cult of this particular Virgin dates back to the 14th century, but it was not until the last century that the *romeria* started to acquire its present popularity, thanks to royal patronage. Nowadays, scores of towns and villages all over Spain – the furthest away being in the Canaries – have El Rocío Brotherhoods who annually process to the shrine.

Processions to the shrine

Each procession consists of dozens of elaborately decorated 'covered wagons', large and small, recalling their Wild West counterparts but smothered in flowers. Some carry little candle-lit shrines, others display their own, full-scale images of the Virgin, all are laden with beautifully costumed participants and the copious wherewithal for their journey. Among them ride traditionally-garbed *caballeros* with black sombreros and heavy leather chaps buckled to their shins and their wives or sisters or girl friends up behind them, brilliantly dressed in frilled *faralae* dresses. There are walkers, too, perhaps penitents, perhaps students giving thanks (or asking) for success in exams; there are followers in jeeps and farm-carts, singing gaily as they kick up the pale sand of the pine and eucalyptus forests.

The *romeria* lasts for days, depending on how far away are the starting points; there are frequent stops to refresh both the pilgrims and their animals, during which the hospitality is unselective and unstinting. At night, throngs of people camp among the trees, playing guitars and dancing far into the night by the light of lamps and flickering fires.

Arrival at El Rocío

Just before Whitsunday itself the processions wend their way into the village and establish themselves either in encampments on the outskirts or in rented houses fronted by hitching-rails for the horses. The broad streets are lined with hastily established open air bars and cafés, and the partying starts in earnest as riders and pedestrians parade about, stopping here and there to drink a *copita* or eat something with friends and strangers alike.

There is an 'official entrance', when the Brotherhoods process into the main square; thereafter many, but not all, make their way briefly into the church to pay homage before the Virgin's image, high above the altar in a silver-gilt tabernacle. The dancing, music, drinking and eating goes on for some 36 hours without a break; no-one sleeps unless he or she absolutely must, and then only as briefly as possible.

The Mass; Festival climax

The climax comes during the final night when a Mass is said in the church and afterwards the Virgin's tabernacle, carried high on the shoulders of members of the Almonte Brotherhood, is borne out into the crowds, a tiny, glittering effigy seeming to toss on a human sea, and carried about the village to the accompaniment of pealing church bells and exploding fireworks and thunderous applause. Gradually dawn breaks, the swallows start wheeling against the pale sky, and the party is over.

Guardians of the shrine
From El Rocío, the way back to Seville is via Almonte, some 48 km (30 miles) from the city, the largish village whose Brotherhood, the oldest in Spain, is charged with the guardianship of the Virgin's shrine.

Cádiz Region

Seville to Cádiz

Cádiz is not much further south of Seville than Huelva is to the west, and a good goal for its own sake as well as a starting point for further exploration; I would not recommend just making a there-and-back excursion. Again, the *autopista* can make short work of the distance, but the old road is more interesting and the minor ones even more so: following these, it would be easy to take a day or longer to cover what by the direct route is only 120-odd km (about 75 miles).

Utrera
Leaving Seville by the Avenida Felipe II, due east from the Maria Luisa Park, a right fork takes you out towards Utrera, an ancient town with a fine, square-towered, restored Alcázar, an attractive Plaza Mayor shaded by orange trees, and several good churches, notably Nuestra Señora de la Consolación with a fine *mudéjar* ceiling.

Lebrija
From here a minor road goes southwest to join the C441, crosses the motorway and reaches the walled town of Lebrija (pop c. 22,000), dominated by a castle that overlooks mile upon mile of marshland, and whose church of Sta Maria de la Oliva endured minimal alteration, beyond the addition of a tower, during its transformation from a 12th-century mosque. Further southwest, the country begins to undulate, the sandy slopes are smothered in the vines from which Manzanilla is made, and the outlines of Sanlúcar de Barrameda can be seen against the glittering sea.

Sanlúcar de Barrameda
Rising above the southern bank of the Guadalquivir estuary, Sanlúcar

(pop c. 48,000) is the centre for the production of manzanilla: its main street is lined with bars selling it and *bodegas* crouch beneath the castle walls in the old part of town. The dome of Renaissance Sto Domingo, in the lower part of town, is well matched by its fine interior vaulting; the earlier Sta Maria de la 'O' has a beautiful *mudéjar* portal, and S Francisco is of interest because it was founded by Henry VIII, originally as a hospital for English sailors.

Magellan; Godoy's zoo
Magellan sailed from Sanlúcar on the first voyage to circumnavigate the world and, Calvert tells us, an important zoological garden was established there by Godoy, Charles IV's chief minister, whose ignominious dealings with Napoleon led to the Peninsular War. "Upon his downfall," Calvert continues, "the intelligent poplace destroyed the buildings and killed the animals in order to express their hatred of the queen's favourite."

Sanlúcar: "Andalusían Brighton"
George Borrow, arriving there early in the last century full of misgivings about a town "in ancient times . . . a rendezvous for ruffians, contrabandistas and vagabonds," was surprised to find none of these. Instead, he witnessed the delightful spectacle of "a multitude of females" engaged in the novel pastime of sea-bathing. Calvert described Sanlúcar as the "Andalusian Brighton", which explains not only why Goya was staying there in the summer of 1798 but also the presence at the same time of the Duchess of Alba.

It was there that the artist made numerous sketches of local *majas* (and *majos*) upon which he later based the famous pair of paintings, now in Madrid's Prado Museum, of the clothed and unclothed lady whose identity has aroused so much speculation.

Chipiona to Rota
Chipiona, a few miles to the west, is a cheery seaside resort thronged with locals throughout the summer, and there are more beaches all the way south to Rota, tidier and more cosmopolitan thanks to the proximity of a huge American naval base. The road then swings inland to skirt the base, and a smaller road off it heads through rolling vineyards for Jerez de la Frontera.

Jerez de la Frontera
Ford called Jerez (pop c. 176,000) or Xerez, "a straggling, ill-built, ill-drained Moorish city", but in fact it antedates the Moors: it was a wine-producing centre in Roman times. Today it is attractive in a restrained, businesslike way, and if its business were something more commonplace than the production of sherry, it might even appear a bit dull. But sherry is its business and this lends it a special

aura, particularly during the September wine-harvest festival when it erupts into gaiety. A brief account of the making of sherry is given in the section on food and drink in the General Information chapter and a visit to one of the *bodegas* is strongly recommended.

Jerez: old town

Apart from the *bodegas*, there are two distinct quarters to the town, which is bisected north to south by a succession of 'main' streets running into one another through handsome palm-shaded squares. To the west is the older part with an 11th-century Alcázar, well restored; there are a couple of good churches and a pretty square, Plaza de la Asunción, bordered on one side by the Renaissance façade of the former Town Hall, now a museum containing a pre-classical Greek helmet found near the Guadalete river.

Visigoth's last battle

Somewhere along the course of the Guadalete, which flows in lazy loops past the southern perimeter of Jerez, is the site of the battle in 711 in which Rodrigo, last of the Visigothic kings, vanished without trace, opening the way for the Moorish invaders to conquer almost the entire Iberian peninsula. His horse, still regally caparisoned, was found after the battle, but not Rodrigo nor his corpse; it is one of history's minor conundrums.

Carthusian monastery

Overlooking the river (and overlooked by the *autopista*) is what H V Morton called "the most interesting non-alcoholic object in the district", the much-restored Cartuja, or Carthusian monastery, whose Baroque-fronted church in honey coloured stone is greatly admired; admission is reserved for men only but, luckily for women, its famous Zurbaráns have been removed to the Fine Arts Museum in Cádiz.

The City of Cádiz

The approach

From the Cartuja the best way of covering the last few miles to Cádiz is via the *autopista*, which ends at the great bridge across the inlet and this ensures that motorists do not miss the turning into it and have to go the long way round. For Cádiz is built at the tip of a headland that thrusts northwards into the Atlantic and is separated from the mainland by its huge, part-marshy bay, now ringed with suburbs and industrial development.

The city (pop c. 158,000) seems to arouse strong feelings of like or dislike, perhaps because it is not, today, architecturally or artistically among the first rank in importance, thanks to its long and embattled history. However, its lack of premier league sights deters the casual tourist and since it is no longer, as it was in Ford's day, "the best starting point for a tour in the Peninsula", it has kept its character very much intact.

Early history: Phoenicians
Historically, of course, as one of Europe's most ancient cities, it is extremely important; Calvert was so impressed by this fact that it inspired one of his best purple passages. "Cádiz is the first-born city of Spain," he wrote, "probably the first foothold of civilisation on the shores of the Atlantic Ocean . . . After heaven knows how many attempts . . . the Phoenicians dared what no people . . . had dared before. The Pillars of Hercules were regarded as the western boundary of the world; beyond was nothingness. And one day, with an easterly wind filling his sails and fear in the hearts of his crew, some forgotten Columbus of Sidon or of Tyre passed through the strait, and turning northward, beached his little galley on the peninsula where we stand."

Catharginians; Romans
Jutting defiantly above the sea, its tall white houses beaten by wind and spray, Cádiz can still induce the same sort of tingle of romance. Standing on one of the promenades that ring the old quarter and looking out to sea, you can visualise Hamilcar of Carthage in 237 AD, beaching his own little galley somewhere down the sandy spit that joins city and mainland; and think of Julius Caesar, so conscious of its strategic importance that he endowed its people with honorary Roman citizenship and important trading rights. Cádiz dwindled in importance after the Romans departed, though it was strong enough to beat off Norman raiders in the early 11th century.

The Moors; Napoleon
Following its reconquest from the Moors in 1262 by Alfonso the Wise, it was re-populated from Cantabria on the Biscay coast of Castile. Its fortunes revived after the discovery of America, but this new wealth attracted predators: among them Drake, who "singed the King of Spain's beard" there in 1587, and Essex who sacked it even more thoroughly nine years later. Subsequent raiders it resisted, and grew fatter over the next 200 years on the lucrative American trade. During the Peninsular War its reputation acquired a new lustre when it became the seat of the anti-Napoleon faction and later the cradle of the new, though short-lived, constitutional movement.

Nineteenth-century opinions
Relics of these heroic chapters of its history are scant, to say the least. Ford considered that Cádiz had "small attraction to the scholar or gentleman", and advised people to see it in a day and leave. Byron was charmed by the beauty of its women but Augustus Hare, having

looked at the painting by Murillo that proved to be his last (he fell from his perch while executing it and died from his injuries) concluded that "there is literally nothing else to see in Cádiz." Nevertheless, it is an agreeable place in which to relax after more strenuous sightseeing.

Parador

The elderly Hotel Atlantico, built as a Parador and again, after a period of ostracism, back in the fold, is ideal for this purpose, being right in the old town, bordered by the Parque Genovese gardens, having a swimming pool and splendid views out to sea.

Main museums; signal tower

And of course there are numerous things to see: the few Phoenician legacies in the Archaeolgical Museum, for instance, which is to be found in the Academia de Bellas Artes, and Zurbarán's 15 magnificent canvases of saints on an upper floor; the 18th-century wooden model of the city in the Museo Historico (both museums are open mornings and afternoons). Not far away, on the way to the market and post office, is the Torre de Tavira, an ancient signal tower. Several churches are also worth attention, including the Sta Cueva and the chapel of the Hospital del Carmen, both with works by El Greco, and S Felipe Neri with a Virgin by Murillo. (His last work, already referred to, is of St Catherine and can be seen in the Capuchines chapel).

The Cathedral

The 18th-century 'new' Cathedral with its enormous yellow-tiled dome merits little praise but does contain the tomb of Manuel de Falla, a native son of the city and perhaps the most Andalusían of modern composers. Near it, the remains of the old Cathedral (burned down during Essex's raid, rebuilt in 1602), dwarfed by its fat tower, is now the parish church.

Seafront promenades

But the real charm of Cádiz lies in its seafront promenades that almost encirle the old town, in some places with pretty gardens, in others punctuated by fortifications, against which the Atlantic perpetually batters. On summer evenings the entire population seems to debouch onto these promenades to laugh and chat and stroll in the cool dusk.

Gardens; restaurants

One of the most attractive sectors is the Alameda de Apodava, in whose gardens stand two colossal, cactus-like drago trees said to be over 500 years old. The gardens are overlooked by the modest but good El Anteojo restaurant, specialising in Andalusían cuisine; for fish specialities, look for El Faro in Calle S Felix on the opposite site of town.

Folly; Hospice

Below the westernmost seafront promenade is a strip of beach with a 19th-century folly of a *balneario,* or spa, on stilts at its centre; opposite, the cream-painted Hospicio, built at the end of the 18th century, was the venue for a ball given in Wellington's honour in January of 1813.

City centre

Huddled inside this circle of promenades is an almost equally attractive grid of narrow white streets, glinting with *miradores,* or balconies glazed over as protection against the wind, and full of animation; Borrow remarked that they were "adorned with many splendid shops . . . in the style of Paris and London." This may not be quite so true today but on the other hand there are masses of cafés, bars and discos: Cádiz is a city where amusement is taken seriously. Its pre-Lent carnival is famous, and during August spectacles and entertainments abound.

City edges

A massive gateway known as the Puerta de la Tierra virtually seals off the old town from the isthmus connecting it to the mainland. The side facing the bay is lined with port installations and suchlike; the Atlantic side has been built over with apartment blocks and hotels that give onto the Avenida Amilcar Barca and the broad beach.

Puerto de Santa Maria

Across the bridge and to the north, turning left on C610, Puerto de Sta Maria (pop c. 61,000), known as El Puerto since before Ford's time and the principal gateway for the export of sherry, sits as the mouth of the Guadalete and is also connected to Cádiz by a ferry. Here are more *bodegas* to visit, as well as an attractive Alameda and a handful of handsome churches.

Local resorts

Beyond it, among a scatter of seaside resorts (the prettiest is Fuentebravia, with a pleasant beach, restaurants and hotels) an ambitious new tourist development is taking place. The Atlantic coast's answer to Puerto Bañus on the Costa del Sol is Puerto Sherry, its first stage opened in 1986, which will eventually become a full-blown resort complete with yacht marina, golf, tennis and other tourist facilities.

Cádiz to Algeciras; La Linea

If you continue southwards along the isthmus as you leave Cádiz, you pass first through S Fernando and then Chiclana de la Frontera, on whose outskirts is the long-established spa of Fuente Amarga.

Medina Sidonia

From Chiclana you can turn inland to Medina Sidonia, passing more of the great, white, pantile-roofed *cortijos* (country estates) so typical of Andalusía, their low-slung buildings ranged almost fortress-like around inner gardens. Seat of the dukes whose luckless scion commanded Philip II's Armada, Medina Sidonia (pop c. 15,000) is a somewhat crumbling but not unattractive town still dominated by the ducal palace and hugged about by the remains of its old walls.

The ducal family

Its historical associations amount to more than the seventh duke's Armada connection, for the Guzmáns (the ducal family name) are among the oldest and most illustrious families in Spain. It was a Guzmán who, when besieged at Tarifa by a Moorish army in 1294, refused to surrender even when the alternative was the murder of his own son: he is said to have retorted that he preferred honour without a son to a son with dishonour. Nicknamed 'el Bueno' (the Good), he was created the first duke and is buried at Santiponce, near Seville.

A later Guzmán, Leonora, was a mistress of Alfonso XI of Castile and bore him twin sons, Enrique and Fadrique of Trastamara. They were older than their legitimate half-brother Pedro (the Cruel) and Pedro was bitterly jealous of them. He had Fadrique assassinated in the Alcázar of Seville and was eventually himself murdered (in 1369) by Enrique, who thereupon assumed the Castilian crown as Enrique II. Blanche of Bourbon, Pedro's French wife, whom he abandoned after two days of marriage, fled for refuge after years of imprisonment to Medina Sidonia, where Pedro had her put to death in 1361; like many another sleepy, sunbaked Andalusían town, it has had its share of dramas.

Vejér de la Frontera

Instead of returning to Chiclana, take the minor C343 south from Medina Sidonia to Vejér de la Frontera (pop c. 8000), one of the prettiest and least spoiled small towns in Andalusía. Crowning a brown hilltop like a spoonful of whipped cream and overlooked by a straggle of windmills on a neighbouring ridge, it has a partly-restored Moorish castle, battlemented walls pierced by stout gateways, and a squarish 13th-century church on the site of a former mosque, all threaded together by brilliantly whitewashed streets of cube-shaped houses cascading flowers from every windowsill. At the heart of it is a palm-shaded Plaza de España with a tiled fountain surrounded by a ring of ceramic frogs.

Cape Trafalgar

From the terrace at the northern edge of Vejér there are glorious views over the Barbate valley, and from the opposite side of the village a road twists down to Cape Trafalgar, a low and undramatic promontory crowned with a lighthouse and surrounded by miles of sand dunes. Too far from any large centre of population to be crowded, even at weekends, it is wonderful for swimming, and as you cool off in the clear sea you can remember Nelson and his final great victory offshore in 1805, and his death on board the Victory as the evening drew in.

Fishing villages; new resort

Cape Trafalgar, Vejér and Medina Sidonia are close enough to Cádiz to visit in a day, but if you continue south you go through the whitewashed fishing port of Barbate de Franco, with its ruined castle at the mouth of the Barbate river, and down the marshy, sand-fringed coast to the smaller fishing village of Zahara de los Atunes (Zahara of the tunafish), where they still net the great fish as they migrate through the Straits of Gibraltar and where *tapas* of fresh tuna and shark are seasonal specialities in the bars. Beyond it are miles of superb beaches, culminating in the newish Atlanterra resort development with hotels and a pleasant restaurant, the Cortijo de la Plata.

Roman Bellone

Inland of it, the main road south from Vejér winds through foothills some way from the coast at first and, as it starts to descend, a turning to the right leads down to the remote seaside ruins of Roman Bellone, or Bolonia, where lizards scatter among the truncated columns at the rare approach of visitors.

Wind-surfing resort

As the main road swoops on southwards, it descends towards another dazzling strip of beach with the Punta de Tarifa headland visible in the distance through the shimmering heat haze. Until recently this windswept coast was shunned by all but the bravest bathers and a handful of dedicated bird-watchers; now the windsurfing craze is bringing it a new clientèle for which it is perfectly suited, and new hotels are making their appearance.

Tarifa

By now there are fantastic views across the Straits to the misty Rif mountains in Morocco, and then the road dips towards breezy Tarifa (pop c. 8,000), its tiny, steep white streets enclosed in Moorish walls and entered through keyhole-shaped gateways. The castle tower, from which the stalwart Guzmán el Bueno (see above) defied the besiegers who threatened to kill his son if he did not surrender (he even contemptuously threw down a dagger to them) has been rebuilt. So have some of the walls, and from the top are marvellous views down towards the gardens at the sea's edge and across to North Africa.

Algeciras

As the road dips and climbs eastwards round the flanks of the Sierra de Ojen there are more staggering views, dominated by the outline of the Rock of Gibraltar across the Bay of Algeciras. Of Algeciras itself (pop c. 86,000) there is little to be said: despite its strategic position and long history, it is undistinguished. Its only compensations are a certain liveliness, deriving from its busy port (ferries and hydrofoils to Ceuta and Tangier, overstretched in August), and the Reina Cristina Hotel, an oasis of beauty from another age. George Borrow likened the view of Gibraltar from Algeciras to the outline of an African lion "who had bounded over the sea bent on the destruction of the rival continent ... A hostile lion it has proved to Spain," he added, "for the most part in the hands of foreigners."

Algeciras: industrial development

As you skirt Algeciras Bay this view is marred now by a fringe of industrial development along the Campo, as the area is called. Set up with great fanfare to provide local employment after the Gibraltar frontier was closed in 1969, these 'new' industries never had adequate backing (in the form of good communications with the Spanish interior as well as cash) and consequently many went bankrupt. The reopening of the frontier and an eventual settlement of the 'Gibraltar question' will doubtless bring a brighter future to the area.

La Linea

A right turn at the S Roque crossroads brings you to Gibraltar through La Linea, which takes its name from the 18th-century Spanish fortifications thrown across it; it did not become a proper town until nearly a century later.

Gibraltar

Gibraltar itself (pop c. 28,000), of necessity transformed from a naval base into a tourist resort for less demanding Britons during the years when the Spanish frontier was closed, has acquired a rather dreary image. It is, however, far from uninteresting, with more assets than duty-free shops and the famous Barbary apes.

Early history

Its early history, of course, parallels that of the rest of Southern Spain; in ancient lore one of the Pillars of Hercules, then at the western edge of the known world, it was inhabited long before the Phoenicians made it a trading post. The Berber chieftain who invaded it in 711 gave it his own name, Jebel Tariq, or Tariq's Hill, and it stayed in Moorish hands until 1462.

British occupation

Britain captured it from Spain in 1704 during the War of the Spanish Succession, her sovereignty twice ratified (by the Treaties of Utrecht in 1715 and of Seville in 1729) but never accepted by Spain which has, down the centuries, besieged it no fewer than 14 times. At least one of these occasions, the Great Siege from 1779-1783 was marked by gentlemanly, civilised interludes of truce. Permission was given to certain of the British defenders to go into Spain to do a little riding and shooting and replenish the larders and their Spanish opposite numbers proceeded across to the Rock for a bit of sightseeing, and to shop for manufactured goods brought to the garrison by sea from London.

View from the top

Evidence of Gibraltar's oddly complicated past abound and the top of the rocky ridge, reached by cable car, makes a good vantage point from which to start looking for it. The 40-acre Admiralty Harbour, probably the most conspicuous landmark, is all built on reclaimed land; at the time of its construction at the end of the 19th century, it was the world's biggest engineering project. The former sea wall is still partly visible near its landward edge, a layer cake of Moorish, Spanish and British fortification. A short way away, a small mole with a stone building at one end was once part of the original harbour, where Nelson's ships docked after Trafalgar.

Below the cable car, amid a profusion of trees and shrubs, you can still see a wall running down the western slope of the Rock, built by the Emperor Charles V to keep pirates at bay (the other faces were too precipitous for marauders to land on). Paralleling Charles V's wall, there also remain fragments of the earlier Moorish wall and of a square-towered Moorish fort.

Cannon rings

Of later fortifications, perhaps the most interesting are the iron rings still embedded at intervals up the face of the Rock, and the famous galleries hollowed out of it. By means of those rings, British cannon were hauled into place on the heights. So heavy were they that it could take three years between the arrival of a gun from England and its eventual installation.

Rock galleries; caves

The galleries were conceived during the Great Siege of 1779 when it was thought necessary to position a gun on an inaccessible outcrop known as the Notch, the better to cover Gibraltar's landward side. One Sergeant-Major Ince had the idea of tunnelling to the Notch, but long before it was reached the plan was modified and the tunnel enlarged to accommodate gun embrasures. By the time they were finished, so was the Great Siege, but they are still impressive. Something like 150 other caves riddle the Rock, St Michael's being the largest. Once a Phoenician temple, it has been used as shelter in times of trouble and as a hospital; nowadays it is furnished with illuminations and piped music.

Museum; Trafalgar Cemetery
Down in the town, two points of interest are the delightful small Museum, housed in a 14th-century Moorish bath, and the small, shady Trafalgar Cemetery. It was in use for some 30 years at the beginning of the 18th century and on its headstones you can read the epitaphs of men who served under Nelson, were wounded and disembarked, and died in Gibraltar.

The Hill Towns

The most spectacular and interesting hill towns of southwest Andalusía are inland from this part of the coast and worth spending several days to explore: more if you enjoy walking or riding.

Almoraima
If you go inland from the S Roque crossroads and head up the valley of the Guadarranque from Algeciras Bay, you climb through cork oak forests first and can detour at Almoraima to see the enormous Moorish castle precinct of Castellar de la Frontera, enfolding the whitewashed hamlet within it.

Jimena de la Frontera; Gaucín
Inland again, surrounded by citrus groves, is Jimena de la Frontera, white-painted and crowned by the remnants of another Moorish castle whose gateway, triple-arched, is partly faced with Roman grave-*stelae.* Off to the northeast is Gaucín, almost as picturesque; to the northwest by some 66 km (just over 40 miles) is Arcos de la Frontera (pop c. 25,000) and its charming Parador.

Arcos
Perched on a sharp spur overhanging the Guadalete with a huge reservoir just behind it, Arcos is one of the gems of the area. It is extremely old, having been settled by the Iberians long before the Romans arrived, and is commanded by two splendid landmarks. One is the fine tower of Sta Maria, with a Plateresque west portal, which stands at one end of a plaza whose opposite side looks straight out over the gorge; between them, one long side of the plaza is flanked by the rigidly battlemented walls of the castle of the Dukes of Osuna, part of it now the Town Hall.

Arcos Parador; S Pedro church
The Parador, just behind the Encarnación building on the opposite side of the plaza, has a terrace with equally stunning views over the river, and so does the other landmark of Arcos, the many-buttressed 16th-century Gothic church of S Pedro with its free-standing tower and cool, tiled interior. Between and below them is a pattern of white alleys, arches and flower-heavy balconies; there are little dark shops and small chapels and glimpses into pretty patios.

El Bosque; Ubrique; Grazalema
A fairly direct and easy road leads from Arcos to Ronda via the picturesque village of El Bosque, 32 km (20 miles) to the east on the edge of good trout-fishing country (its hotel-restaurant Las Truchas specialises in trout). Here, however, there are endless opportunities for digression before Ronda. Another road branches south to Ubrique (pop c. 16,500), also picturesque, whose tanneries and workshops produce much of the leatherwork sold in shops along the Costa del Sol.

You can come back to the direct Ronda road from here via Grazalema, perhaps prettiest of all the hill villages, "plastered like a martlet-nest on a rocky hill," said Ford. Its inhabitants are no longer the "smugglers and robbers" he deemed them to be, but instead organise riding holidays in the surrounding mountains.

Zahara
Just 24 km (15 miles) north of Grazalema is Zahara, yet another entrancing village with yet another Moorish castle that eyes sated with castles might merely glance at. However, its history is more dramatic than most, for in 1481 it provided the tinder for the flames of reprisal that culminated in the reconquest of Granada 11 years later. Just after Christmas, Washington Irving relates, Moulay Aben Hassan "at the head of a powerful force, had hurried from Granada . . . in the obscurity of a tempest" and annihilated the town. Those citizens still alive were taken back to Granada in chains and there, while Aben Hassan and his generals were congratulating themselves on this coup, a seer denounced him, predicting that "the ruins of Zahara will fall upon our heads: . . . the end of our empire is at hand."

Olvera; Setenil
Some 25 km (just over 15 miles) to the northeast of Zahara is Olvera, its stone fortress pinned to an outcrop above the village. During the Peninsular War, even the women of Olvera, Ford recounts, resisted the French: on one occasion giving them donkey flesh instead of veal when compelled to provide rations to a detachment of Napoleon's troops. The semi-troglodyte hamlet of Sentenil is 15 km (10 miles) southeast of Olvera, and from there Ronda is another 18 km (just over

12 miles) further south.

Ronda

Even after so many other charming hill villages and despite its increasing popularity as a day-excursion from the Costa del Sol, Ronda (pop c. 31,500) does not disappoint. The town, occupying one of the most sensational settings imaginable, rides the summit of a wide rock-escarpment between 150 and 300 metres high, commanding fantastic views of the surrounding *sierras,* which is dramatic enough in itself; what is unique to Ronda is that this cliff is split by a huge chasm, El Tajo, through which tumbles the Guadalevín river.

Approaching the town

Arriving from the north, you take Ronda by stealth, so to speak, coming in through modern suburbs to the Mercadillo, the part of town built after its reconquest by Ferdinand and Isabella in 1485. Until then Ronda, capital of a remote *taifa* which, says Washington Irving, "was the most virulent nest of Moorish depredators in the whole border country", consisted only of the section on the south side of the gorge, partly built with stones removed from Roman Acinipo, to the north, now known as Ronda la Vieja.

You want to dispose of the car as soon as possible: Ronda's streets are best explored on foot; if you are coming up from the Costa del Sol, there are regular public bus services.

Alameda garden; bullring

The Calle de Jerez runs parallel to the cliff-face, and halfway along it is the early 19th-century Alameda garden, with wide views. Beyond this is the bullring, the second oldest in Spain (built in 1784) after that of Seville, and exceptionally large and graceful, with slender columns supporting its decorative arcades and a beautiful entrance. Pedro Romero, third generation of a famous family of bullfighters, was born in Ronda in 1754 and there laid down the rules of classical bullfighting.

Hotel Reina Victoria

The venerable Reina Victoria, where the Austrian romantic poet Rilke stayed (a more recent guest suggested that it had not been repainted since), stands at the edge of the Plaza de España. British-built just after the turn of the century, when the well-to-do would ride up to Ronda from Gibraltar, it is comfortable enough, marvellously situated on the edge of the gorge, and has parking as well as a swimming pool.

Tourist office; market; shops
Opposite the hotel is the Tourist Office, the Town Hall and the market, just behind it, is perched on the edge of the cliff. Behind the hotel are traffic-free streets full of shops selling antiques and ceramics, among other things. In one street, Espinel, is a birdcage-shaped balcony that even in this land of intricate balconies is exceptional.

Puente Nuevo
The south side of Plaza de Espana opens on to the 18th-century Puente Nuevo which spans the gorge, and here you can peer down through the railings into the abyss below. The architect, who had the somewhat sinister idea of building a prison cell directly beneath the bridge (now transformed into a restaurant), fell to his death from there just after the bridge was finished.

Old Moorish town
Across the bridge are the tiny streets of the old Moorish town: whitewashed façades with old walnut doors and ironwork balconies, cobbled alleys and flights of steps. From the Plaza Campillo, to the west, are more cliff-edge views, likewise from the gallery of the Mondragón Palace nearby. Below, a path leads down to one of the Moorish-built mills, where you can look up at the Puente Nuevo and the precipice and recall Gustave Doré's illustrations for Dante's 'Inferno', which it inspired, and Hemingway's passages in 'for Whom the Bell Tolls', which were taken from an actual incident during the Spanish Civil War when prisoners of the Republicans were made to hurl themselves into the chasm.

Sta Maria church; Moorish baths
At the heart of the old town is the 16th-century church of Sta Maria, converted from a mosque, and on the other side of the main street a solitary minaret is all that remains of another mosque. Down the hill behind it, the little street called Marqués de Salvatierra leads to the Renaissance mansion of the same name and thence through an archway to the early 17th-century Puente Viejo, on Roman foundations. Just upstream are the ruins of Moorish baths and, if you climb the 400 steps back to town on the other side of the old bridge, you arrive in the garden of the so-called House of the Moorish King – in fact of later date than the last Islamic ruler.

Pileta Cave: rock paintings
You need to stay in Ronda for two or three nights to get the feel of the place – in the early mornings before the tourist buses arrive, and in the evenings when they have gone. There is at least one excursion to be made, to the huge Pileta Cave, some 28 km (about 17 miles) to the southwest, first taking C339 and turning off it to the left; its rock paintings of animals in black and rust-red are said to be earlier than

those of Altamira, dating back more than 25,000 years.

A Detour before Málaga

Alora

Leaving Ronda, take C344 east to its junction, at Pizarra, with C337, and turn left for Alora (in all about 72 km, or 45 miles). High above the valley, with the remains of a castle, a beautiful wood-roofed 16th-century church and several other fine buildings, this little town has great charm.

Guadalhorce Valley

You can make another tour from here of 52 km (about 33 miles) through some dramatic *sierra* country (punctuated, it is true, by a few power stations) by forking right to start with and following the valley of Guadalhorce northwards. A side turn takes you to the river-gorge called the Garganta del Chorro; further on, passing beneath the ruins of a castle, you come to the remains of the early 10th-century church of Bobastro.

Carratraca

After Bobastro the road parallels the shore of the huge Guadalhorce reservoir as far as Ardales, with another ruined castle. Here you turn left on MA441 and come first to Carratraca, in the last century an exclusive spa patronised by Doré, Rilke and Dumas. Ferdinand VII came to take its waters and built himself a miniature palace that is now a *hostál.* Despite its feel of remoteness, it is within quick and easy reach of Málaga, only 40-odd km (about 25 miles) southeast of Alora.

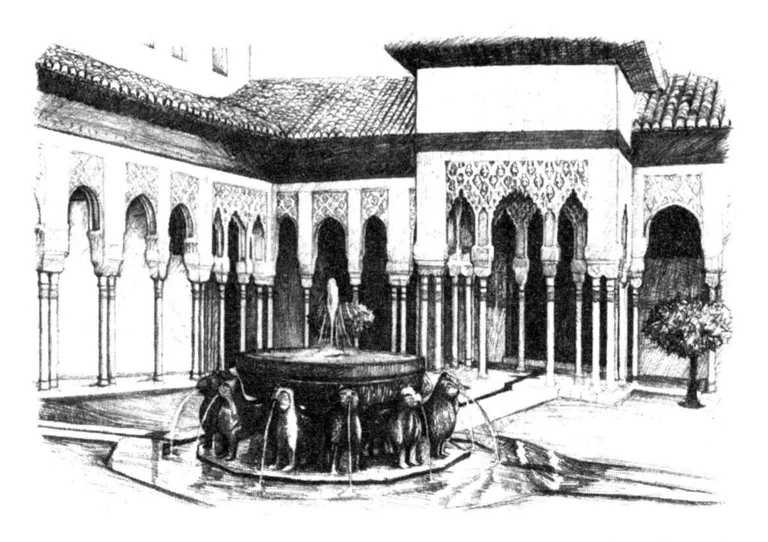

Lion Court, Alhambra, Granada

Eastern Andalusía

Málaga Region

The City of Málaga

As with Western Andalusía, so Málaga city (pop c. 504,000) is the most usual gateway into Eastern Andalusía; so much so, in fact that it is more often than not completely overlooked as a city. Yet its winter climate is one of the best in Southern Spain, vying with that of Valencia, and its position splendid. Ford dismissed it: "One day will suffice. It has few attractions beyond climate, almonds and raisins, and sweet wine." But if you battle successfully with the spaghetti junction of highways and forests of high-rise apartment blocks and factories outside it, the old part is surprisingly pleasant.

History: Romans to Reconquest

It is an old city: founded by Phoenicians and enlarged by the Romans into a major port, in which role it continued under the Moorish kings of Granada. Its capture by Ferdinand and Isabella in 1487 was one of the more unpleasant episodes of the Reconquest: the Catholic Monarchs, perpetually short of funds, allowed the richer citizens to believe they could ransom themselves for huge sums, and relieved them of their more portable valuables as down payments. When they failed to produce the rest of the ransom-monies their entire properties were confiscated and they themselves deported, sold (in the case of the young girls) or put to the sword.

19th and 20th centuries

In more recent times, along with a reputation for immorality and crime, it acquired notoriety as a fount of liberal thought and ideals, rebelling against the government twice in the 19th century and strongly supporting the Republican cause in the Civil War, which may explain the violent anti-Nationalism of its most famous son, Pablo Picasso, who became self-exiled after Franco gained power.

The Parque; hotels

Although it boasts nothing very outstanding in the way of art or architectural monuments, there is plenty to keep the visitor interested; if, at worst, a crisis involves a visit to Málaga's British Consulate and keeps you there for a couple of days, there are compensations. The city centre lies east of the partly-canalised Guadalmedina, and all roads into it lead eventually to the long, shaded Alameda garden, or Parque, which extends behind and parallel to the port. The pleasantest town centre hotel is Casa Curro, just back from the Parque; nearby is the modest but very acceptable Derby. Out of the centre, up the hill on which the castle stands, the modern Parador has magnificent views but only 12 rooms.

Market; shops

In the western part of the city is the market, a wrought-iron and glass confection incorporating a Moorish gateway and lively with raucous housewives and stallholders. East of the market, the principal shopping street is Marqués de Larios, running between the Parque and Plaza de la Constitución, and off it lead narrow alleyways, mostly pedestrianised, with patterned pavements and flowers trailing from grille-protected windows; the El Chinitas restaurant is on one of them. To the traveller setting out to explore Andalusía from Málaga, these alleys are a foretaste of the prettier quarters of Seville and Córdoba, yet if you look closely you see weeds sprouting from between roof pantiles and cracks in door lintels, hinting at the shabbiness of other streets only a few hundred yards away.

Cathedral; Sagrario

Running parallel with Marqués de Larios, the next major street to the east is, confusingly, Molina Larios, which leads to the Cathedral. Facing its west door is a small, pretty square flanked by the facade of the Bishop's Palace and with a fountain at its centre. The Cathedral looks lopsided from outside, for the second of its twin towers was never built, and its interior is chiefly distinguished for an extraordinary shell-studded ceiling carved to resemble palm fronds.

North of the Cathedral, a little garden separates it from the Sagrario, an oblong brick building converted from a mosque; it has a rather lovely, weather-beaten Isabelline (Flamboyant Gothic) north door, best seen from across the street.

Art Museum
The narrow Calle S Augustín leads away from the Sagrario to the Bellas Artes Museum, housed in an early 16th-century *mudéjar* mansion with a central courtyard and fine wooden *artesonado* ceilings (open mornings and afternoons). Roman mosaics have been relaid here and there in its garden and the house contains a good collection of Spanish paintings (Zurbarán, Ribera, Murillo, Morales) and also features local artists, including Picasso, a few of whose works are grouped in one of the galleries. There is also some beautiful old furniture and a motley collection of ecclesiastical treasures.

Picasso's birthplace; Plaza de la Victoria
Beyond the museum is Plaza de la Merced, where Picasso was born at No. 15, and to the north, Avenida de la Victoria leads through the seedier part of town, where cinemas show semi-pornographic films with names like 'America de Noche Prohibida'. Plaza de la Victoria, with a church, is said to occupy the site where Ferdinand and Isabella camped during the long and terrible siege in which the inhabitants were eventually starved into negotiating a surrender in 1487, and then stripped of their valuables and taken captive.

Gibralfaro fortress
Above this area looms the Gibralfaro fortress, where the diminished and equally starved military defenders of Malaga held out against the Catholic Monarchs for two days after the city had surrendered; when they finally capitulated, Ferdinand took up residence in Gibralfaro while Isabella made her quarters in the city.

Moorish Alcázaba
The Moorish Alcázaba, which you reach from the Calle Alcázabilla, running between Plaza de la Merced and the Parque, sits on a lower spur of the Gibralfaro hill. The wall that shores it up on the seaward side is pitted with holes that have been commandeered by myriads of pigeons; if you sit on one of the benches in the garden below it, you are serenaded by gentle cooing noises. The Alcázaba entrance is near the partly-excavated remains of a Roman theatre, rather incongruously marked by a Roman column topped by a wrought-iron crucifix and four lamps.

Rather drastically restored, the old Moorish citadel with its succession of horseshoe arches is nonetheless pleasant and peaceful, its gardens smelling of lavender and rosemary.

Archaeological Museum

At the summit of the citadel, in a series of Arabesque pavilions, is the Archaeological Museum, with a heterogeneous collection of Neolithic pots and implements from Nerja; Phoenician and Roman fragments, and some lovely tenth- to 14th-century Islamic glass and ceramics.

Parador

To the east, a path climbs the Gibralfaro hill through pines and eucalyptus to the ruined eighth-century fortress, still connected to the Alcazaba by walling; it is here that the Parador is situated and its terrace is a fine place for lunch. The view over the harbour from here is splendid even though it is no longer "lined with charming villas, each standing in gardens which abound with . . . tropical flora", as it was when the 'Cook's Handbook' was written in 1921.

Protestant Cemetery

But if you go east along the harbour front road, past the hospital and the bullring, you can still glimpse a garden on the opposite side of the road. It is the Protestant Cemetery, the first of its kind to be permitted in Spain, and was founded in 1830 by the then British Consul, William Mark. Previously, according to Ford, "heretical carcases . . . used to be buried in the sea sands like dead dogs, and beyond the low watermark, and even this concession offended orthodox fishermen." Hans Christian Anderson felt at home there, reading the worn headstones "inscribed in Danish, Dutch and German"; in fact most are memorials to long-gone Britons and Americans, the majority probably connected with the wine trade.

West of Málaga: the coast

West of Málaga the Costa del Sol highway hugs the coast, passing a string of heavily built-up beach resorts and marinas. Almost at Málaga's back door is the most famous, the high-rise capital of honky-tonk, Torremolinos. Further along the coast is Fuengirola, which has a pleasant beach.

Marbella

Marbella (pop c. 68,000) is the oldest of the Costa del Sol resorts: it was in fact a walled stronghold in the 15th century as you can see from one of the beautifully-detailed choirstall carvings in Toledo Cathedral that chronicle the stages of the Conquest of Granada. Parts of the walls can still be seen in the thoroughly-restored old part of Marbella, which has managed to retain an element of quality among the general hotch-potch development scarring this coast.

S Pedro de Alcántara; Estepona
S Pedro de Alcántara has a good beach and vestiges of Roman buildings; just east of it is Nueva Andalusía with its studiedly quaint-chic yachting marina, Puerto Bañus.

West again is Estepona, perhaps the least over-developed of these resorts, then the road by-passes the secluded, luxury resort of Sotogrande before reaching the S Roque crossroads and the turn-off for Gibraltar (see previous chapter).

Hill villages
Minor roads wind into the hinterland behind the Costa del Sol, to once-typical Andalusían hill villages whose characters are steadily being eroded by the demands of tourist coachloads on half-day outings. Casares, grouped beneath a Moorish fort behind Estepona, is the least accessible and thus still the most delightful; Ojen, on a sharp spur surrounded by beautiful scenery above Marbella, is known for producing the best *anis* in Andalusía.

Mijas, above Fuengirola, is now almost Disney-esque, with hardly a house not given over to a bar, crafts boutique or restaurant. Few of its present inhabitants probably know that it is the village whose mayor, a latter-day Rip van Winkle, went into hiding during the Civil War and did not re-emerge until the general amnesty some 30 years later.

Córdoba Region

North to Córdoba

The road from Málaga to Córdoba is fairly direct with not much inducement to detour – though if you have missed it earlier, Antequera (see previous chapter) should not be bypassed. Olive groves stretch in every direction, occasionally interrupted by fields of sunflowers, as you come towards Lucena. Ford described this as "another of these large towns which no one visits," and since the road bypasses it widely, you are not encouraged to do so. But this sprawling little town is of some interest as the manufacturing centre of decorative copper and brassware.

Aguilar; Montilla
Aquilar (pop c. 12,500) has a delightful plaza at the top of the town that makes an agreeable place to pause for a cup of coffee, and Montilla (pop c. 22,000) also repays a brief detour. A large wine village where Amontillado is produced, it is ringed with large,

whitewashed *bodegas* and the slopes to the east of it are covered with vines.

Montilla's 'Gran Capitán'

The 'Gran Capitán', after whom so many Spanish streets and plazas are named, was born here in 1453: he was Gonzalo Fernandez y Aguilar, perhaps the most distinguished soldier in Spanish history, who swept the House of Bourbon off the Neapolitan throne and became the first Spanish viceroy there. His monetary rewards were, however, hard-gained: Ferdinand the Catholic, always stingy, was ungracious enough to demand from him a full account of his military expenditures, to which he responded with his famous *cuentas* (accounts). The statement reads, in part: "200,736 ducats . . . paid to the clergy and the poor who prayed for the victory of . . . Spain. 100 millions in pikes, bullets, and entrenching tools; 100,000 in powder and cannon-balls; 10,000 ducats in scented gloves to preserve the troops from the odour of the enemies' dead left on the battlefield; 100,000 ducats . . . in the repair of bells . . . worn out by . . . announcing fresh victories . . . and 100 millions for the patience with which I have listened to the King, who demands an account from the man who has presented him with a kingdom."

The City of Córdoba

A little further, a tall tower signals the ducal castle of Fernan Nuñez, a hilltop town also bypassed by the main road, and then you join the principal highway between Seville and Madrid and sweep into Córdoba across the Guadalquivir and past the walls of the old Alcázar. After the rash of unlovely suburbs and despite the choking traffic, this approach manages to produce a tingle of anticipation.

Early history

For two and a half centuries from 756, when the Ummayed ruler Abderrahman I captured it, until the early 11th century when the excesses of the usurper, Almansor, began to undermine it, Córdoba was the most brilliant capital in Europe, civilised and wealthy, the Athens of the Dark Ages, with a population almost twice as big as today's 285,000-odd. It had been the principal city of the peninsula for long before that, developing from an Iberian market town to become the capital of Roman Baetica; both Senecas were born there. Some 250 years later it was the bishopric of Osius, adviser to the Emperor Constantine and presiding prelate over the Council of Nicaea, and it continued to be a bishopric under the Visigoths.

Centre of learning

Only after the disintegration of the Caliphate of Córdoba did the city begin to decline, but although it lost political power to the kingdom of

Seville it still continued to be a centre of learning: it was where a Moorish scholar known as Averroes introduced the works of Aristotle to the west, while his Jewish contemporary, Maimonides, was a no less distinguished theologian and philosopher. The list of Córdoba's other famous sons includes poets and painters (notably Valdés Leal) as well as the great bullfighters Manolete and El Cordobes.

The Reconquest and after

After the Reconquest, the city sank to the ranks; the Christian conquerors were bent on eradicating its brilliance and bringing it to heel and this they did, driving new streets through its old quarters and repopulating it with Christians from the north. Thus it degenerated for centuries; despite a reputation for fine leather- and silver-work. Ford called it a "dirty, benighted, ill-provided, decaying place" and Hare, in the 1870s, writes that "there are no shops apparent, no animation whatever, nor any sign of life in the houses . . . only miserable beggars wrapped in their mantas . . . Córdoba is a city of the dead."

Later prosperity

But that was over 100 years ago, and Córdoba has prospered and expanded since, not only acquiring the inevitable barricade of new factories and high-rise flats and the inevitable street crime problems, but also a tendency to over-embellish its more saleable assets. Even so, it is an unmissable city for the tourist, smaller than either Seville or Granada and less demanding in terms of the number of things to see; less feverishly gay than Seville, less romantic, perhaps, than Granada, but better enshrining the feel of Islamic Spain.

Hotels; restaurants

There is a fair choice of hotels; in high summer the Parador on the outskirts or the Melía, just outside the old city walls and the Almodóvar gate, have the advantage of swimming pools; in cooler weather the Maimonides, almost next to the Mezquita and with a garage next door, or the smaller Marisa, equally close, are alternatives. The nicest restaurants are all near by: the Almudaina, between the Alcázar and the Mezquita, is among the best; the Bandolero a close second; the El Churrasco not far behind, and all have patios for summer eating.

The Mezquita

George Borrow, no admirer of Spain's Catholic churches, conceded that the Mezquita of Córdoba was "perhaps the most extraordinary place of worship in the world", and it is unthinkable to start exploring anywhere else. The former mosque of Córdoba, open mornings and afternoons every day, was built in stages between 785 and 990 and from the outside is now as massively walled as a fortress; its former minaret, with a hideous Baroque casing, is equally off-putting.

Patio de los Naranjos

The main entrance door, the Puerta del Perdón, is faintly uninviting too, its much later double-arched Moorish style gateway topped by a Baroque frivolity that is entirely out of character. It leads into the colonnaded Patio de los Naranjos, where the layout of the orange trees corresponded with that of the rows of columns within the mosque; originally there was no wall between this ablution-courtyard and the interior.

Columned interior

Once inside, the cool, dim, petrified glade of columns and arches literally takes the breath away with its exquisite perspectives (though at the time of writing restoration work has resulted in roped-off areas that spoiled the overall effect). Like the trees in a forest, the columns are all different and come from all sorts of places, some from as far afield as France and North Africa. Their heights have been levelled off and most are Roman, but the capitals are often Byzantine, Moorish or Visigothic as well as Roman.

The two-tiered Moorish arches that spring from them to link them and support the roof are boldly striped in red brick and white stone and, while parts of the ceiling above were stone-vaulted after the Reconquest, much of the original carved and painted woodwork remains.

Prayer niche

Wandering through this astonishing mirage of vistas, you come to the glorious *mihrab* (prayer niche) of 965. Its outer façade of three arches decorated with subdued Byzantine-style mosaics is superb, and above are three small cupolas supported on overlapping arches, the centre one covered in more mosaics, predominantly gold, blue and green.

Inside, the shallow recess is roofed with a shell-shaped cupola and lined with trefoil arches framed in intricate plasterwork and separated by small marble columns with gilded bases and capitals, repeating the theme of the arches along the top of the façade. The more often one looks at it, the more one sees in the exquisite juxtaposition of lines and curves and in the delicacy of the mosaics.

Mezquita into Cathedral

The first essay in introducing a Christian place of worship into this ensemble took place against the southwest wall in the 13th century and paid its surroundings the compliment of faintly echoing its style, with *mudéjar* features between restrained pointed arches. The somewhat later *capilla real*, immediately east of it, almost opposite the *mihrab* was also decorated with arabesque plasterwork. Neither of these disturbed the balance of perspectives, but in the 16th century some 200 columns and the roof above them were brutally cleared away in order to construct something more grandiose.

The resulting Cathedral, which you come across almost accidentally after working your way wonderingly around it, contains the inevitably enclosed *coro* and *capilla mayor*, and its roof has been raised above that of the mosque, but otherwise its walls are non-existent and the transition comes as a jolt. Charles V told the builders that they had destroyed something unique to build something commonplace, but with hindsight this was probably preferable to pulling the whole mosque down, as was done in Seville.

To sit inside the Cathedral, near the transept crossing, and look out at the patterns made by the columns and arches outside it, is a curious sensation, like viewing a masterly stage set through a ponderous proscenium. Other unhappy intrusions are the Christian altars and carvings erected within Moorish archways without thought for the harmony of those aisles, and the walling-off of the arches between the mosque and the Patio de los Naranjos, which many consider to be the worst piece of aesthetic vandalism.

Mezquita to the river; Alcázar

Outside again, the west wall of the Mezquita has a lovely Moorish brickwork doorway (not in use as such) facing the partly 15th-century Archbishop's Palace and near the annexe to the Bellas Artes Museum. The street between them leads down towards the river where a neo-Classical 16th-century archway, on the site of the Moorish gate, stands before the ancient bridge, largely Moorish but with Roman piers. A clumsy Baroque pillar stands at this end of the bridge, topped with a statue of S Rafael; on the opposite bank is the imposing Calahorra Tower.

The Alcázar

West of the Mezquita is the Alcázar, built in the early 14th century by Alfonso XI of Castile on the site of an Ummayyad palace and rather austere within – a reminder that it was used by the Inquisition – though relieved with some good Roman mosaics on the walls, and by cool, interconnecting patios and corridors. Its gardens are lovely, full of pools where lazy carp undulate among the waterlilies, fountains and flowers, shady walks bordered with clipped hedges, and secret corners where lovers sit clasping each other in the dusk.

The Jewish Quarter

The narrow alleyways of the Judería, the former *aljama,* or Jewish quarter, whitewashed to a fault and so overflowing with flowers and the massed displays of the souvenir shops that it is sometimes difficult to pass without disturbing them, hug three sides of the Mezquita. They have, arguably, been over-prettified, nevertheless they afford constant glimpses of beautiful interior patios that are outstanding even in the land of beautiful patios.

The little 14th-century synagogue (open mornings and afternoons), last relic of the scores that flourished in the city's heyday and remarkable for its magnificent plasterwork and still-intact women's gallery, is just inside the Almodovar Gate.

Municipal and Archaeological museums
The Municipal Museum (open mornings and afternoons), chiefly devoted to bullfighting and with mementoes of Cordoba's great *toreros,* is housed in a delightful mansion close by. A short way to the east is the Plaza Jeronimo Paez, surrounded by delightful facades, where a former palace houses the Archaeological Museum (open mornings and afternoons), full of well displayed exhibits dating back to Roman times and earlier, including Iberian stone carvings and Roman mosaics and, of particular interest, superb examples of Andalusían Islamic art.

Anti-clockwise round Córdoba

Plazuela del Potro
Eastwards again, a gateway known as the Portillo marks the eastern perimeter of the old city walls: a few sections can be seen along Calle S Fernando. Opposite is the church of S Francisco, with a tiny plaza in front of it, and behind this church is the Plazuela del Potro, with a beautiful Renaissance fountain surmounted by a rearing colt *(potro),* mentioned in 'Don Quixote'. Cervantes is said to have stayed at the much-restored inn alongside (now partly converted into a handicrafts bazaar).

Arts Museum
Facing the fountain is the Bellas Artes Museum, installed in the old convent of La Caridad; its collection of paintings of the Spanish school is small but exceptionally representative – not many provincial museums have two such good Goya portraits, for instance. In a twin building across the street are displayed the works of the local, early 20th-century portraitist, Julio Romero de Torres.

Plaza Mayor; market

North of Plazuela del Potro a succession of alleyways, hardly less attractive and certainly less crowded with tourists than those of the Juderia, lead past the market and Plaza de la Corredera or Plaza Mayor, a harmonious ensemble of 17th-century brick houses rising to three storeys from arcades. At one time it was used for bullfights and other spectacles and then it housed the market; now it has been cleared and restored without becoming too manicured and the market is to one side of it.

Shopping centre

Northwards again, and westwards, the commercial part of the city begins, its traffic-snarled heart the Plaza de las Tendillas, off which the main shopping streets (Jesus y Maria, Conde de Gondomar) radiate, but even here you can turn off into little white lanes that end in cul-de-sacs or erupt into small plazas.

Roman temple

To the east, near the dilapidated gateway fronting the church of S Pablo, a Roman temple has been recently excavated and partly enveloped in the brand new, glass and brass Town Hall, one side of whose entrance lobby is entirely of Roman stonework. Behind the Town Hall (reachable through it on weekday mornings, also visible from outside) eleven columns of the temple have been put back *in situ* and excavations are continuing.

Churches; Viana Palace

San Pablo itself is perhaps the most beautiful of Córdoba's churches, late Romanesque behind the crumbling Baroque façade, with a marvellous *mudéjar* ceiling. San Lorenzo, further to the east still, also has a fine *mudéjar* ceiling, and some good frescoes around the apse, and the area north of it is another maze of alleyways that tourists seldom penetrate. At its heart is the superb Viana Palace, with a breathtaking succession of 14 patios; it can be visited in the mornings. Just north of it is the mellow Gothic church of Sta Marina with a statue of the great bullfighter Manolete outside the west door.

Capuchinos convent; Plaza de Colon

Turning westwards, a flight of steps leads from Puerta del Rincón into the quiet white square of the Cristo de los Farioles, flanked by the façade of the Capuchinos convent and containing a Calvary surrounded by crooked wrought-iron lamps. Just north of this is the Plaza de Colón with the early 15th-century Malmuerta tower.

Avenida del Gran Capitan

To return to the Judería, either take Avenida Cruz Conde or Gran Capitán (with a tree-shaded Alameda and cafes down its centre; the charming small church of S Nicolás at its southern end has a minaret converted into a bell tower with no Baroque additions to mar it).

West of Córdoba: a day trip

Medina Azahara

A pleasant day's outing westwards starts with Medina Azahara (open mornings and afternoons except on Tuesdays). An enormous palace, more like a small city, it was built in the 10th century by a Byzantine architect for Abderrahman's favourite, Zahara, and sacked very soon afterwards. For a long time it was thought to have disappeared altogether, but about 50 years ago the royal apartments were discovered beneath collapsed masonry and since then it has gradually been excavated and lovingly reconstructed. It is immensely evocative, with a magnificent Throne Room, courtyards and other chambers, and beautiful gardens.

Almodóvar del Rio; Posadas

If you continue westwards on the Seville road (C431), which hugs the north bank of the Guadalquivir, you get a splendid view across the river of the Moorish castle of Almodóvar del Rio, its battlements and towers rising from a cone-shaped hill on the opposite bank; Pedro the Cruel used it at one time as a repository for his loot, and it has now been restored.

Next comes Posadas, on the north bank, its towers rearing above the rooftops against a shimmering background of the Sierra Morena.

Meandering back to Córdoba

If time allows, keep on westwards for another 45 km (just under 29 miles): the quiet minor road curves and dips along gentle undulations just above the river's course where, in the heat of summer, children paddle and wallow and you can find picnic-spots. The fresh-looking mountains seem to advance and retreat in the hazy distance to the north of you; there are more glimpses of castles on ridges and the road is punctuated by little white villages with attractive churches like Palma del Rio, just across the Guadalquivir; Peñaflor, marked by a noble tower; Lora del Rio with its ruined castle. From here you can turn south across the river, join the main NIV road in 16 km (10 miles) and return to Córdoba in 105 km (about 65 miles) via Ecija (see previous chapter).

Granada and Jaén Regions

Córdoba to Granada

Granada is, of course, the heart of eastern Andalusía, but it is still some way from Córdoba, and with many a stop to be made en route; indeed there is a host of distractions along whichever road you take. If you come direct from Córdoba, then the N432 is as good as any to start out on, with a succession of hilltop castles to enhance the views.

Espejo; Castro del Rio

Espejo is the first of them, a really splendid affair built for the Dukes of Osuna, with fat turrets at the corners and a big square keep; the little town lives, like Montilla to the west, by producing the amontillado wines grown on the surrounding hillsides.

Castro del Rio is the next castle, and between these landmarks are more of the *cortijos* so typical of the region: vast, whitewashed farmsteads standing like islands in their widespreading domains.

Baena

Next comes Baena (pop c. 17,000), up a steep hill beside the main road with another huge castle at its top; I happened to spend a night there once, being in the vicinity towards the end of a hot summer afternoon and noticing in the Michelin Red Guide that it had a hotel of sorts. The Iponuba turned out to be spotless and welcoming and the town full of handsome Renaissance houses.

The pretty Plaza Mayor has an old arcaded brick building flanking it and, high above, the remains of the castle that, at the time of the Reconquest, belonged to the Count of Cabra, one of Ferdinand and Isabella's most intrepid co-belligerents; it was from this stronghold that he rode out in April of 1483 to intercept an attack on Lucena by Boabdil, the boy-king of Granada, whom he captured.

Inside the castle walls, where Boabdil was then interned, are more handsome mansions with carved portals and a couple of churches, including the Madre de Dios with a restored cloister full of ancient columns.

Doña Mencia; Cabra

A delightful minor road, C327, that runs south from Baena, climbing among hills thick with olive groves, reveals more castles, many of them evoking other episodes in the ten-year campaign to drive the Moors from Granada. The first is that of Doña Mencia, beyond that is Cabra's, rather severely truncated. But the little town (pop c. 20,000) is charming, and from its marble quarries came many of the columns in the Mezquita of Córdoba and in its own churches.

Priego de Córdoba; Alcalá la Real
You can come back to the main road from here via Priego de Córdoba, with riotously Baroque churches and fountains, after which the next of the hilltop castles is at Alcaudete, grouped about its church tower, and then Alcalá la Real, equally fetching, at the junction with the N432.

Illora
Illora, with Roman columns in its church and yet another ruined castle, is 11 km (7 miles) off this main road to the right: here the odious Godoy, chief minister to Charles IV and lover of Maria Luisa, his queen, had his country estates. Disgraced and exiled after allowing Napoleon's troops to set foot on Spanish soil, his estates were confiscated and later presented to the Duke of Wellington; the family still owns them. Back on the main road the final landmark is the ruined ancient city of Elvira, off to the left as you approach Granada; it has as yet not been fully excavated.

A Northern route to Granada

Before coming to Granada itself, there is another approach to look at: the one from the north, which people would take if they came direct from the ferry terminal at Santander, or from Madrid.

Despeñaperros; La Navas de Tolosa
This road crosses La Mancha and arrives at the mountain barrier of the Sierra Morena. Here it winds through the pass of Despeñaperros and down along grey rocky gorges to bypass the village of Las Navas de Tolosa, just off the road to the left. This was the site of a historic victory over the Moors in 1212 by Alfonso VIII of Castile, husband to Eleanor of England (whose brothers were Richard Coeur de Lion and King John). To this battle, whose date every Spanish schoolchild knows, Alfonso and his army of knights from all over Europe were guided by a mysterious apparition in the form of a shepherd, suspected to have been Santiago (St James) himself in disguise; his statue in Toledo Cathedral is said to have been designed by Alfonso himself.

Bailén
A later battle, in some ways no less significant, took place further south, at Bailén (pop c. 15,600) where, among other comfortable roadside hotels, there is a Parador. The date was July, 1808, and the chief protagonists Napoleon's commander General Dupont, fresh from having sacked Córdoba, versus a Spanish force under General Castaños backed by an English army under General Reding. Castaños's victory over Dupont was one of the major Spanish successes in the Peninsular War and gained him the dukedom of Bailén.

The main road does not go through Bailén itself, which is far from unattractive, but instead bypasses it and forges down to Jaén. But at Bailén I would turn east, past the mining town of Linares where Manolete was killed in a bullfight, and make for Úbeda.

Úbeda

The little Parador of Úbeda (pop c. 29,000) is inside a beautiful 16th-century palace with an exceptional patio, worth going some way to see even if it were not so well placed for sightseeing in these sierras.

Originally a Moorish stronghold to which the force defeated at La Navas de Tolosa retreated to lick its wounds, Úbeda is enchanting; most of the animation and the good shops have gravitated into its newer quarter, leaving the old part in a time-warp.

Úbeda: Plaza Vasquez de Molino

Now mostly Renaissance and Baroque, its heart is the Plaza Vasquez de Molino, in which the Parador stands. The Town Hall, on the south side, was originally built by Vandelvira in the 16th century for Philip II's uxorious secretary, Francisco de los Corbos; opposite it, past the trees that shade the statue of Vandelvira (Andalusía's most prolific architect) is the late 15th-century Sta Maria church and the square-towered Mancera Palace. A few remains of the old Alcázar and the Bishop's Palace complete this end of the plaza; beyond the Parador to the west is the ornamental façade of the church of El Salvador, with a sacristy by Valdevira. Behind it, alongside the remains of a *hospicio,* is a belvedere.

Úbeda: Church of S Pablo

North of Plaza Vasquez de Molina is another square with the handsome La Vela de Los Cobos palace façade at one corner, and north again is the church of S Pablo. Its south door is Isabelline and the north and west doors more restrainedly Gothic; the interior is quite plain, with no *coro* to block the view and lovely chapels protected by fine wrought-iron screens, one of them (by Vandelvira again) surmounted by stone death-heads.

Úbeda: museum and other sights

Behind S Pablo are superb mansions and one of the few reminders of Úbeda's Moorish past: the Casa Mudéjar, a museum ranged around

Opposite: Plazuela del Potro, Córdoba (top left)
Semana Santa procession, Baeza (top right)
Lagunas de Ruidera, Albacete (below)
Overleaf: The Alhambra, Granada

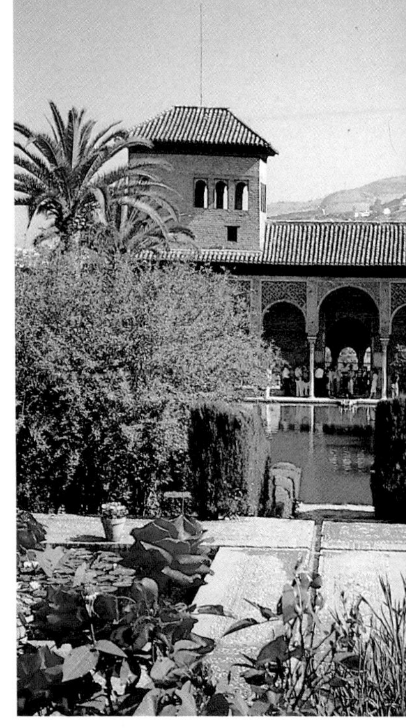

its patio. Notable are a couple of good Ibero-Roman stone heads and some Moorish pots. Other churches to look for include S Pedro, basically Romanesque; Sto Domingo with a Renaissance doorway and S Lorenzo, on the southern edge of town, with views over the surrounding countryside. Look, too, for the Casa de los Torres, with a fine patio; Casa de La Ramble, with reliefs of two warriors drooping over their ceremonial shields; the medieval clock tower in Plaza General Saro and the 16th-century hospital of Santiago, opposite the bullring on the way to Baeza, with a warlike relief of the Moor-slaying saint over its door.

Baeza

Baeza (pop c. 15,000), where the younger Scipio defeated Hasdrubal in 545, is another architectural gem only nine km (just over five miles) southwest of Úbeda and the road leads straight into its main square, surrounded by arcades. The far end of it gives onto the tiny Plaza de los Leones, named after the old fountain at its centre, two of whose stone-carvings are of horses, not lions. To one side is the mellow 16th-century former abattoir and to another the former courthouse, now the Tourist Office; the archway next to it is said to have been built in honour of the Emperor Charles V, who stopped here on his way to Seville to wed Isabella of Portugal.

Baeza Cathedral

A street at the top of this plaza leads up to the Cathedral, standing sideways on to another square; it, too, owes its design to Vandelvira. Its interior is refreshingly free of ornamentation except for one gilded chapel alongside the *capilla mayor;* on its south side some of the cloister arches were once part of a mosque. Alongside the north door of the cathedral, a massive stone building bears the stone-carved arms of Charles V's unhappy mother (Juana the Mad) and her husband Philip of Burgundy, and opposite it is the 17th-century seminary, covered with scholarly *graffiti* which graduating students traditionally executed in ox-blood.

Baeza: palace, church, town hall

Downhill of this is the superb façade of the late 15th-century Jabalquinto Palace, incorporating oddly-tilted coats of arms, and opposite is the small Romanesque church of Sta Cruz. Downhill again is the old university, bringing you back again to the arcaded main square, the Paseo, on whose north side, past the Casa Consistorales Bajas, is the magnificent 16th-century Town Hall. This was once the prison but was transformed with ornate Plateresque windows and sculptured

Previous page: The Generalife, Granada
Opposite: Explanada de España, Alicante (top)
The port of Javéa, Alicante (below)

figures beneath the overhanging roof, executed in the manner of ships' figureheads.

Sierra de Cazorla: National Park

To the east of Úbeda, cut by the Guadalquivir, rises the Sierra de Cazorla, cool and wooded, watered by countless streams and full of flowers and wildlife: deer, ibex, moufflon and other creatures. In Roman times its silver mines were famous; now it is partly preserved as a national park and idyllic for walkers and bird-watchers, for whom there is a Parador in the style of a mountain lodge some 25 km (just over 15 miles) above Cazorla. It is riding country, too, scene of part of Penelope Chetwode's delightful equestrian odyssey, 'Two Middle-Aged Ladies in Andalusía', but for the less energetic it can also offer a splendid circuit of some 240 km (150 miles) into the remotest reaches of Andalusía.

Sabiote to the Tranco Reservoir

Start with the pretty hill-village of Sabiote, just east of Úbeda, and come back to cross the N322 on to the J314, which takes you up to Cazorla, watched over by a pair of Moorish castles. Unless you have planned to stay at the Parador above it, turn north at the fork to follow the course of the Guadalquivir inland until it widens into the huge Tranco reservoir and follow this to its other end, where there is a turn-off to the right for Hornos, a high-perched mountain village with a ruined castle and wonderful views. The northbound road has another turnoff a little further on, this time for Segura de la Sierra, even more dramatically perched and still walled. After this you can turn left to rejoin the main N322.

Jaén city

Leaving Úbeda for the last time and heading south towards Granada, Jaén (pop c. 96,000), capital of Jaén province, is the chief place of interest en route, though it must be admitted that it is somewhat dull. It produces delicious olive oil; otherwise its twin claims to fame are the enormous castle on the hill overlooking it, beside which a Parador, with wide views over the mountains and surrounding olive groves has discreetly been installed, and a cathedral by Vandelvira of almost equally monumental proportions at the top of the town. "Jaén of the ugly Cathedral", Sacheverell Sitwell called it, but in fact its size is its chief defect, dwarfing everything around it.

The City of Granada

Granada (pop c. 262,000) is 94 km (just under 60 miles) to the south, and there is an important basic decision to make on the question of an hotel: to stay up on the hill, close to the Alhambra, or down in the town. I would recommend the first option, which is cooler in summer and more peaceful at any time of year.

Parador; hotels

The Parador, in an old convent in the Alhambra gardens, is the most desirable but tends to be booked months, if not years, ahead; the tiny Hostál America at its gates is perfectly charming but also booked up well ahead. The best compromise is to stay just outside the Alhambra gates where the Alixares is big and caters for groups but is pleasant enough and has a swimming pool on the roof. The Washington Irving, slightly lower down the hill, is smaller, more old-fashioned and atmospheric. There are a couple of uninspiring but convenient restaurants nearby if you want an alternative to going into town or eating at your hotel.

Early history

Spilling down from the three hills of the Sacromonte, the Albaicín and the Alhambra in the foothills of the Sierra Nevada, Granada is not an old city by Spanish standards: the original Ibero-Roman settlement was to the northwest, at Elvira, and this the Moslems probably used as a quarry when they started to build, as was their custom, in a more commanding position.

A provincial capital during the Caliphate of Córdoba, it began to grow in importance as a kingdom in its own right as Córdoba's Ummayyad kingdom declined in the middle of the 11th century, and became a stronghold of Berbers from North Africa.

Moorish period: Nasrid dynasty

Various factions ruled and strengthened it for 200 years and in 1238, two years after Córdoba had fallen to the Christians, one Ibn el-Ahmar became its king. Internal problems were occupying the Christian kings of Castile and Aragón at the time, enabling him to consolidate and even expand his *taifa.*

When the wars of reconquest started again, he cunningly ceded Jaén to Castile in return for certain safeguards that allowed him to entrench himself even more strongly at Granada, where the Nasrid dynasty that he founded was to rule for 250 years.

Nasrid-Castile treaty

The price of peace with Castile was that Ibn el-Ahmar should provide assistance for its anti-Moorish campaigns elsewhere in Andalusía; he even took part, albeit heavy-heartedly, in the capture of Seville. But at the same time he continued to fortify his own kingdom, which extended for many miles around the city in all directions and provided a refuge for fellow-Moslems fleeing from other captured cities, burgeoning and prospering to such an extent that under the Nasrids Granada produced the last and perhaps the greatest flowering of Islamic art in Spain.

Nasrid feud and fall

Its decline was precipitated by a bitter family feud sparked off when Moulay Aben Hassan, who ruled from 1462-1482, became besotted in his old age with Isabel de Solis, a Christian prisoner. He gave her the Moorish name of Zoraya, ('morning star'), and pride of place in the palace hierarchy, displacing his longer-standing wife Ayesha, who had borne him a son, Boabdil. When Zoraya herself produced two sons and was scheming to have them given precedence over their older half-brother, Ayesha spirited Boabdil away at dead of night to Guadix and from there proclaimed him the Boy King (El Rey Chico).

Boabdil, the Boy King

Boabdil, who commanded a good deal of popular support, dethroned his father in 1482, but although courageous in battle he lacked strength of character and the continuing family feud contributed to his irresolute behaviour. On occasions he continued to honour the long-standing family oath to support the cause of the Catholic Monarchs elsewhere in Andalusía, on others he felt obliged to prove his worth to his people and break it. He was twice captured by the armies of Ferdinand and Isabella and twice redeemed himself by ceding portions of his kingdom to them.

The Siege of Granada

When he lost Guadix and Almeria, in 1490, the Catholic Monarchs demanded his surrender. He refused, and they proceeded to devastate the fertile *vega* up to the city walls and then to lay siege to it. Preferring to starve Granada out rather than to storm it (a costlier operation, and Ferdinand and Isabella were always short of funds), they took from April to November of 1491 to accomplish the task, during which time countless forays and counter-forays took place, all vividly recounted by Washington Irving in 'The Conquest of Granada'; the keys of the city were finally handed to them on January 2, 1492.

Ferdinand and Isabella's campsite

The probable site of Ferdinand and Isabella's camp was on the banks of the Genil at Los Ojos de Huescar, just west of the city, though as the winter approached they moved away from the river and built more weather-resistant quarters, more like a miniature city, whose name is commemorated in the suburb of Sta Fé.

The end of Boabdil

In the end, it was at a point not far from the Puente de Genil, today on Granada's southern edge, that Boabdil took leave of the Catholic

Monarchs and rode off to the small kingdom they had given him in the Alpujarras, to the south. He did not stay there long, but crossed to Africa and died some 40 years later, fighting for the King of Fez.

Decline of Granada
It was a sad finale to nearly 800 years of Moorish supremacy, and all the sadder because the Christian conquest spelt the beginning of a long twilight for Granada and for Southern Spain as a whole. It unleashed a terrifying torrent of religious intolerance: in that same year, the Jews were expelled by the Inquisition and when the *Moriscos* (Christianised Moslems) were sent packing in their turn just over a century later, Granada and all of Spain lost huge numbers of its most talented and energetic citizens. Only comparatively recently have industry, commerce and tourism revived the city's fortunes.

Washington Irving's 'Tales'
Even more than Swinburne, who visited and made drawings of Granada's Alhambra in 1775, it was the American writer Washington Irving who rekindled interest in the city. He came to Granada in 1829 and lived for some months in the Alhambra (then privately owned, and inhabited by all manner of people) and, following his account of the Conquest, went on to write his celebrated 'Tales of the Alhambra' about his fellow residents.

The Alhambra

Suddenly the eyes of the world were focussed upon this romantic, pink-walled Moorish fort whose desecration (described in all its awful detail by Richard Ford, who spent two summers in it) was already far advanced, thanks in part to Napoleon's forces who also nearly succeeded in blowing the whole place up. As a result of the huge upsurge of public interest, attempts at repair began in about 1840, gaining momentum towards the end of the 19th century. Reading Ford, it is difficult not to wonder how much of the "restoration" is in fact sheer reconstruction, but perhaps it is best not to dwell too much upon such thoughts and simply enjoy it. It is not only the point of supreme interest in Granada, but unique in the world.

Getting to the Alhambra
One word of warning: it is essential to get there as the gates open (0900 in summer, 1000 in winter, everyday) before the onslaught of the coach tours. Apart from anything else, the Nasrid palaces that are the crowning beauty of the Alhambra (there are several palaces, and other buildings and gardens, too) can only hold 500 people at a time and queues start to build up for them by about 1100 in summer. If you are staying down in the city, it is pleasant to walk slowly up the morning coolness but it is a steep walk; the alternative is to take the #2 bus

from the huge, circular, fountain-embellished plaza just south of the Puerta Real, which leaves every 40 minutes from 0800 onwards.

The Alameda
Once through the Puerta de las Granadas, topped with the pomegranates *(granadas)* that have been adopted as the city emblem, the shady Alameda, in a depression between the summit and the Torres Bermejas, or Vermilion Towers, gives respite to walkers before the final ascent to the main entrance. This deliberately zig-zagged corridor, designed to confuse enemies, opens onto the space called Plaza de los Aljilbes after the cisterns built beneath it. If you come from one of the Alhambra Hill hotels, you enter along a broad path bordered by tall cypresses that ends at the same place.

The Alcázaba
From here, I would not follow the advice of the older guide book writers and take the buildings in chronological order (".. restrain your curiosity," urges the 'Cook's Handbook' author, "... and first visit the old Alcázaba ... to your left.") In this day and age, even if you are a student of Islamic architectural development, you start with the Nasrid palaces, otherwise the crowds, already hard on your heels, will soon engulf you. The coach tours are often on tight schedules and many of their passengers will not visit the Alcázaba at all.

Not a great deal remains of this 13th-century fort in any case, apart from its walls and a gateway with a simple dome in decorative brick above it, and it is agreeable to visit later; it is a reminder of the Alhambra's embattled history, for on its Torre de la Vela Ferdinand and Isabella watched the Christian flag being unfurled on that January day in 1492. You can climb it and see the bell that is rung on every anniversary, and admire the sensational views of the snow-dusted Sierra Nevada from its summit. (An even better view opens up from the belvedere in front of the Alcázaba, at the tip of the spur, from where you can also look straight down into the Plaza Nueva at the heart of the city below.)

Nasrid palaces
Of the rooms and the courtyards of the Nasrid palaces, most dating from the 14th century and the most beautiful example of Mahgreb (North African) Islamic art anywhere, much has been said and written but none of it quite prepares you for their almost ethereal grace and harmony. The decoration takes the breath away: the glowing *azulejos* and the delicate, filigree plasterwork that Washington Irving describes as the "fairy tracery of the peristyles and the apparently fragile fretwork of the walls" which, one feels, might simply take off and vanish, so insubstantial does it look. (In fact the beauty is literally skin-deep, for the basic construction was flimsy and it is a miracle so

much survived.)

The mass of detail in the decoration is almost dizzying: honeycomb ceilings touched with colour, walls covered in myriad abstract patterns and inscriptions (in which the motto *"Wa la ghaliba Ill-Alla"* or "There is no victor but God", is endlessly repeated; the slender columns and subtly-shaped arches of doorways and windows; intricate *artesonado* ceilings; the contrasts of light and shade, chambers and courtyards, unyielding marble underfoot and quivering jets of water shooting into the air. In contrast to the still-enduring sense of devotion that irradiates the Mezquita of Córdoba, this is purely a pleasure-dome to relish with the senses.

The Palace Courts
To give a few practical pointers, the Court of Myrtles and sumptuous Hall of the Ambassadors with its magnificent, stellar-patterned *artesonado* ceiling, multi-patterned stucco and *azulejos,* belong to the earliest period of the palace, between 1334 and 1354. The Court of the Lions with its charming fountain and slender pillars and the Hall of Two Sisters (note its octagonal, honeycomb cupola) were built by a later king, Mohamed V. It was in the Abencerrajes gallery, across the Court of the Lions that Boabdil caused the leading members of that family, who still supported his aged father, to be murdered. In the pool in which their heads were supposedly piled you can see the reflection of the star-shaped cupola of the ceiling.

The King's Chambers
In the King's Chambers, alongside, the arches above the alcoves are painted with courtly scenes that were probably executed after Granada had been conquered, since Islamic law does not permit representation of the human form.

Daraxa and Partal Gardens
Below are the Daraxa Gardens, leading into the Partal Gardens, smelling of clipped box and tinkling with water running along narrow channels; not many crowds bother with them and there are benches on which to sit and admire the views of the mountains. Alongside the Daraxa Gardens is the original suite of rooms that Charles V converted to live in while his own palace was being built and it was here that Washington Irving lodged.

On the lowest level are the charming Torre de las Damas, with more delicate plasterwork, and the tiny Torre del Mirhab prayer tower.

Charles V's Palace
Charles V's palace (1526), from the outside a ponderously inappropriate structure for which parts of the Alhambra were razed (which makes

you wonder if he really did deplore the desecration of Córdoba's Mezquita), stands on what was probably the site of the harem. Inside, it is surprisingly elegant with a circular courtyard surrounded by a double colonnade in restrained neo-Classical style, but it was never finished.

Museums; church

The palace houses two museums: the Hispano-Moorish collection, which includes the wonderful, blue, 15th-century Alhambra Vase (temporarily closed at the time of writing), and the Bellas Artes Museum with a number of religious paintings by Spanish artists of the 16th-18th centuries. There is also a 16th/17th century church, Sta Maria, on the site of the former mosque.

Covent and Towers

East of the palaces, the Alhambra gardens stretch right round the former convent (now the Parador) that Isabella founded, and in whose chapel her body and that of Ferdinand lay until they could be buried in the Capilla Real.

Beyond the Parador, the Torre de las Infantas is named for the Moorish princesses who once lived there; its lush decoration belongs to the early 15th century. The Torre de la Cautiva, about a century older, was reputedly the prison in which Isabel de Solis was held before she caught the eye of Moulay Aben Hassan.

Generalife Palace and Garden

A gateway in this wall leads to a footbridge across the ravine known as the Cuesta del Rey Chico to the Generalife Palace, once the royal summerhouse and older than the Alhambra. In some ways its decoration is more beautiful than that of the Alhambra, but it is more altered and decayed.

The gardens, also reached by a pathway from the Avenue of Cypresses, are sheer magic, with a grassy, open-air theatre, fountains and pools and rills of water tumbling like miniature waterfalls, riotous pergolas of roses and more clipped box hedges, and the views across to the Alhambra are lent perspective by the dark outlines of cypresses.

Casa del Carbón to Capilla Real

Chateaubriand wrote that it was impossible to scratch the surface of Granada without discovering Moorish remains, but that is no longer true. The notable exception, down in the city centre near the Cathedral, is the 14th-century Casa del Carbón, so called because it was used until quite recent times as a coal depot. Now restored, it is a perfect example of an Arab caravanserai, the only one of its kind in Europe. (In the southern part of the city, near the church of Sto Domingo, is a tightly shuttered Moorish palace which, according to local folklore, retains a wealth of original features, but it cannot be visited.)

Alcaiceria shops

Leaving the Casa del Carbón and crossing Granada's main artery, Avenida de los Reyes Catolicos (built above the course of the river Darro), you have only to follow the signs to the Alcaiceria, a crass, 19th-century copy of the Moorish silk-souk that formerly stood there, and now occupied by craft and souvenir shops, to realise how far you have left Islamic art behind. However the Sevilla, one of the city's most agreeable and typical restaurants, is in the northeast corner of the Alcaiceria.

The Capilla Real

Just opposite is the square in front of the Capilla Real, the Christian glory of Granada, built in the early 16th century as the mausoleum of Ferdinand and Isabella.

Royal effigies

The white Italian marble effigies of the Catholic Monarchs, and of their ill-fated daughter Juana the Mad and her Burgundian husband Philip, are separated from the body of the chapel by an exquisite ironwork screen. Ferdinand wears the Order of the Garter, conferred upon him by Henry VII of England; Isabella the Cross of Santiago. Isabella's face is fixed in a stiff, suffering look, as well it might be: when she died in 1504, 13 years before her husband, she was only 53 and her triumphs had been followed by a series of tragedies. Her only son, the adored heir, had died in 1497; her eldest daughter, Queen of Portugal, died the following year; the year after that, her daughter Catharine of Aragón left Spain forever to marry the English Prince of Wales, only to be widowed a year later; her last years were blighted by the creeping insanity of poor Juana.

Altarpiece

The wonderful *retablo* behind the effigies bears fine, high-relief panels in painted wood depicting less unhappy scenes from the life of the Catholic Monarchs and, if you take a few steps towards the altar and look down to the vault below, you glimpse the plain coffins in which the four royal corpses rest, escaped from both triumphs and tragedies.

Sacristy

The sacristy contains some priceless paintings: Memlings, van der Weydens, a Botticelli, a Perugino and more besides, and in a glass case are Isabella's crown and sceptre, Ferdinand's sword, and other mementoes of this remarkable couple.

Cathedral to Hospicio Real

Cathedral

By contrast, the Cathedral is a disappointment, a ponderous structure whose chief merit is the *capilla mayor* with lovely stained-glass windows ranged above a series of paintings by Alonso Cano, a native of Granada, who is buried in the nave.

Market; churches

To the north of the cathedral is the market, separated from the buildings of the university by some charming narrow streets, and beyond the university are two notable churches, Renaissance S Jeronimo, the oldest in Granada, where 'El Gran Capitán' is buried, and Baroque S Juan de Dios, named for the Portuguese-born saint who founded the Order of Knights Hospitallers that still bears his name. He died in Granada in 1550 and his relics are enshrined in a silver urn.

Hospice; Carthusian monastery

The street in which this church stands leads up to the gardens that flank the Hospicio Real, founded by Ferdinand and Isabella and now part of the university; about a kilometre to the northeast of it is the early 16th-century Cartuja, or Carthusian monastery, whose lavishly-stuccoed sacristy Jan Morris called "a marvel of Churrigueresque (that) looks as though its decoration had not been carved, or even daubed, but rather squeezed out of a tube." Just to the south, off Plaza del Triunfo, an old Moorish gateway, the Puerta Elvira, leads into a narrow street of the same name, lined with crumbling houses, some now antique shops, that brings you back to the heart of the city at Plaza Nueva.

Plaza Nueva to Sacromonte

The rest of Granada's attractions grow on you slowly: the shopping streets, if you are not struggling through them in a car, are pleasantly lively and at the far end of Plaza Nueva, where the insignificent Darro river is banished underground, a narrow street follows its course eastwards past Sta Ana church and some resplendent but unrestored Baroque-fronted houses. Little pebble-paved bridges arch across the stream and there are views of the Alhambra walls rising from the surrounding trees directly above you.

Moorish baths

On the left is the Balneario, the 11th-century Moorish baths, behind the flowery patio of the guardian's house and open until 1800 – later, if she feels like it. Four chambers, two with star-shaped holes pierced in the barrel-vaulting and one with columns, some of whose capitals are Visigothic and Roman, catered for steam baths, massage and relaxation, and there are remains of the hot water conduits and the furnace that heated the water.

Convent; Archaeological museum

A little further, the 16th-century Convent of Sta Catalina de Zafra is being restored and, a little further still, opposite the 16th-century S Pedro church, is the handsome Casa de Castril, housing the Archaeological Museum (open in the mornings).

The Albaicín

Above this rises the Albaicín, second of Granada's three hills, to which Boabdil's mother Ayesha repaired during one of his periods in Christian captivity, and defiantly set up court in full view of the temporary incumbent of the Alhambra. It is the oldest part of the city, a web of secretive, narrow streets steadily being gentrified and winding up to the church of S Nicolás. Here there is a broad terrace with sensational views across to the Alhambra, especially at sunset when the walls seem to light up and smoulder in the last rays. Just behind the church to the north is the agreeable Zoraya restaurant and, to the west of it, a stretch of old Moorish walls.

The Sacromonte

The last of Granada's three hills is the Sacromonte, where the gypsies live in a honeycomb of semi-troglodyte houses; a visit to one of the caves to hear gypsy music and watch the dancing is best arranged through your hotel.

South of Granada

Alhama de Granada

There is a mass of exploration to do outside Granada. To the southwest, on a charming minor road (C340) that eventually brings you down to Málaga, the village of Alhama de Granada (pop c. 6,000) is 53 km (33 miles) from the city centre. It is immensely picturesque, clinging as it does to the edge of a steep gorge, and a spa hotel, the Balneario, lies just downhill of it.

It also features strongly in the annals of the Reconquest as the first outpost of the Kingdom of Granada to be taken by the Christians, in furious reprisal for the sacking of Zahara. The scaling of its walls at dead of night for a successful surprise attack marked the start of the 10-year campaign to win Granada itself and, in Washington Irving's account, also marked the first milestone in the dazzling military career of the leader of the attack, Rodrigo Ponce de León, Marquis of Cadiz. This knight, born in 1443, "noble in his deportment towards his equals; loving . . . to his friends; fierce and terrible, yet magnanimous, to his enemies" emerges from Irving's pages as a perfect paragon; in Alhama, he protected the wife of the castle's commander (who was absent at the time), and her female servants, from the licentious pursuit of the Spanish soldiery, "for he had a soul full of honour . . . towards her sex."

Solynieve ski resort
The Sierra Nevada, in summer a paradise for walkers and bird-watchers, also cradles a fast-developing winter resort, Solynieve, South-east of Granada and reached by one of the highest mountain roads in Europe. At the resort you are within sight of the Mediterranean and on a good day the snow can be almost the best in Europe: light powder. The pistes are above the resort, reached by cable car, and although most are best suited for beginners and intermediates, more advanced terrain is being developed in the hope that Solynieve will be chosen to host the 1995 Winter Olympics.

Armilla; Ultimo Suspiro del Moro
Heading south from Granada on the Motril road, N323, you come to the suburb of Armilla, from which Ferdinand and Isabella watched their standard being broken from the Alcázar after Boabdil's surrender. A little further south is the pass known as the Ultimo Suspiro del Moro, where Boabdil is said to have paused and wept for his lost kingdom, causing his mother to snap at him: "Thou dost well to weep like a woman for that which thou did not defend like a man." Industrial haze and high-rise apartment blocks unfortunately all but obscure the view nowadays.

Motril
After the Lanjarón/Alpujarras turnoff (see below) there are great fields of sugar cane to be seen as you near the sugar-exporting port of Motril (pop c. 40,000) and, if you turn right, you eventually reach Málaga, 92 km (just under 58 miles) away.

The coast road west
The corniche road to Málaga passes through a succession of little towns that briefly became battlegrounds in the campaign to conquer Granada: Salobreña, still dominated by a Moorish castle; El Capricho, where the first Caliph of Córdoba, Abderrahman I, is said to have set foot on Spanish soil; and Almuñecar.

It also passes through Nerja (pop c. 12,000), a dramatically situated former fishing village (with a well-placed Parador), now a full-scale resort hemmed about by new development; above it are stalactite caves, quite recently discovered, and the prettified hamlet of Frigiliana.

The coast road east

The coast east of Motril is less developed than that to the west, with little places like Calahonda, Castell de Ferro and La Rábita that still keep much of their original character.

South-east of Granada

Back on the southbound N323 out of Granada the road twists and winds through the hills and there is a turning left to pretty Lanjarón, on the edge of the sierra of Las Alpujarras, in which lay Boabdil's last kingdom.

Lanjarón

Lanjarón (pop c. 4,000) is famous as the spa from which Spain's best known bottled mineral water comes; it is also a curative resort, many of whose little hotels boast pools fed by the thermal water; there is also a public *balneario* and the views from the edge of town, across the gorge on which it perches, are tremendous.

Orgiva

Orgiva, a little further east, is smaller and simpler but also has a few hotels and, having seen a copy of The Financial Times on sale there, I suspect it is only marginally less sophisticated.

Between the mountains to Cádor

After Orgiva the country becomes more rugged and the hamlets more remote. To the north, across the Guadalfeo valley, rise the bare flanks of the Sierra Nevada, patched with snow; to the south the Sierra de la Contraviesa cuts you off from the sea, with just one road through it to join the coast at La Rábita. Cultivation is patchy, evidence of modern civilisation scant.

Even Yegen, set on a mountain shelf, where Gerald Brenan lived for many years and wrote 'South from Granada', seems to have remained impervious to the famous who visited him there (though a sign advertising rooms suggests that pilgrims still pass that way).

From Cherin another road leads down to the coastal highway near Adra, but it is perfectly practicable (and much prettier) to keep to the mountains; almost every village has a café-bar or two that serves *tapas;* petrol stations are scarcer. As you approach the main N340 Almeria road at Gádor, via Alhama de Almeria, the country becomes barer and the hills are eroded into strange shapes that give a foretaste of the Wild West landscape to be encountered later.

East of Granada

Viznar; Purullena

Leaving Granada for the last time, due east, a turning off the main road to the left shortly after you leave the city takes you to Viznar, where the poet and playwright Federico García Lorca is buried. There is then no alternative to the main road, which climbs and dips beneath the Sierra Nevada towards Guadix. Just short of it is the pottery village of Purullena, where showy displays of wares are heaped in front of whitewashed troglodyte dwellings scooped into the tufa to either side of the road and, alongside the whitewashed chimneys, the owners' doubtless equally necessary TV aerials protrude from the soil.

Guadix

The origins of Guadix (pop c. 20,000) are ancient, antedating the Romans who first mined the seams of silver in its vicinity, but like Granada it did not stand on its present site until the coming of the Moors, who rebuilt the city where it is today and whose castle still looks down on it. It has a large, pinkish sandstone Cathedral, dating from the 16th century and with a Renaissance belfry, but later given a Baroque façade from which the statues are missing. The other interesting church is Santiago, with a Plateresque portal and *artesonado* ceiling, its tower topped by an *azulejo*-covered pyramidical steeple. The Plaza Mayor is pleasant enough, and the hill above is also riddled with troglodyte houses.

Baza: ancient statue

You can fork left at Guadix for Murcia and come in 47 km (just over 30 miles) to Baza (pop c. 20,000) through country that has been queerly eroded into spiky, dry hillocks. "Fragments of antiquity are constantly found on the Vega, and are as constantly neglected or broken to pieces by the peasants," wrote Ford. But less than 25 years ago the *vega* of Baza yielded more than a fragment: the great and beautiful seated stone figure, dating from that 4th century BC, that is called the Dama de Baza and is displayed in Madrid's Archaeological Museum.

Almeria Region

Lacalahorra to Almeria city

If you fork right at Guadix, the Almeria road passes beneath the theatrical-looking castle at Lacalahorra, with four domed corner towers, comes within sight of the more ruinous castle of Fiñana, followed by that of Gergal, and eventually joins the main Murcia-Almeria road. By this time the landscape is a succession of eroded, *mesa*-like hills and rolling dunes, cut by sharp ravines; for years it was a popular location for the shooting of Western and other films – part of 'Lawrence of Arabia' was shot in the area. Now that the film industry is less active in these parts, many of the old sets that used suddenly to come into view and as suddenly disappear have been collected in one spot, christened 'Mini Hollywood' and turned into a tourist attraction.

Tabernas; prehistoric necropolis
To the east of the main road junction Tabernas, partly restored, is among the most majestic of Moorish castles, and to the west is the huge prehistoric necropolis of Los Millares.

Almeria City

Then the road, having been joined by the one through Las Alpujarras, runs through the fertile Andarx valley down to Almeria (pop c. 141,000). Increasingly prosperous nowadays, thanks to iron mines in the neighbourhood and its convenience as a tourist gateway, it is somewhat unjustly neglected for its own sake.

History
Almeria is very old: an important Roman port and, under the Moors, even more powerful, with a pirate fleet that ravaged coasts as far afield as Northern Italy and Galicia. When it fell to the Catholic Monarchs in 1488 and its inhabitants were expelled shortly afterwards, it went into a decline and only began to revive at the end of the last century, when the railway was built.

It lies in a sort of amphitheatre, its highest point the hill on which the Alcázaba sits, with a palm-shaded Paseo skirting the harbour and a bright, busy main street, Pas de Almeria, running inland almost at right angles to it.

Hotels, Cathedral, Alcázaba
A short way up this street the Hotel Costasol, by no means Almeria's grandest, is very acceptable for an overnight stop and the Club de Mar, on the seafront, is excellent. Between the Pas de Almeria and the Alcázaba is a network of agreeable streets and the massive 16th-century Cathedral. Above this the old Alcázaba has been carefully restored and filled with gardens, pools and fountains. From the top are superb views of a massive curtain wall that runs down behind it and up the next hill, which is crowned with a large modern statue.

West of Almeria
To the west of Almeria much tourist development is taking place between Aguadulce and Roquetas de Mar and beyond; to the northeast it is much the same story. The main road, after 'Mini

Hollywood' referred to above, swings north for Murcia and stays well inland.

East of Almeria

A secondary road, N332, being greatly improved, goes east out of Almeria past the airport and stays closer to the coast. A turnoff to the left leads to the white hill-village of Nijar, where they weave thick striped blankets, and another turnoff to the right, just past the dramatically-perched pottery village of Sorbas, leads down to the coast at Carboneras.

Carboneras

This once simple, straggling fishing village on a gritty beach has fairly recently acquired a power station for a neighbour and is also going through an unattractive adolescent development stage as it is dragged into the 20th-century resort scene. Beyond it to the north, a narrow road sometimes runs *en corniche* above the sea and sometimes swings inland through dark, barren hills and in 21 km (about 14 miles, arrives at the increasingly built-up new resort that has spread south from the astonishing hill-village of Mojácar.

Mojácar

Mojácar (pop c. 1600) was "discovered" about 25 years ago and, from one oversized hotel that was built in the village at the time, followed by a Parador and a few restaurants and pensions on the beach below, has swollen hideously – with more grandiose plans in the pipeline for which it is clear, from correspondence in the local paper in May of 1989, that the infrastructure was still inadequate. It is a pity: Mojácar's situation is sensational, wrapped around a half-detached mountain spur so steep that you have to corkscrew up it, but its little white alleys are now crammed with discos, bars and souvenir shops and its secretive atmosphere, that so impressed Sacheverell Sitwell, is long since gone.

The road to the Levante

Leaving Mojácar, the coast road north passes through the unpretentious port town of Garrucha, almost on the borders of Murcia, with a fort, a marina and a long beach. It is hardly worth continuing on the coast road after this: Vera Playa is being energetically and unimaginatively developed and beyond it are miles of tomato-cultivation. Beyond them, the few ruined watchtowers that squat among the dark foothills look down on nothing more inspiring than uninviting small beaches. Better to leave the coast just after Garrucha, where the road swings inland to Vera; from there you can either return to Almeria or go on north to Lorca and so into the Levante.

Remains of 14/15th century aqueduct, Morella

Levante

The Land

As the name implies, the Levante forms the easternmost edge of the south of Spain: a long, mountainous coastal strip extending at its broadest point barely 150 km (under 100 miles) inland. It suffers, in current jargon, an image problem: it is home to almost the brashest of all Spanish resorts, Benidorm, and to the best-known of all Spanish dishes, *paella;* beyond that, few people know much about it and its byways, unlike those of Andalusía, Castilla-La Mancha and even Extremadura, are only lightly trodden. Yet in many ways it is the most truly Spanish part of Southern Spain and full of untrumpeted pleasures for the enquiring to discover. Paradoxically, too, that little-known hinterland is one of the easiest to explore from a base on the coast, thanks to its very narrowness; indeed, from the beaches of the Costa del Azahar (orange-blossom coast) in the north and the Costa Blanca in the south, you can thrust as far inland as, say Alarcón and Cuenca in Castilla-La Mancha, with surprising ease. You need only buy a large-scale map to see how many desirable inland sights and beauty spots are accessible on a circuit of two or three days.

History

Two former kingdoms make up much of the Levante: Valencia and

Murcia. Palaeolithic man lived there, leaving as evidence rock paintings in many of the caves that riddle the mountains, and his Ibero-Celtic successors were the artists who bequeathed to Spain some of the magnificent stone figures in Madrid's Archaeological Museum, notably the majestic 2,400 years-old lady known as the Dama de Elche.

Phoenicians to Romans
Eventually, Phoenicians arrived in Murcia and Greeks in Valencia, both later to give way to the Carthaginians who exploited Murcia's gold and silver deposits and made the region a launching-pad for Hannibal's assaults upon the Roman Empire. Once Rome had beaten off Carthage, it ruled both provinces until the Empire disintegrated in the fifth century and the Visigoths moved in its wake. Their conquerors, 300 years later, were of course the Moorish invaders in 711.

Moorish rule
After the brilliant Caliphate of Córdoba collapsed at the end of the 10th century, Valencia and Murcia became independent *taifas,* or mini-kingdoms, two out of nearly 30 throughout the south, and both reverted to this state of semi-independence following the short-lived attempts of two invading North African Berber tribes, the Almoravides and the Almohades, to reunite Moorish Spain in the 12th century. Meantime the Reconquest, by the kingdoms of the Christian north, was gradually gathering momentum, although it often happened that Christians and Moslems combined against more threatening common enemies. When, for instance, Valencia was briefly taken by that medieval Knight-at-arms the Cid, who captured it in the name of Alfonso VI in 1094, half the members of his victorious army were Moslems. Two years after his death in 1099 it was again under Moorish rule and the two kingdoms did not finally fall to a Christian conqueror, Jaime I of Aragón, until the middle of the 13th century.

Christian conquest
Even then the Moors remained: in the fertile *huertas* (plains) around Valencia, they had refined and expanded a system of irrigation first devised by the Romans that is in use, scarcely changed, to this day, and *Moriscos,* or Christianised Moors, continued to cultivate the *huertas* of both Valencia and Murcia until ill-advisedly expelled by Philip III in 1609. Although their irrigation methods were not lost with their departure, the gradual decline of both Valencia and Murcia dates from this period, the early 17th century.

War of Succession
Both former kingdoms suffered further during the War of Succession 100 years later when most of Europe banded together and fought

France and Spain in an unsuccessful attempt to prevent a Bourbon monarch, Louis XIV's grandson, from inheriting the Spanish throne. Valencia misguidedly sided with the anti-Bourbon opposition, whose claimant was the Holy Roman Empire candidate.

Peninsular and Civil Wars; modern economy
Valencia and Murcia were again battered, this time by the armies of Napoleon, in the following century, and in this one paid dearly for supporting the Republican cause in the Civil War. Today, the revived fortunes of Valencia are partly due to tourism (at some sacrifice to the beauties of its coastline) and agriculture; renewed prosperity in Murcia, driest of all the regions of Spain, has depended less upon these two sources of income (though it is rich in cunningly-irrigated orchards and rice-paddies) and more upon commerce and industry, such as the development of Cartagena as a naval base, the oil refineries at Escombreras, metallurgy and fruit-canning.

The Arts; Cuisine

Levante has produced more famous names in the field of visual arts than of literature. Baroque is the recurrent style throughout these regions: although they have contributed their share of Gothic and Renaissance artists, notably Ribalta and Ribera, the delight of Levantines in decoration purely for its own sake has smothered many a basically Gothic building in exuberant embellishment. It is no coincidence that Spain's foremost Baroque sculptor, Salzillo, was born in Murcia.

Like their neighbours, the Andalusians, the people of the Levante revel in music. "They have wine, grapes, and melon, ices, songs, dances and the guitar," wrote Richard Ford, going on to add that "their great joys and relaxations are religious shows." These are indeed to be found everywhere, among the most important of them being the ancient mystery play of Elche, the *fallas* of Valencia, elaborate Holy Week celebrations and processions in numerous other places, plus scores of local *Moros y Christianos* festivals, re-enacting actual or imaginary battles between believers and infidels.

Edible specialities
Gastronomically speaking, the great dish of Levante, now almost the adoptive Spanish national dish, is the *paella Valenciana,* based originally on the rice grown around the huge, salt-water La Albufera lagoon and the eels and other fish that thrived in it, and now more likely to contain a mixture of chicken, snails, shellfish and vegetables. Traditionally it is cooked in big shallow pans over wood fires in the open, when the combined smells of the woodsmoke and cooking ingredients are irresistible. Several other good rice dishes are native to both Valencia and Murcia (more heavily spiced in Murcia) and fish is,

of course, omnipresent. One fish chowder that is impossible to reproduce elsewhere is *sopa de datiles,* made with the dark-coloured mussels from the coast north of Castellón de la Plana; it can sometimes be found in restaurants at Peñiscola and in the Parador at Benicarló. Other specialities include wild mushrooms, hams and other cured meats, and a cheese called *tronchon.*

Marvellous fruit is grown all along the fertile Levante coastal plain and in the foothills: all sorts of sweet oranges and mandarins and other citrus, plus more exotic fruit like pomegranates, passion fruit, figs, loquats and the muscatel grapes from which the delicious local raisins are made. Almonds grow in abundance, too, and are the basis for the famous Alicante and Jijona *turron,* not unlike nougat.

Wine

Wines tend to be red, heavy and strong (some as high as 18 per cent) and most come from Murcia province, which also produces a palatable *moscatel* dessert wine. The best of Valencian wines, some of them very smooth indeed, come from the district of Requeña-Utiel, straddling the way to La Mancha.

Valencia: Castellón Region

Routes from the north

People intent on touring, and coming from the north, usually approach the Levante either from Madrid or along the Mediterranean coast – or use one route coming in and the other going out, as I propose to do. The Mediterranean route is mostly motorway now; in fact you can join an *autopista* just under 90 km from the car-ferry terminal at Santander and stay on motorways all the way to the northern border of Levante, just short of the fishing port of Vinarós: 700-odd km (450 miles). It is, however, both a shorter and far more interesting route if you cut inland or, when you actually approach the Levante border, follow the old diligence road, now the main N340. Richard Ford dismissed it as "not particularly interesting" but there are two places along it of more than passing interest, and an exceptionally agreeable hotel that makes a good base.

Benicarló

The Parador at Benicarló (pop c. 16,500), is one of the most tranquil Paradors I know, perhaps because the town itself is primarily a workaday fishing port, pleasant to stroll along in the afternoons, watching the boats come and go. Although there is a town beach, there are better ones out of town and it has thus escaped too much tourist development.

Peñiscola

Just south of it the rocky promontory, once an islet, of Peñiscola (pop c. 3,200), first colonised by the Phoenicians, fortified by the Carthaginians (it is where the young Hannibal dedicated himself to the destruction of Rome) and presented to the Knights Templar after its reconquest from the Moors.

Massive holiday developments along the beaches to either side of it have robbed it of some of its drama and transformed its steep, winding alleyways into picturesque tourist souks, but for all that it is not unimpressive and has some pleasant seafront restaurants, Simó among them. The castle at its summit, built by the Templars, was the refuge in old age of the Avignon-nominated Anti-Pope, Pedro de Luna, who clung to the title of Benedict XIII and refused to step down in favour of the Rome-elected pontiff. He died there in 1422.

Sierra de Maestrazgo

Inland, most easily reached from Vinarós, is the lovely, wild hinterland of the Sierra de Maestrazgo with dozens of hamlets that were once fortified outposts, first of the Moors and then of the conquering Christians – in particular, the Knights of Montesa, an order founded by Jaime II of Aragón in the early 14th century.

Morella

Most dramatic of the Sierra's small towns is Morella (pop c. 3,400), just 64 km (40 miles) from the coast on N232 yet light-years away in ambience and a good base from which to explore these mountains. It has several small hotels, notably the Cardinal Ram, converted from an old mansion; the Elias is a more conventional alternative.

As a fortress, it goes back to Roman times but most of its monuments and many of the houses lining its steep streets date from the days of the Knights of Montesa. At its summit is the castle, with wonderful views of its mile-long girdle of walls punctuated by towers and gateways, and the remains of an aqueduct. Its church of Sta Maria, earlier than the castle and walls, has beautiful carved doors, a raised *coro* reached by a minutely-carved spiral staircase, and a small museum of paintings.

Just north of Morella, Morella la Vieja has prehistoric cave-paintings; beyond, more fortified villages dot the sierras: Forcall, Todolella, Ortells.

Hill route to Castellón de la Plana

Since both the *autopista* and the main coast road run well inland south of Peñiscola, and the high rise coastal developments are of little interest (Benicasím is the biggest), you could turn south on C238 on the way back from Morella and keep to the hills: it is only about 72 km (45 miles) from the turnoff to Castellón de la Plana, so there is time to dawdle and follow signposts (not always predictable) to see more prehistoric cave-paintings that lie up the side roads.

A turnoff to the right at Puebla Tornese takes you up to yet another charming, castle-topped village, Villafames, popular with artists; there is an excellent Museum of Modern Art (open mornings and afternoons) in one of its 15th-century mansions, and from the citadel you can see over miles of rolling hills and orchards where almonds and peaches grow.

Castellón de la Plana

A sea of orange groves surrounds the provincial capital, Castellón de la Plana (pop c. 126,000), from whence the region's fruit and wine is exported. Badly damaged in the Civil War, its Cathedral with a free-standing belfry looks old but in fact has been lovingly rebuilt down to the last detail. Castellón is also the centre of a ceramics-producing area and there are glimpses all along the road of village church-domes set with blue and red *azulejo* tiles.

Valencia Region

Sagunto

A hill topped by the ruined castle of Almenara signals the approach to Valencia, whose borders it once guarded, and then the sprawling acropolis of Sagunto (Saguntum) comes into view, covering the length of a sharp ridge and spilling down the hillside. Once it was a seaport, founded by Iberians, colonised by Greeks and Romans, and besieged by Hannibal for eight months in 129 BC to spark off the Second Punic War; the resistance of its citizens is legendary. Now silting has marooned it some three miles inland and the modern port lies untidily at its feet.

Roman Saguntum

The town gets prettier the further uphill you go and the ancient site itself, open mornings and afternoons, is splendid: a well-preserved 2nd-century AD Roman theatre, where festivals are still occasionally held and an engaging small museum with a few statues and mosaics. Above it the fortress walls are mostly Moorish, but beneath them sections of Roman and earlier walls have been uncovered. It is vast, and difficult to decipher, but the breezes are cool, the views magnificent and the associations heroic: rather than surrender to Hannibal alive the inhabitants, according to Livy, flung themselves and their treasures upon a huge pyre in the public square.

Segorbe; Onda; Alcora; Jerica
Inland, and dipping briefly back into Castellón province, lies Segorbe (pop c. 7,600), an ancient walled town whose remodelled Cathedral is best glossed over; the Diocesan Museum, on the other hand, contains some beautiful examples of church paintings by Valencian Gothic and Renaissance artists. Onda, just north of it, together with Alcora, slightly north again, are known for their fine ceramics. Further up the same road (N234) is picturesque Jerica, again walled and with a Moorish castle.

Liria to Ademuz
You can wind back down to the coast again from Segorbe along the C224 which, at the old town of Liria, joins the C234. Inland of Liria is the valley of the Turia, with the two great Turia dams that hold Valencia's water and are watched over by ruined castles at Domeno and Pueblo de Loriguilla; Chelva, just beyond, has a Roman aqueduct and beyond that the prettiest of roads curls up to Ademuz and eventually into the Serranía de Cuenca. If you turn south, instead, the C234 joins the main road into Valencia: a circuit of just over 100 km (63 miles) from Sagunto.

The City of Valencia

By the direct road the provincial capital Valencia (pop c. 752,000) is only 22 km (14 miles) south of Sagunto. It is renowned for its *ferias,* and in particular for its March *fallas* when huge wood and *papier maché* caricature effigies of everyday people are processed through the streets and eventually consumed by enormous bonfires to the accompaniment of a fusillade of fireworks.

History: El Cid
Founded by the Romans, prosperous under the Moors, Valencia's other chief pride lies in its association with Spain's great folklore hero, El Cid, who in the name of Alfonso VI of Castile captured the city from the Moors in 1094 after a somewhat half-hearted 20-year siege; his loyalties tended to waver in direct proportion to his rewards and, for part of the time anyway, he was helping the King to conquer Toledo. Half of his army that took Valencia was in fact Moslem and he only ruled it for five years, dying in his bed in 1099 surrounded by his family (Ximena, his wife, and two daughters, Sol and Elvira) and even his favourite charger, Babieca. To discourage the Moors from trying to reoccupy the city after his death, they placed him upon Babieca and paraded him out of the city to his burial sitting upright, as if still alive. This bit of sorcery did not succeed for long, and Ximena lost the city again soon afterwards.

Hotels; restaurants

Augustus Hare, arriving by train in the 1870s from Tarragona, "a most fatiguing journey of 11 hours" and finding at the railway station "a truly southern mob . . . shrieking out the merits of the (opposing) hotels", offered a warning of the subject: "Woe betide the traveller who on such occasions has not chosen his resting place!" The one he chose, because of its romantic associations, was the Fonda del Cid ("the first thoroughly comfortable hotel we had met with in Spain"), where Hans Christian Andersen had stayed a few years earlier. It appears no longer to exist but the Reina Victoria ("new, with central heating," Baedeker noted in 1913), is still extremely good and, like the homelier Inglés, very central.

Good restaurants in the same area include the Comodoro and the Venta del Toboso; there are masses more restaurants only slightly further afield.

The Cathedral

Chief point of interest is the Cathedral, a basically Gothic building on the site of many an older place of worship, much altered and added to. No fewer than five of its bishops in the 15th and 16th centuries were Borjas, better known to us as Borgias, thanks to the notoriety of the family's Italian branch.

The west door, overshadowed by the octagonal Gothic Miguelete tower ("El Micalet"), covered in fine tracery, is a curious, concave Baroque confection much maligned by all except Sacheverell Sitwell who called it "one of the prettiest of Valencian buildings."

The interior is less captivating but its *sala capituler* (chapterhouse), with lovely vaulting, contains a glorious Roman goblet in deep purple agate, adorned with gold and pearls and theatrically displayed against pale alabaster reliefs; it is venerated as the Holy Grail.

The Water Court

The cathedral's south door is Romanesque, the north one is Gothic and opens onto the circular Plaza de la Virgen. Here, beneath the gaze of the 12 Apostles and their attendant saints and angels carved upon the portal, the eight black-clad farmer members of the ancient Water Court meet every Thursday at noon to rule on all matters relating to the irrigation of Valencia's *huerta.* All proceedings of this "rare court of common sense", as Ford called it, are verbal and no appeals may be made against its decisions; water was (and is) too precious to waste time on normal legal procedures in cases of dispute over its use. This unique court goes back at least 1,000 years as, indeed, does the complex system of irrigating the *huerta.*

Around the Plaza de la Virgen

A covered way connects the Cathedral with the high-Baroque church of Valencia's patron saint, Nuestra Señora de los Desamparados (the helpless) on the eastern edge of the plaza. Behind it is a medieval former granary, the Almudín (open mornings and afternoons), somewhat incongruously housing dusty skeletons of long-extinct Argentinian fauna. Beyond that is S Esteban, where the fanatical preacher of the Inquisition, S Vicente Ferrer, was baptised (he was born in Valencia) and where by tradition the daughters of the Cid, Sol and Elvira, married. Across the Plaza de la Virgen to the west is the 15th-century Palacio de la Generalidad (open in the mornings) with an attractive patio and some sumptuous rooms, two of which have breathtaking coffered *mudéjar* ceilings, glowing in gilt and painted decoration.

Puente Serranos

Past the Palacio, Calle Serranos leads east to one of the remaining city gateways, the Serranos Tower, ". . the whole of the grand old walls having been pulled down . . . in 1871 . . . in order to give 'employment to the poor'", scoffs Augustus Hare, who arrived shortly afterwards. A bridge leads across the old course of the Turia (now canalised around the other side of the city).

Old Silk Exchange

Calle Caballeros, lined with some of Valencia's handsomest mansions, leads westwards from the Plaza de la Virgen. South of it is another remarkable Gothic building, the Lonja, or Old Silk Exchange; mulberries were cultivated in Valencia in former times, and silk woven. The roof vaulting springs from gracefully twisted columns; there is a pretty garden alongside and a handsome upper room with an *artesonado* ceiling. Opposite the Lonja, a row of vendors selling the traditional flat vessels for cooking *paella* partly obscures this side of the enchanting market building, all wrought iron and glass and *azulejos,* with miles of food stalls radiating away from a central dome and water butt.

Plaza del Ayuntimiento

South of the market Avenida Maria Cristina leads to Plaza del Ayuntimiento and its flower-sellers, with the Town Hall and Tourist Office on one side and a network of pedestrian streets off it; east of the market, an alley opposite the Sta Catalina church threads into the circular Plaza Redonda, once perhaps a bullring.

S Martín; ceramics museum

Leaving by the alleyway to the south, you are close to S Martín and its splendid bronze statue, over the door, of the saint dividing his cloak; a little further on is the grotesque Baroque front of the Palacio de Dos Aguas, its doorway flanked by two enormous, stone-carved water carriers drooping over their overflowing water jars. Above them is a welter of caryatids carrying elaborate cornices, stone balconies and turrets; inside is the marvellous Ceramics Museum (open mornings and afternoons), with a collection dating back to Roman times of pottery from all over Spain – including a fantastic reproduction of a typical Valencian tiled kitchen.

Colegio del Patriarca museum
Beyond this museum, and opposite the university, the Colegio del Patriarca is a Renaissance former seminary whose museum, open weekend and holiday mornings, has good paintings by the Valencian school, notably Ribaltas. There are also tapestries in the chapel and diamond-pattern *azulejos* in the vestry. Beside the university the street called Comedias leads up to Palau and the Casa de los Almirantes de Aragón, with a beautiful Gothic doorway and patio, and eventually back to the Cathedral.

Palace of Justice; Plaza de Tetuan
Going south-east from the Patriarca, two enormous shady squares sandwich the Palace of Justice between them; they come alive in the evenings when those Valencians not strolling in the main square come to stroll here instead. Northwards is Plaza de Tetuan, flanked by the church of Sto Domingo on one side and radiating streets packed with discos and bars on the other.

Gardens; Arts Museum
Beyond the Plaza the Puente del Real crosses the old river-bed to the Jardines del Real and the excellent Bellas Artes Museum (open mornings and afternoons except in July, August and September, when it is open only in the mornings). It contains, among other things, works by painters who lived and worked in Valencia: Juanes, Espinosa and Orrente as well as Ribalta and Ribera.

Environs of Valencia

Pottery; local crops
In the immediate neighbourhood of Valencia is its seaport, El Grao, and the pottery town of Manises, near the airport, with a number of factories that can be visited. But the *huerta* is of overriding interest, a patchwork of meticulously divided fields, cut and cross-cut by the intricate canals along which long, narrow boats drift. Each owner's patch is watched over from his house, no longer always the traditional peak-roofed whitewashed *barracas* but more often conventional cottages from which entire families emerge to work in the *huerta*. The combination of good soil, water, sunshine and hard work enables some to get as many as four crops a year: fruit, vegetables and rice.

Salt-water lagoon

Much of the rice is grown south of Valencia, alternating with citrus in the area around the great salt-water lagoon of La Albufera which is separated from the sea by a sandy spit, La Dehesa, cut by inlets called *goleras* which are full of eels and other fish, and a resting-place for migatory birds. The seaward edge of the lagoon is a ribbon of not always pleasing development but there is a Parador there, a racecourse and a golf course.

Cullera

South of it, at the mouth of the Júcar river, sits Cullera (pop c. 20,500), rapidly burgeoning with high-rises but still quite pretty, with a hilltop castle ruin and a yacht marina wedged into the river mouth beneath it.

A round trip to the west

Due west of Valencia, the main N111 Madrid road can bring you swiftly to Castilla-La Mancha by way of more of Levante's inland surpises: Chiva, with a Moorish castle; Buñol, with a majestic fort in which François I of France was held for a time, after his capture in Italy in one of the many wars he had with the Emperor Charles V. Here you can choose to continue on the main road to Requeña and Utiel, at the heart of the wine-producing area, or turn south along N330 for Cofrentes, with another castle, coming back to the coast on C322 via Játiva (see below) to Gandía.

Gandía

If you go to Gandía (pop c. 48,000) directly from Valencia, the old road and the motorway run almost parallel after Cullera, and the total distance to Gandía is just under 70 km (44 miles) from Valencia. An old town, still partly walled, from which the Borjas took their ducal name, it has a Borja palace, now a Jesuit college, with a succession of splendid rooms that are shown on guided tours, two in the mornings and one in the afternoons.

The Borgias

An old Aragonese family, the Borjas, branched into Italy when two of its members became popes; it was the second one in the late 15th century who became Pope Alexander VI and sired, among other off-spring, the notorious Cesare and Lucrezia Borgia. His grandson, descended from another son, was Duke Francisco, who retired to Gandía after taking to a life of monastic holiness; he was eventually canonised and perhaps has atoned for the family sins. Playa de Gandía, below the town, is a well-developed resort with hotels and fish restaurants.

Alicante Region

Coast road to Benidorm

Beyond Playa de Gandía a side-road branches left to follow the coast of Cape de la Nao and its lesser capes, punctuated by the ancient port towns of Denia, Javea, Calpe (huddled at the foot of the Gibraltar-like Peñon de Ifach) and Altea. In all can be found picturesque corners and a few relics of their past, but all are now more or less dedicated to tourism, which has peppered the hillsides between them with endless gentrified developments.

Benidorm

The tourist resort that dwarfs them all, however, is Benidorm, just down the coast, once a smugglers' harbour and now a near-endless vista of towers that stab the sky and host, with streamlined efficiency, millions of package tourists every year.

Guadalest

Inland of all this, the mountains rise like stiff, petrified waves above troughs of villa-strewn olive groves. On the crest of one of them sits the once-noble castle of Guadalest, the village houses wrapped within its walls and the village cemetery tucked into the castle keep; it is exactly the right distance from Benidorm to make a popular excursion and has suffered accordingly.

Inland: Játiva to Alicante City

Játiva

Further inland still, however, you are off the tourist track and the air is less humid as well as more peaceful. Játiva (Xátiva, pop c. 24,000), lying almost directly west of Granada and also associated with the Borjas, who moved here from Aragón in the 14th century, is a fine old town once you are through its modern outskirts. The first paper to be made in Spain (possibly the first in Europe) was made here in the 12th century (Valencia holds the distinction of having had Spain's first printing-press) and it was also the birthplace of the painter Ribera.

The twin-peaked hill, ringed by the largely 15th-century walls of the half-ruined castle (fantastic views) was the site of a series of cities going back to Roman times. Hannibal's wife is said to have given birth there and, in the 13th century, it served as a prison for Spain's equivalent of England's Princes in the Tower: the young de la Cerda princelings, whose uncle had usurped the throne of Castile. In the early 16th century Cesare Borgia (Borja) was also imprisoned there by

Ferdinand the Catholic.

Játiva's treasures

Whatever the faults of the Borjas, they were all connoisseurs of the arts and enriched the churches with which they were connected: the chalice of Duke Alfonso (Pope Calixtus III) and a custodia given by Duke Rodrigo (Pope Alexander VI) are among the treasures of Játiva's Colegiata church, the building itself was extensively remodelled in the 18th century when it was damaged (as indeed was the whole town) during the War of the Spanish Succession, and again following the Civil War. Opposite it is the Plateresque façade of the Municipal Hospital; uphill is the chapel-museum (open mornings and afternoons) displaying some fine Valencian primitive paintings.

Augustus Hare described Játiva as "full of fountains – a perfect city of clear rushing waters . . . fragrant with fruit and flowers" and would have stayed but for "the extreme wretchedness of the inn." Nowadays the Vernisa makes an acceptable overnight stop if you are not inclined to continue for another 37 km (just under 24 miles) south to Alcoy (pop c. 66,000) and the grander Hotel Reconquista.

Alcoy

The outskirts of Alcoy are predictably awful but the old part of town, on a steep ridge between two ravines, is delightful; it is one of the many places that stages a *Moros y Cristianos* festival, in April, and is known for its sugared almonds (as well as paper factories).

Inland castles

A minor road runs westward from it to Villena, capped with a Moorish castle, and there are other castles to see along almost every road: Biar and Castalla, flanking the road between Alcoy and Villena; at Sax; at Petrel, and above Elda; at Monóvar (the oddly conical Castillo de Luna).

You could make a fine tour of them by turning inland at Monóvar on C3213 to Jumilla (pop c. 21,000), 51 km or just over 32 miles away; its castle, well restored, looms above a church with a blue and white *azulejo* dome and some handsome old streets. Between it and Yecla (pop c. 25,000), with a more ruinous castle, C3314 runs across a high plateau smothered in vineyards, for both are wine-producing townships.

Carrasqueta Pass; Jijona

Both towns are gateways into La Mancha, via Hellín and Almansa respectively; both are equally accessible to Alicante, reached from Alcoy via the dramatic Carrasqueta pass and Jijona (pop c. 9,000), with yet another stupendous castle, where they make a version of the celebrated Levante *turron.*

The City of Alicante

History

Alicante (pop c. 246,000), just a few miles further south and capital of the province, is one of those gateway cities through whose airport throngs of tourists pass each year, hardly aware that the city exists. In package holiday terms, it is probably only a half-day shopping excursion for the more adventurous, yet its history goes back to the Romans and for centuries it was the southernmost guardian fortress of the Moorish Kingdom of Valencia. When it was reconquered by the Christian King Jaime of Aragon, it turned its energies to trade, apart from a brief period when it supported the losing candidate in the War of the Spanish Succession – and its castle was razed by the winner, Philip V, in reprisal.

British wine merchants

At one time it had a British colony of merchants, largely engaged in exporting wines ". . . rich, with a rough taste combined with sweetness . . .used to doctor thin clarets for the British market", says Ford. It still has a British Consul, who is nowadays more likely to concern himself with tourists who have got into trouble than with the problems of wine exporters.

Old town; hotels and restaurants

Sacheverell Sitwell thought Alicante delightful but uninteresting, which sums it up pretty accurately, yet despite its rapidly growing industrial areas it is not to be despised for a couple of nights, with a pleasant old quarter and many good hotels and restaurants: the Gran Sol hotel, on Rambla Mendez Nuñez, has fine views of the harbour and the much simpler Maisonnave is close to the Cathedral; the Delfín on the waterfront esplanade is the best restaurant and La Goleta, further up the same street, a fair alternative. The port is lively and busy and the climate, particularly in winter, is enviable.

Castle; Esplanade

What remains of the Castle of Sta Barbara, on a hilltop to the east, is the most compelling sight: more for the views it affords than for itself, though it has been tidied and planted with flowers and shrubs. A walk along the palm-shaded Esplanada de España, mosaic-paved in an attractive, wavy pattern, is an agreeable way of passing the early evening, watching everybody else doing the same.

Markets; churches

The market area – there are two covered markets, close to one another, further into town – is full of life and colour; S Nicolás Cathedral and

Baroque Sta Maria both stand on the sites of mosques.

Elche

Augustus Hare travelled from Alicante to Elche by diligence in the 1870s, charmed by its comfort and speed, by comparison with the trains he had used; charmed, too, by the coachman "in his quaintly decorated velveteen suit" who urged the horses by alternately talking to them and pelting their tails with stones "from a little hillock prepared already on the coach box."

Dama de Elche

You are more likely to cover the 24 km (15 miles) to Elche (pop c. 165,000) by car or bus, perhaps noticing a sign on the outskirts that reads (or used to read) "City of mystery, the Dama and palms." If you have been to Madrid's Archeological Museum and seen the enigmatic, stone-carved, 5th century BC beauty called the Dama de Elche, you will appreciate that reference.

Mystery play

The "mystery" is a centuries-old re-enactment of the events of the Assumption of the Virgin, in which all the female parts are played by boys. Spain's oldest mystery play, dating from 1370 when the script and a miraculous image of the Virgin were delivered in a chest, according to legend, by a mysterious stranger who immediately disappeared, is the centrepiece of a solemn annual two-day festival on August 14 and 15.

Phoenician palm grove

If you do not know the Dama and are not there in August, take heart: the palms alone are worth the visit. Originally planted by the Phoenicians, Europe's biggest palm grove encloses the town on three sides, invading the extremities of many a street, and make an extraordinary sight. The dates they produce are not of prime quality, though they are assiduously cultivated by artificially pollinating the female trees. Even more lucrative is the trade in palm branches, harvested from the barren female trees and less prolific males, and the oddest sight in Elche is not so much the waving palm fronds as those that cannot wave because they are tightly bound to bleach them. They look like up-ended paintbrushes but their end product, when the sap has receded and the leaves turn pale, is much in demand for Palm Sunday rituals.

Palm "museum"; Dama site

Anyone interested in learning more about palms and seeing a very odd, 150-years-old mutation with seven "branches", can tour the Huerta del Cura (open day-long, except on Mondays), opposite the very plush hotel of the same name. Those more intrigued by the town's prehistory can go to the estate of La Alcudia, about two km (one mile) away, where the Dama was unearthed at the end of the last century and where there is a small site museum open mornings and afternoons.

Town Museum
There is also a town museum in the municipal park, open at weekends, which houses a splendid stone lioness only slightly younger than the Dama, perhaps 2,000 years old, and displays of local, palm-based handicrafts.

Moorish Elche
As you zigzag about the old part of Elche, bisected by a deep river gorge that runs past the walls of the former Moorish Alcázar, now known as the Altamira Palace and largely 15th-century, there is still a feeling of being in one of the more sophisticated North African oasis towns where homely factories and apartment houses rub shoulders with traditionally flat-roofed houses, and stray palms are everywhere.

Sta Maria church
But at the enormous, Baroque-style church of Sta Maria (rebuilt in 1936, though the 17th-century portals are original), Christian Spain reasserts itself, for this is the venue for the annual "mystery" festival that erupts into the streets when the Virgin's funeral is enacted.

Orihuela

Another and considerably smaller palm grove fringes the outskirts of Orihuela (pop c. 50,000), south-west of Elche along the N340. An extremely ancient settlement it is now rather overwhelmed by a carapace of new development.

Glorieta Park; Cathedral
At the heart of the old quarter is the shady Glorieta park, from which you can look upwards at the ruins of the castle, and it has a number of interesting churches (Ford called Orihuela "over-churched"; Hare was greatly taken with "all the handsome girls . . . with fresh roses stuck jauntily behind their ears"; the 1913 Baedeker dismissed it curtly with "the Cathedral is uninteresting.") In fact the Cathedral has some fine Gothic vaulting enhanced by twisted, corkscrewing ribs and, in the pretty cloister, a Diocesan Museum (open in the mornings) contains works by Velázquez, Morales and Ribera.

Churches; Calle Mayor
The Baroque front of Sta Justa is studded with undressed stone blocks that were never carved into statues; Santiago, with a fine

Gothic doorway, has Salzillo statues in some of the chapels; the College of Sto Domingo, or former university, has a Renaissance façade and two fine cloisters. Calle Mayor, running between the Cathedral and the Episcopal Palace, is charming: narrow and pedestrianised with mosaic paving, projecting wrought-iron lamp brackets and balconies, and a number of attractive streets leading off it lined with dignified façades.

Murcia Region

The southbound N340 runs along the valley of the Segura, which waters the *huertas* of both Orihuela and Murcia, some 24 km (about 15 miles) further, passing the castle-crowned eminence of Monteagudo.

The City of Murcia

The Segura flows through the centre of the provincial capital of Murcia (pop c. 289,000) and gives it serenity and sparkle, all the more welcome after the problems of negotiating road-works and new suburbs on the approach. Fountains throw droplets into the air in the riverside Glorieta gardens, where beautifully turned-out children play and their elders saunter and gossip.

Hotels; restaurants

There are a number of good hotels: a Meliá and the Rincón de Pepe at the top end; the Fontoria and the Hispano, more modest but conveniently central. Many of the good restaurants are near the Cathedral: Rincón de Pepe with a Michelin rosette; Los Apóstoles and Baltasar, all on or near Plaza de Apóstoles.

History

Founded as a Moorish stronghold in the ninth century on the site of older settlements, Murcia fell in the 13th century to Castile and was re-populated with Christians from the north. It was saved from sacking during the War of Succession by the expedient of flooding its approaches and, until the early 18th century, prospered on its silk industry. Earthquakes shook it in the 19th century and it was badly damaged in the Civil War, but today it is again prosperous thanks to fruit canning, and remarkably attractive.

Salzillo Museum

One normally starts to explore a city from the Cathedral, but in Murcia you should save this until late afternoon and, if you arrive after dark, start your morning sightseeing elsewhere. This is no problem: Spain's premier Baroque sculptor, Salzillo, was born there and a museum at the opposite (western) end of town is devoted to his works and open mornings and afternoons.

Although Baroque art may be out of fashion, Salzillo's work is compelling by its sheer technical excellence, quite apart from its dramatic quality. The montage of the Nativity and Infancy of Christ, lining one room, is a succession of meticulously carved miniature figures, some of them on turntables that can be activated by flipping switches. And the enormous *pasos,* multi-figure compositions that are processed through the streets during Holy Week, are alarmingly lifelike.

Botanical Gardens; Archaeological museum
Just east of the museum a web of narrow old streets leads to S Nicolás and, if you follow this southwards towards the river, you come to the market and the charming Botanical Gardens beyond. From the river, where it is crossed by the Puente Viejo, the lively Gran Via runs north from Plaza Tornel; if you turn right at Aciscio, some eight short blocks up it, and left into Plaza Alfonso X, you come to the Archaeological Museum (open mornings, until 1400), with some fine ceramics. The charming, narrow and partly pedestrianised Calle Trapería leads back south again, crossed by Platería and other atmospheric streets.

The "Casino"
An unmissable building on Trapería is the ornate 19th-century Casino, through whose windows can be seen elderly gentlemen dozing over their newspapers or engaging in conversation: casinos, a feature of most Spanish cities, are the equivalent of London's exclusive men's clubs.

The Cathedral
Trapería emerges opposite the bell tower and north portal of the Cathedral; make your way round to the west, preferably towards sunset, to see the fantastic Baroque façade, framed by a fountain and the 18th-century Bishop's Palace, glowing deep pink in the evening light. It is amazingly theatrical, with carved angels and prelates in swirling draperies striking dramatic attitudes between columns and above cornices; Sitwell called it "a masterpiece of decadent architecture."

Cathedral's Velez chapel; relics
The interior is largely Gothic, with a *coro* that overwhelms the nave; the fine Capilla de los Vélez, with a carved stone screen and interior, is off the ambulatory. (Its octagonal exterior is equally fine; the Vélez family were powerful hereabouts and many of the castles in the surrounding hills were their strongholds.) An urn to the left of the high altar contains the bowels of Alfonso the Wise of Castile, 13th-century

conqueror of Murcia; "Coals to Newcastle," Ford observed waspishly; "had he bequeathed a portion of his brains, this Dunciad see and city might have profited."

The coast: Sta Pola to Cartagena

It is no hardship to spend a few nights in Murcia, exploring the vicinity. There is a string of resorts along the coast to the east, where salt-pans vie with tourism as the local industries: Sta Pola, with good fish restaurants, a few Roman remains, and excursions to the islet of Tabarca; Guardamar at the mouth of the Segura; fast-growing Torrevieja; smaller Cabo Roig on its peninsula, and Campoamor. Then comes the Mar Menor, a huge, shallow, salt-water lagoon, its placid surface broken by numerous islets and almost cut off from the sea by long, narrow spits; an ambitious new luxury resort development, La Manga, majoring on sporting activities, lies along the southernmost spit. The road skirts the inland edge of the lagoon via Los Alcazares, also bidding for the tourist trade, and ends in Cartagena.

Cartagena

The appeal of Cartagena (pop c. 173,000), 49 km (just over 30 miles) from Murcia by the main N301, lies largely in its name and its associations. New Carthage, founded by Hannibal's antecedents and developed for its gold and silver deposits, became the springboard for the Carthaginians' assaults on Roman Spain; it was eventually captured by the elder Scipio in 208 after a long siege. Later a Moorish stronghold, later still raided by Sir Francis Drake on one of his 16th-century forays to "singe the King of Spain's beard", it is today a major port and naval base, prosperous and busy, reflecting little of its chequered past beyond some scant Roman excavations.

The view from the Castillo is impressive, the Archaeological Museum displays some good Roman pieces, and there is a very early submarine, invented by a native of the city, on show in the main square.

About 28 km (18 miles) to the west is the resort of Puerto de Mazarrón, with fish restaurants and small hotels.

North-west of Murcia

There are more things of interest to see inland: Murcia's lush *huerta* is full of citrus and soft-fruit orchards; to the north-west the N301, parallelled by a prettier minor road on the other bank of the river, follows the Segura inland through a valley that remained a Moorish enclave even after the conquest of Granada, in 1492, officially ended the Moorish occupation of Spain.

There are old towers in the hills, Moorish baths in Archena that were patronised (the waters are curative) by the Romans before them, and a ruined Moorish castle above Cieza (pop c. 30,000). Here you are on the threshold of La Mancha again and, just before Hellín, the prehistoric painted rock-shelter of Cueva de Minateda is just off to the right.

South-west of Murcia

Alcantarilla: folk museum
On the N340 west of Murcia is Alcantarilla (pop c. 24,000), where a folk museum called Museo de la Huerta focuses on the local country life and includes a huge Arab water-wheel, or *noria.* South-westwards, this main road follows the Guadalentin valley, bypassing the old spa town of Alhama de Murcia and its Moorish fort.

Sierra Espuña nature reserve
Above Totana the medieval hill village of Aledo, with its battlemented castle walls, is the gateway to the wild Sierra Espuña nature reserve, where mountain goats and other wildlife still abound; satisfying territory for walkers and climbers.

Lorca
Back on the main road, Lorca is a big, busy market town that boasts one of Spain's most theatrical Holy Week celebrations. It also boasts some splendid Baroque façades: Casa de los Guevara, with its corkscrew columns, where the Tourist Office is; Casa de los Musso Valenta, across the street; Palacio S Julián, further on, and several good churches.

Lorca's old quarter
Off the main street and uphill, in the older quarter, are more imposing houses, many of them grouped around the sun-bleached Plaza de España, surrounded by the Baroque façades of the Town Hall, the S Patricio collegiate church and the law courts. And above that again is a castle dating back to the 12th century and the Moorish occupation.

Pantano de Puentes dam
Ford goes into some detail about the financial scandals attendant on the building of the Pantano de Puentes, the dam from which comes Lorca's water supply; dams were rare enough in his day to warrant description for their own sake, but this one had the added distinction of bursting within months of being filled, in 1802, and half-inundating the town below.

Puerto Lumbreras Parador
If you are looking for somewhere to stop nearby, the Parador at Puerto

Lumbreras is only 18 km (11 miles) further west, flanked by other hotels, and a useful staging point. There are masses of interesting little places to see in the hinterland.

An Inland Detour

Vélez Rubio; prehistoric caves

A marvellous inland detour starts from Puerto Lumbreras, taking first the main road towards Baza and Granada and branching off it northwards at Vélez Rubio, where a ruined castle stands on the opposite side of the valley. There are prehistoric caves (Los Letreros) nearby.

Vélez Blanco

A few kilometres beyond Vélez Rubio, past neatly cultivated terraces, the splendid 16th-century castle stands at the summit of the charming old village of Vélez Blanco, on the edge of the Sierra de Maria nature reserve. It is, strictly speaking just over the Andalusían border, but Vélez family castles fairly pepper the Levante countryside; this one is being gradually restored but you can drive up to it and admire the coats of arms set into its walls, the massive merlon-capped crenellations, an arcaded patio high on one tower, and fine views over the pantiled roofs of the village below.

Pueblo de Don Fadrique

The road continues northwestwards, skirting the wooded lower slopes of the Sierra de Maria massif, and crosses a high, saucer-shaped plateau, barely populated, where olives and almonds and vines are cultivated. Pueblo de Don Fadrique lies at the eastern edge of the remote Sierra de Segura, cobwebbed with tiny roads curling along its flanks.

Caravaca de la Cruz

If you turn east here, you come to Caravaca de la Cruz, with a picturesque old quarter beneath its much-truncated castle walls. Rising above them is the huge church of Sta Cruz, whose pink, red and pale grey Baroque portal glows in the sun.

The Holy Cross for which the church is named was brought down from heaven by an angel during the Moorish occupation, when a 13th-century priest wishing to say Mass before the local Moslem ruler lamented that he had no crucifix. When it appeared, the Moor was converted at once and the cross assumed miraculous properties, but this did not prevent it from being stolen just before the Civil War. The interior of the church emphasises the continuing veneration of the miraculous cross with a gilded replica and tabernacle; beside the church, across an attractive patio, is a museum housing paintings by the Master of Caravaca.

Calasparra; Mula; Socovos
Northeast of Caravaca is Calasparra with yet another (sadly ruined) castle, and if you are not yet sated with castles you can either come back to Murcia via Mula, which also has a splendid example, or go northwest into the hinterland for the red sandstone beauty piled above the hamlet of Socovos – at which point you are back again in Eastern Andalusía and well on your way to Albacete, La Mancha and Madrid.

Glossary

Acotado - private shooting or fishing reserve; also *Coto*
Ajimez - twin-light Moorish window divided by a slender column
Alameda - promenade, often planted with trees, shrubs
Alcázaba - Moorish citadel
Alcázar - Moorish fort or fortfied palace
Alicatado - glazed-tile mosaic
Artesonado - coffered wooden ceiling
Avenida - avenue
Ayuntamiento - town hall; also *Casa consistorial*
Azulejo - glazed tile
Balneario - spa
Barranco - ravine
Barrio - district
Bodega - wine-cellar or warehouse, sometimes a wine-bar
Calle - street
Calleja or *Callejon* - alley
Camino - road
Campo - countryside, field or plain
Capilla - chapel
Capilla mayor - chancel
Carretera - main route, highway
Cartuja - Carthusian monastery
Castillo - castle
Cerrado - shut
Churrigueresque - 17/18th century exuberant Baroque architectural details, named after the Churriguera family
Circunvalación - bypass
Ciudad - town
Claustro - cloister
Colegiata - collegiate church
Coro - choir in a church
Cortes - Parliament
Cortijo - farm or estate
Cueva - cave
Desfiladero - pass or defile
Embalse - artificial lake, dam
Ermita - hermitage or chapel
Ferrocarril - railway
Finca - farm
Feria - annual fair
Fuente - fountain or spring
Garganta - gorge
Huerta - highly cultivated market garden area
Iglesia - church
Infanta - princess
Infante - prince
Isabelline - Spanish equivalent of the Flamboyant (Gothic) architectural style
Judería - Jewish quarter; also *Aljama*
Lago - lake
Lonja - trade-exchange building
Mercado - market
Meseta - plateau
Mirador - belvedere or viewpoint
Molino - mill
Morisco - Christianised Moor
Mozárabe - Christian subject to the Moors
Mozarabic - architecture of Christians subject to the Moors
Mudéjar - Moslem subject to the Christians; also their architecture
Obispo - bishop
Palacio - palace
Pantano - dam, dammed reservoir
Paseo - promenade
Pasos - religious sculptures processed at festivals
Patio - courtyard
Peaje - toll

Peña - rock or summit
Plateresque - finely detailed stone carving, named because of its affinity with silversmiths' work (*plata* - silver)
Playa - beach
Plaza - town square or place
Plaza mayor - main square in town or village
Posada - inn
Pueblo - village
Puente - bridge
Puerta - gate or doorway
Puerto - mountain pass or port
Reja - ornamental iron grille
Retablo - altarpiece
Río - river
Salida - exit
Sierra - range of hills or mountains
Sillería - choirstalls
Torre - tower
Travesía - lane, alleyway
Vega - alluvial plain

Evolution of Art and Architecture

Roman, Visigothic and Romanesque

During the five centuries that elapsed between the waning of Roman power (from the late 2nd century AD) and the arrival of the Moors, the Visigoths with their capital at Toledo were masters of most of the Iberian peninsula. But Southern Spain, though rich in Roman remains (particularly in Extremadura), is short on Visigothic and later Romanesque ones: a few primitively carved column-capitals here, a fresco or two there – notably in the Church of S Román in Toledo – and a handful of Romanesque church portals, among them the East door of Valencia Cathedral. It is highly unlikely that the Moorish invaders systematically destroyed Christian buildings; more likely that these either fell into disuse and crumbled away over the centuries, or that they were partly demolished to make way for Gothic successors erected during the later stages of the Christian reconquest.

Moorish and Mudéjar (8th-15th centuries)

These unique styles are discussed on pp 41-42; briefly, their principal architectural features are the horseshoe arch and the more elaborate multi-lobed or 'scolloped' arch, and the cupola, either single or grouped. Decorative elements are achieved by alternating white stone with red brick, by relief-patterns in brick on brick backgrounds, and by intricate wood- and plaster-work. Since Islamic tradition forbids the depiction of human and animal forms, artists instead interplayed lines, angles and curves to produce almost abstract geometrical effects, or produced lacelike designs by using formalised plant motifs or inscriptions in the angular Cufic script. Much of Moorish decoration work is thus in the natural colours of brick, stone, wood and plaster, but they were also masters of painted designs on wood and, above all, of achieving brilliant polychrome effects with tiles, often set at subtle angles to one another to reflect light.

Gothic (13th-16th centuries)

Largely an import from France, the Gothic style was introduced by Christian monarchs as they gradually reconquered the country. Most of the craftsmen they employed, however, were still *mudéjars,* or Christianised Moors, who were never entirely at home with the new form, whose hallmarks are flying exterior buttresses and soaring pointed arches embellished with carved stone; thus Spanish Gothic churches, such as Seville Cathedral, are frequently ponderous rather than uplifting and retain many *mudéjar* features, notably minarets converted to belfries. Only with the emergence of the florid Isabelline style, a development of Flamboyant Gothic, did Spain achieve an authentically national idiom. In the fine arts field, however, influenced by Italian and, later, by Flemish masters as well as the French, Spaniards developed a highly personal style in the carving and painting of austere statuary and altarpieces *(retablos).*

Renaissance (16th century)
A more confident, more truly Spanish style now emerged in which foreign influences were not merely adopted but subtly adapted. Among the best examples from this period are the *capilla de los Reyes Muevos* in Toledo Cathedral, by Covarrubias; the Hospital de Tavera, also in Toledo, by Bustamente; Jaén Cathedral by Vandelvira; Granada Cathedral by Siloe and, although it sits uncomfortably among Granada's glorious Nastrid palaces, Charles V's palace by Machuca. The greatest architectural influence, however, was that of Herrera the Elder, leader of the classical movement, whose supreme contribution was to incorporate Classical forms and to perfect the style of architectural decoration known as Plateresque: detailed and finely-chiselled carving and moulding that echoed the art of silversmiths (*platero*=silver) that had started under Machuca and Bustamente; most of his best work, however, is to be found in the north. In painting, a more dramatic sense of colour and perspective evolved in the works of Berruguete, Borgoña, Alonso Coello, Llanos, Morales and Moro, reaching their apogee in the masterpieces of El Greco, newly arrived from Italy.

Classical and Baroque (17th and 18th centuries)
Classicism dominated architectural form to begin with, and Herrera the Younger continued to work in the Plateresque idiom, but gradually a more exuberant style of ornamentation developed, reflecting the rise of Baroque in other countries but again imprinted with a wholly Spanish character. Mora's Plaza Mayor in Madrid is a superb example of the transition between the two; not so successful is Bautista's S Isidro Cathedral, also in the capital. More emphatically Baroque are the facade of Murcia Cathedral and the elaborate *trasparente,* by Tomé, in Toledo Cathedral. In time, another peculiarly Spanish and even more elaborate rococo style superseded the Baroque: it is known as Churrigueresque after the Churriguera brothers who developed it and is exemplified by Vergara's Dos Aguas palace in Valencia; much of the prodigious output of Pedro de Ribera; by several of the palatial facades in Ecija; and by Arévalo's and Hurtado's contributions to the Cartuja in Granada. In the field of painting and sculpture, the scope became broader, moving towards secular as well as religious subjects, especially in portraiture. Great names include those of the Valencians

Ribalta and José Ribera, the Murcian sculptor Salzillo, the Andalusians Murillo, Valdes Leál and Zurbarán, Claudio Coello and, head and shoulders above the rest, Velasquez and Goya.

Nineteenth century to the present day
Inevitably, the lavishly decorative fashion exhausted itself and there was a return to basic classical disciplines, albeit overlaid with traces of earlier exhuberance; many of Madrid's monuments and public buildings date from this era, notably the Cibeles fountain, the Prado Museum building, the Alcala Gate and the layout of the Botanical Gardens. Probably the less said the better of much of the building work executed during the present century, varying as it does from the brutally functional to the Disney-esque neo-vernacular, but there are signs of the emergence of a more authentic contemporary style. Prominent Southern Spanish painters of this period include the Valencian artist Sorolla, whose brilliant seaside canvases can be seen in the Madrid museum that was his studio home. Pablo Picasso, although born in Málaga, worked mostly in Barcelona in the north before moving to France and other great Spanish modern artists such as Miro and Dalí were also northerners.

Castles down the ages

Being primarily military in purpose, these need to be considered separately, although many of the later ones incorporated palatial apartments. The Moorish *alcazaba,* or citadel, such as the one that looms over Málaga from the slopes of the Gibralfaro hill, was the hub of a town's defenses, as were the *castillos,* with their massive keeps, erected by the Christian conquerors, *Alcazares,* on the other hand, whether purely Moorish (as in Granada) or raised later by Christian monarchs (as in Toledo), enclosed royal dwelling quarters, courtyards and gardens. The later palaces and royal residences of the Hapsburgs and Bourbons, such as Charles V's final home at Yuste and even the more Classical structures of Aranjuez, often thematically echo the design of the *alcázar.*

Applied and decorative arts

The field of ceramics, both vessels and glazed earthenware tiles, or *azulejos,* is probably the oldest: Moorish craftsmen practised in it from the 10th century onwards, and their *mudéjar* and Spanish successors followed in the same traditions to the present day. Best known centres for this work were ancient Elvira, in the neighbourhood of Granada, Málaga, Seville, Valencia and Talavera.

Furniture, especially richly-carved and often intricately inlaid chests and tables, and chairs that incorporated embossed Córdoba leather work, is also typically Spanish. Metalwork is yet another craft on which Spanish masters stamped their own imprint, notably three generations of the 16th-century Arfé family who executed exquisite silver and gold mostrances, including the magnificent examples in the Cathedrals of Toledo and Seville. At about the same time, other craftsmen (Francés, Bartolomé, Villalpando, Cespedes, Fray Francisco de Salamanca) were developing and refining the skills of wrought ironwork and producing the delicate masterpieces that make up the choir- and chapel-screens in the Cathedrals of Toledo, Granada and Jaén.

Finally there is tapestry, which was invariably Flemish or French until the 18th century, when Philip V created the tapestry workshop that still exists in Madrid, for which Goya and other artists designed cartoons.

Lexicon of Food and Drink

General

Almuerzo - breakfast
Cena - dinner
Desayuno - breakfast
Una mesa - a table
El menú, el menú fijo - the menu, set menu
Un plato - a plate
Una servilleta - a table napkin
Un vaso, un copa - a glass
Un tenedor - a fork
Un cuchillo - a knife
Un cuchara - a spoon
La cuenta - the bill
Frio, fria - cold
Caldo, calda - hot
Pan - bread
Mantequilla - butter
Mostaza - mustard
Sal, pimiento - salt, pepper
Azúcar - sugar
Aceite, vinagre - oil, vinegar
Gracias, por favor - Thank you, please

Food and cooking methods

Ahumado - smoked
Asado - roast
A la brasa - spit-roasted
Braseado, braseada - braised
Brochetas (en brochetas) - on skewers
Cazuela (en cazuela) - casseroled
Cocido, cocida - boiled (literally, cooked)
Escalfado, escalfada - poached
Estofado, estofada - stewed
Frito, frita - fried
Al horno - baked
(a la) parilla, plancha (parillada, planchada) - grilled
Rellenos - stuffed (literally, filled)
Salteado, salteada - sautéed
Tostado, tostada - toasted
(al) vapor - steamed

Starters and vegetables

Sopa, caldo - soup, broth
Entremeses - hors d'oeuvres
Aceitunas - olives
Ajo, ajillo - garlic
Alcachofas - artichokes
Berenjena - aubergine
Calabacín - courgette
Cebolla - onion
Col, repollo - cabbage
Coliflor - cauliflower
Ensalada - salad
Espárragos - asparagus
Espinacas - spinach
Guisantes - peas
Habas - broad beans
Judías verdes - green beans
Lechuga - lettuce
Patatas - potatoes
Pimientos - sweet peppers
Verduras - green vegetables

Lexicon of Food and Drink

Egg dishes *(huevos)*

Huevos fritos - fried eggs
Huevos reveueltos - scrambled eggs
Huevos a la flamenca - fried eggs with tomatoes and peas
Tortilla - omelette
Tortilla Español - Spanish omelette, with potato filling

Seafood

Abadejo - fresh cod
Almejas - clams
Anchoas - Anchovies
Anguila, angulas - eel, baby eels
Atun, bonito - tunafish
Bacalao - salt cod
Besugo - bream
Calamares - squid (calamares en su tinta - squid in their ink)
Gambas - prawns
Lenguado - sole
Lubina - sea bass
Mariscos - seafood (usually mixed, as in a soup or grill)
Mejillones - mussels
Merluza - hake
Mero - grouper
Pez espada - swordfish
Rape - hake
Salmonete - red mullet
Trucha - trout

Meat, cuts of meat

Albóndigas - meat balls
Biftec, bistec - beefsteak
Buey - beef (in stews)
Butifarra - spiced sausage
Cabrito - kid
Callos - tripe
Cerdo - pork
Chorizo - spiced sausage
Chuleta - chop
Conejo - rabbit
Cordero - lamb
Higado - liver
Jamón - smoked ham
Lacón - boiled ham, gammon
Lomo - loin (of pork)
Pollo - chicken
Rabo - tail (rabo de buey - oxtail)
Solomillo, filete - tenderloin, fillet steak
Ternasco - baby lamb
Ternera - veal
Venado - venison

Puddings and desserts *(dulces)*

Flan - caramel custard
Frambuesas - raspberries
Fresas - strawberries
Fruta - fruit
Helado - ice cream
Manzana - apple
Melocotón - peach
Melon - melon
Naranja - orange
Sandia - watermelon
Uvas - grapes
Queso - cheese

Drink

Vino, lista de vinos - wine, wine-list
Vino de la Casa - house wine
Vino tinto, blanco, rosado - red, white, rosé wine
Dulce, seco - sweet, dry
Botella, media botella - bottle, half-bottle
Jarra - carafe
Cerveza - beer
Agua mineral gaseoso/sin gas - mineral water, sparkling/still

Limonada - lemonade
Naranjada - orangeade
Zumo de fruta fresca - fresh fruit juice
Café - coffee
Café con leche - with milk
Café solo - black
Café con agua caliente a parte - with hot water (to dilute it) on the side
Chocolate - chocolate
Leche - milk
Té - tea

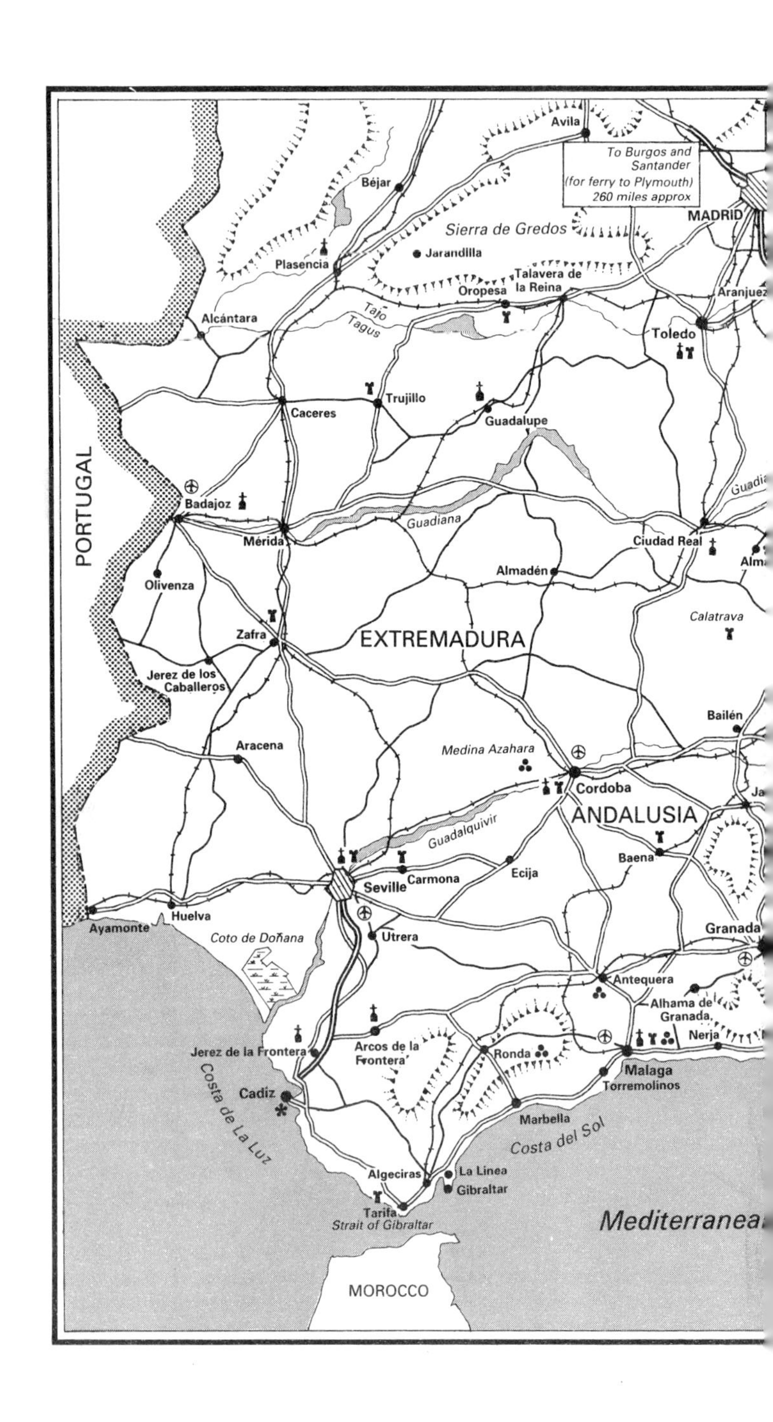
Avila
To Burgos and Santander (for ferry to Plymouth) 260 miles approx
MADRID
Béjar
Sierra de Gredos
Jarandilla
Plasencia
Talavera de la Reina
Oropesa
Aranjuez
Alcántara
Tajo
Tagus
Toledo
Trujillo
Caceres
Guadalupe
PORTUGAL
Badajoz
Mérida
Guadiana
Ciudad Real
Almadén
Olivenza
Calatrava
Zafra
EXTREMADURA
Jerez de los Caballeros
Bailén
Aracena
Medina Azahara
Cordoba
ANDALUSIA
Guadalquivir
Baena
Seville
Carmona
Ecija
Ayamonte
Huelva
Coto de Doñana
Utrera
Granada
Antequera
Alhama de Granada
Nerja
Jerez de la Frontera
Arcos de la Frontera
Ronda
Malaga
Torremolinos
Cadiz
Costa de La Luz
Marbella
Costa del Sol
Algeciras
La Linea
Gibraltar
Tarifa
Strait of Gibraltar
MOROCCO

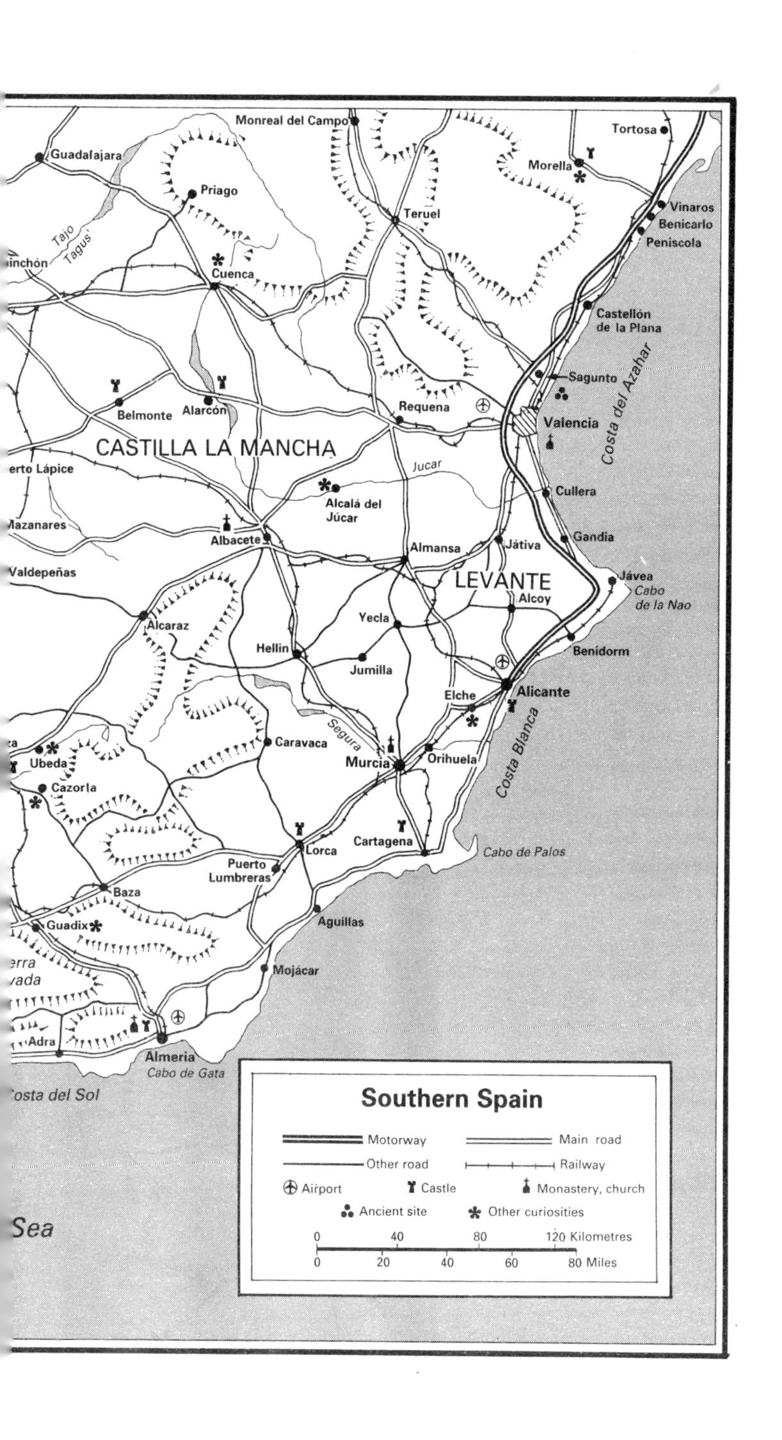
Monreal del Campo
Tortosa
Guadalajara
Morella
Priago
Teruel
Vinaros
Benicarlo
Peniscola
Tajo
Tagus
Cuenca
Castellón de la Plana
Sagunto
Costa del Azahar
Belmonte
Alarcón
Requena
Valencia
CASTILLA LA MANCHA
Jucar
Alcalá del Júcar
Cullera
Albacete
Gandia
Almansa
Játiva
Valdepeñas
LEVANTE
Jávea
Cabo de la Nao
Alcoy
Yecla
Alcaraz
Benidorm
Hellin
Jumilla
Alicante
Elche
Segura
Caravaca
Ubeda
Murcia
Orihuela
Costa Blanca
Cazorla
Cartagena
Lorca
Cabo de Palos
Puerto Lumbreras
Baza
Aguilas
Guadix
Mojácar
Adra
Almeria
Cabo de Gata
Sea
Southern Spain
Motorway
Main road
Other road
Railway
Airport
Castle
Monastery, church
Ancient site
Other curiosities
0 40 80 120 Kilometres
0 20 40 60 80 Miles

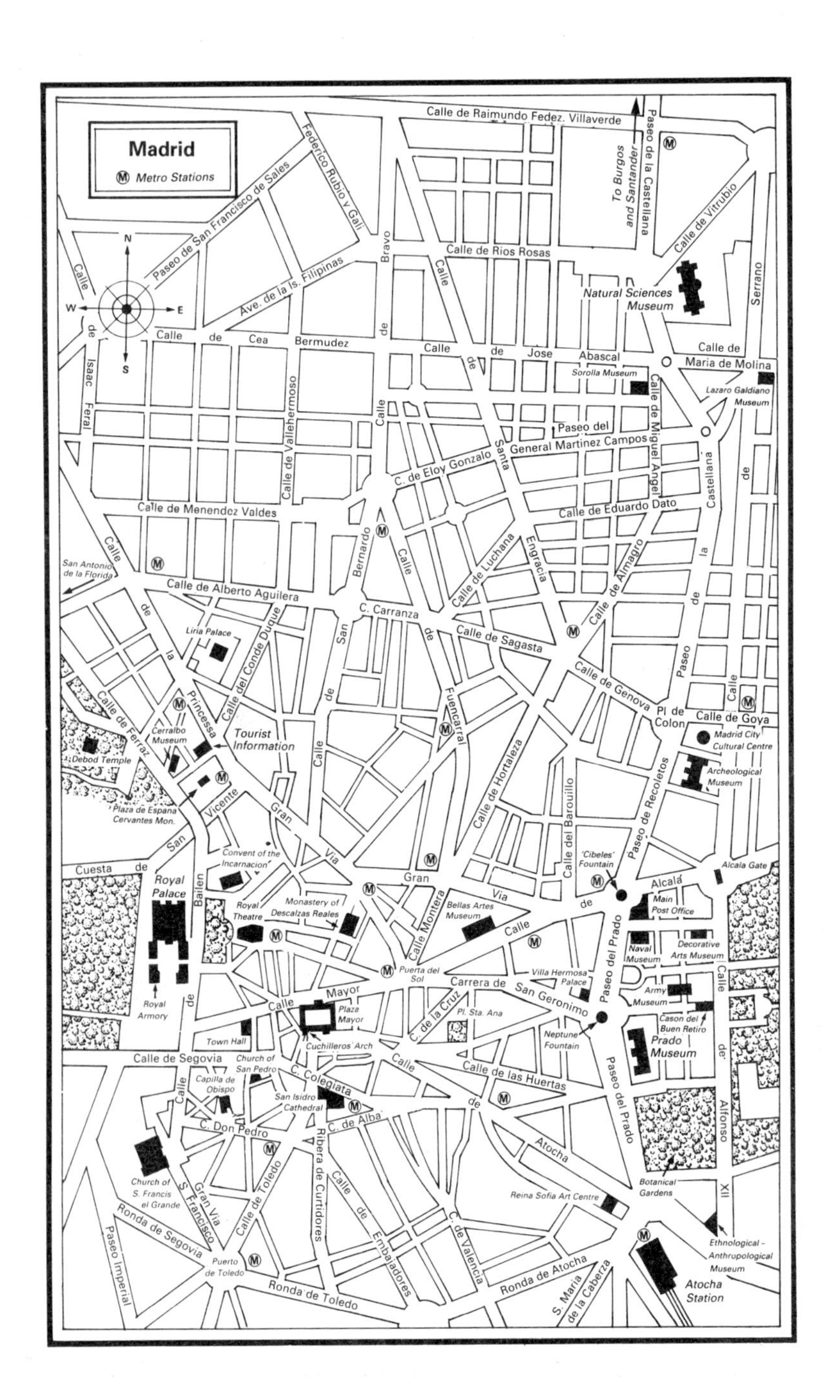

Madrid
Metro Stations
N
S
E
W
Calle de Raimundo Fedez. Villaverde
To Burgos and Santander
Paseo de la Castellana
Federico Rubio y Gali
Paseo de San Francisco de Sales
Ave. de la Is. Filipinas
Calle de Rios Rosas
Bravo
Calle de Vitrubio
Natural Sciences Museum
Serrano
Calle de Isaac Feral
Calle de Cea Bermudez
Calle de Jose Abascal
Calle de Maria de Molina
Sorolla Museum
Lazaro Galdiano Museum
Calle de Vallehermoso
Paseo del General Martinez Campos
Calle de Miguel Angel
C. de Eloy Gonzalo
Santa Engracia
Calle de Eduardo Dato
Calle de Menendez Valdes
Castellana
Calle de Bravo Murillo
San Antonio de la Florida
Calle de Alberto Aguilera
Calle de Luchana
Calle de Almagro
Paseo de la Castellana
C. Carranza
Calle de San Bernardo
Liria Palace
Calle de Sagasta
Calle de Fuencarral
Calle de Genova
Calle del Conde Duque
Calle de la Princesa
Pl de Colon
Calle de Goya
Calle de Ferraz
Cerralbo Museum
Tourist Information
Madrid City Cultural Centre
Debod Temple
Calle de Hortaleza
Archeological Museum
Plaza de Espana Cervantes Mon.
San Vicente
Gran Via
Calle del Barquillo
Paseo de Recoletos
Cuesta de San Vicente
Convent of the Incarnacion
'Cibeles' Fountain
Alcala Gate
Royal Palace
Bailen
Calle de Alcala
Main Post Office
Royal Theatre
Monastery of Descalzas Reales
Calle Montera
Bellas Artes Museum
Paseo del Prado
Naval Museum
Decorative Arts Museum
Puerta del Sol
Villa Hermosa Palace
Carrera de San Geronimo
Army Museum
Royal Armory
Calle Mayor
Plaza Mayor
C. de la Cruz
Pl. Sta. Ana
Casen del Buen Retiro
Town Hall
Cuchilleros' Arch
Neptune Fountain
Prado Museum
Calle de Segovia
Church of San Pedro
Calle de Atocha
Calle de las Huertas
Calle de Alfonso XII
Capilla de Obispo
C. Colegiata
San Isidro Cathedral
C. Don Pedro
C. de Alba
Ribera de Curtidores
Botanical Gardens
Church of S. Francis el Grande
Gran Via S. Francisco
Calle de Toledo
Calle de Embajadores
Reina Sofia Art Centre
Ronda de Segovia
C. de Valencia
Ethnological - Anthropological Museum
Paseo Imperial
Puerto de Toledo
Ronda de Atocha
S. Maria de la Caberza
Atocha Station
Ronda de Toledo

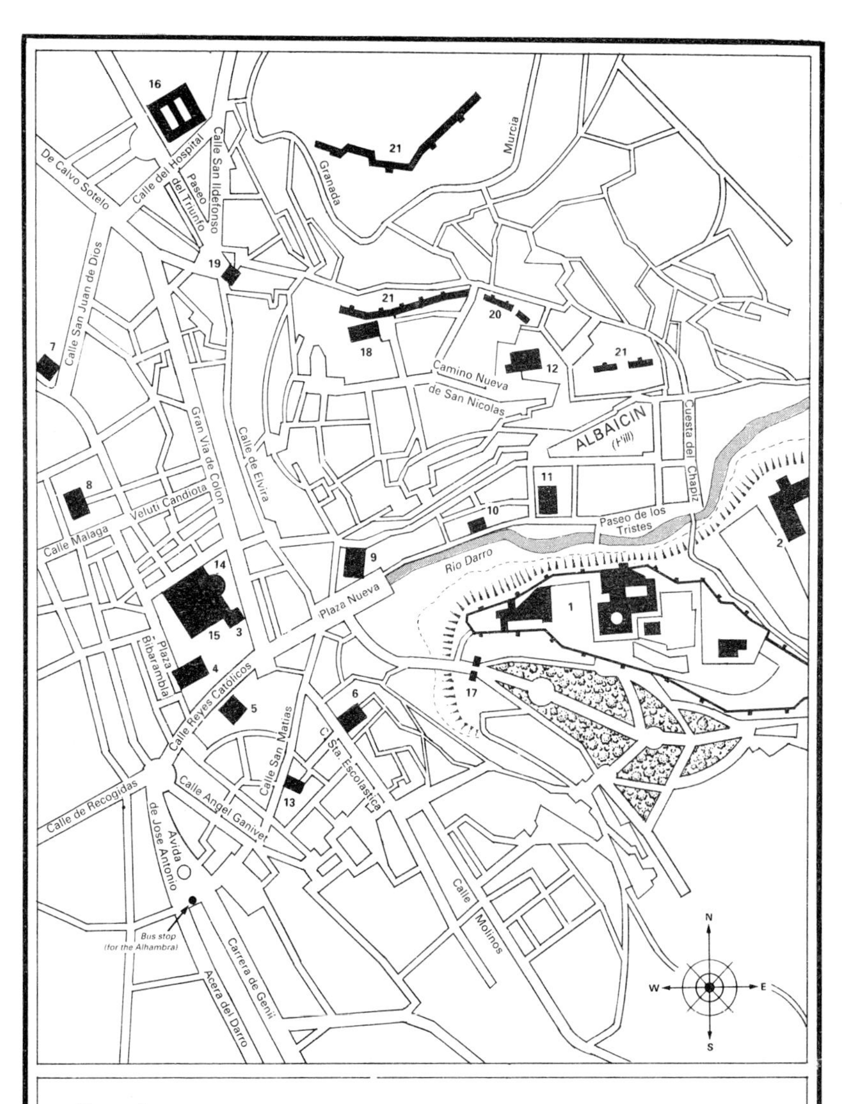

Granada

1 *The Alhambra*

2 *The Generalife*

3 *The Royal Chapel Capilla Real*

4 *The Alcaceria (Silk Exchange)*

5 *Corral del Carbón*

6 *Casa de los Tiros (Tourist Office)*

7 *Church of San Juan de Dios*

8 *University*

9 *Law Courts*

10 *El Bañuelo (Moorish Baths)*

11 *Casa del Castril (Archaeological Museum)*

12 *Church of San Nicolás*

13 *Church of San Matias*

14 *Casa de los Cabildos (Chapter House)*

15 *The Cathedral*

16 *Hospital Real (Royal Hospice University)*

17 *Puerto de las Granadas*

18 *Daralhorra Moorish houses*

19 *Elvira Arch*

20 *Las Pesas Arch*

21 *Ruins of Moorish walls*

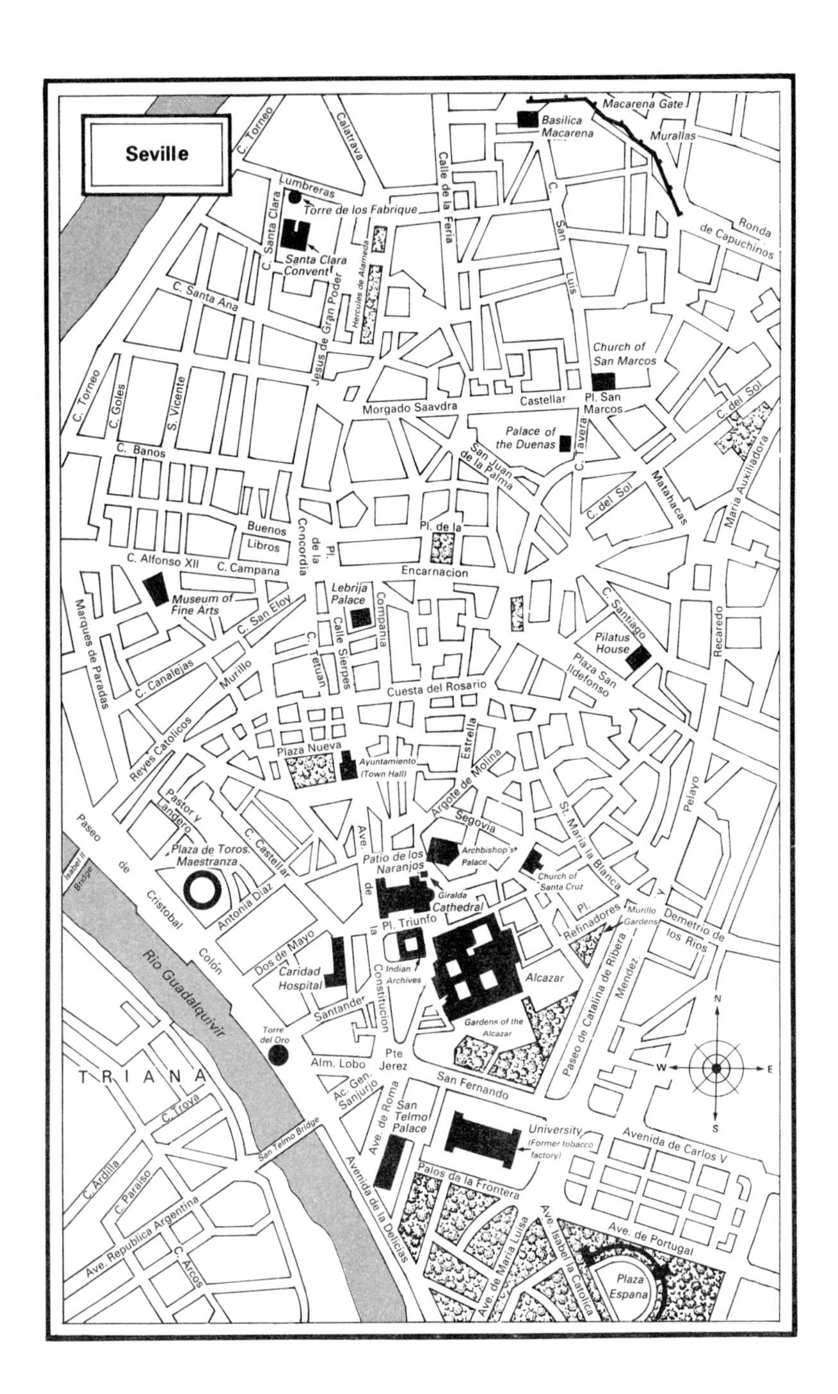
Seville
Macarena Gate
Basilica
Macarena
Murallas
C. Torneo
Calatrava
Lumbreras
Torre de los Fabrique
C. Santa Clara
Santa Clara
Convent
Calle de la Feria
C. San Luis
Ronda de Capuchinos
Hercules de Alameda
Jesus de Gran Poder
C. Santa Ana
Church of
San Marcos
Castellar
Pl. San
Marcos
C. Torneo
C. Goles
S. Vicente
Morgado Saavdra
Palace of
the Duenas
C. del Sol
Maria Auxiliadora
C. Banos
San Juan
de la Palma
C. Tavera
Matahacas
C. del Sol
Buenos
Libros
Concordia
Pl.
de la
Pl. de la
Encarnacion
C. Alfonso XII
C. Campana
Museum of
Fine Arts
Lebrija
Palace
Compania
C. San Eloy
C. Santiago
Pilatus
House
Recaredo
Marques de Paradas
Calle
Sierpes
C.
Tetuan
C. Canalejas
Murillo
Plaza San
Ildefonso
Cuesta del Rosario
Reyes Catolicos
Estrella
Plaza Nueva
Ayuntamiento
(Town Hall)
Argote de Molina
Pastor y
Landero
Pelayo
Segovia
Paseo
de
Cristobal
Colon
Ave.
de
la
Constitucion
St. Maria la Blanca
Plaza de Toros
Maestranza
C. Castellar
Patio de los
Naranjos
Archbishop's
Palace
Church of
Santa Cruz
Isabel II
Bridge
Antonia Diaz
Giralda
Cathedral
Pl.
Refinadores
Murillo
Gardens
Demetrio de
los Rios
Pl. Triunfo
Rio Guadalquivir
Dos de Mayo
Caridad
Hospital
Indian
Archives
Alcazar
Paseo de Catalina de Ribera
Mendez
N
Santander
Gardens of the
Alcazar
Torre
del Oro
W
E
S
Pte
Jerez
Alm. Lobo
TRIANA
San Fernando
Ac. Gen.
Sanjurjo
C. Trova
Ave. de Roma
San
Telmo
Palace
University
(Former tobacco
factory)
Avenida de Carlos V
San Telmo Bridge
Avenida de la Delicias
Palos de la Frontera
C. Ardilla
C. Paraiso
Ave. Republica Argentina
Ave. de Maria Luisa
Ave. Isabel la Catolica
Ave. de Portugal
C. Arcos
Plaza
Espana

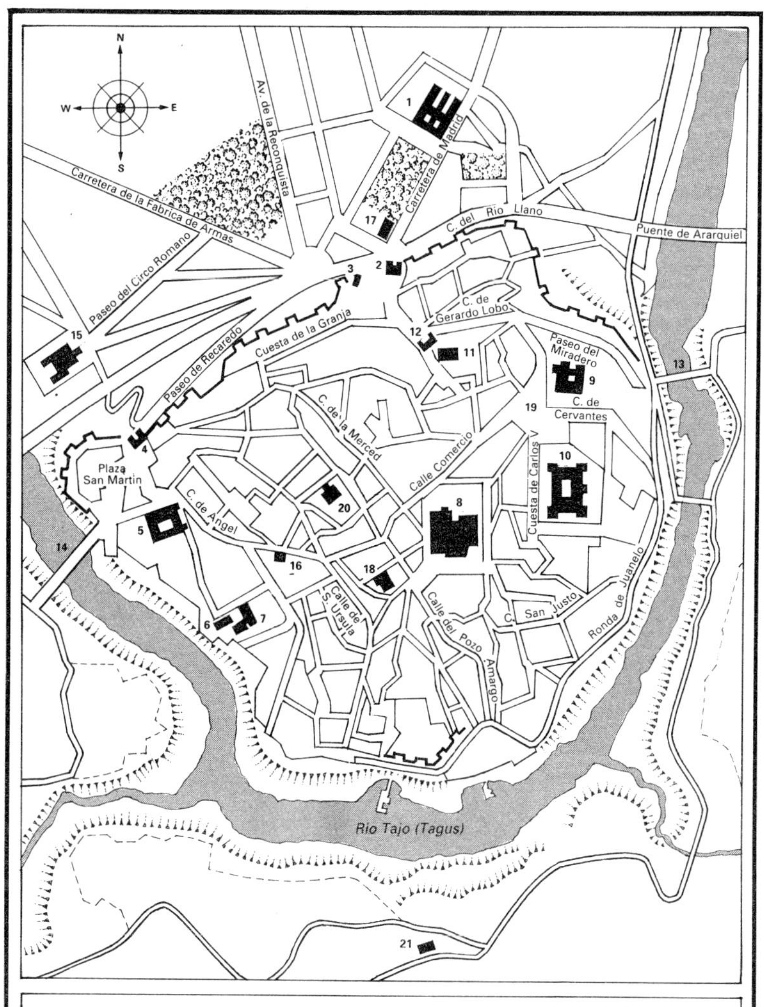

Toledo

1 *Tavera Hospital*
2 *New Bisagra Gates*
3 *Old Bisagra Gates*
4 *Cambrón Gates*
5 *San Juan de los Reyes*
6 *Tránsito Synagogue and Sephardic Museum*
7 *El Greco House Museum*
8 *The Cathedral*
9 *Santa Cruz Museum*
10 *The Alcázar*
11 *Cristo de la Luz*
12 *Puerta del Sol*
13 *Alcántara Bridge*
14 *S Martin Bridge*
15 *Cristo de la Vega Hermitage*
16 *Santo Tomé*
17 *Tourist Information*
18 *Ayuntamiento (Town Hall)*
19 *Plaza de Zocodover*
20 *San Roman – Visigothic Museum*
21 *Parador*

Index